19542

BEYOND THEISM

D0765247

Library
Oakland S.U.M.

19542

Library
Oakland S.U.M.

BEYOND THEISM

A Grammar of God-Language

Theodore W. Jennings, Jr.

New York   Oxford
OXFORD UNIVERSITY PRESS
1985

Oxford University Press

Oxford New York Toronto
Delhi Bombay Calcutta Madras Karachi
Kuala Lumpur Singapore Hong Kong Tokyo
Nairobi Dar es Salaam Cape Town
Melbourne Auckland

and associated companies in
Beirut Berlin Ibadan Nicosia

Copyright © 1985 by Oxford University Press, Inc.,
200 Madison Avenue, New York, New York 10016

All rights reserved. No part of this publication may be reproduced, stored in a
retrieval system, or transmitted, in any form or by any means, electronic, mechanical, photocopying, recording, or otherwise, without the prior permission of
Oxford University Press.

Library of Congress Cataloging in Publication Data

Jennings, Theodore W.
Beyond theism.

Bibliography: p.
Includes index.
1. God—Knowableness.   2. Languages—Religious
aspects—Christianity.   I. Title.
BT102.J46 1985   231'.042   84-27269
ISBN 0-19-503613-1

Printing (last digit): 9 8 7 6 5 4 3 2 1

Printed in the United States of America

For my teachers

Preface

Rather than attempting to perform the astonishing gymnastic feat of saying at the beginning what it has in fact taken me many pages to say I will content myself with a few remarks about the way the book has been written.

When I began this book I started at the middle (chapter six) and worked my way out. Many other projects (including two or three books) were begun and finished while I valiantly struggled to bring this book, if not to a conclusion, at least to an end.

The form which it now takes is dictated by pedagogical considerations, simpler issues first, then more complex ones. Each of the three parts considers the question of our talk about God from a distinctive perspective. The first is a consideration of the theological crisis occasioned by the rise and collapse of theism as a way of talking about God. The second attempts a phenomenology of experience and of our way of speaking about experience in order to determine how the term 'god' is situated in the language of experience and the experience of language. The third part investigates the different kinds of discourse within which the term 'god' appears: explaining, proclaiming, praying, and praising. In the last chapter I suggest ways in which the perspective thus attained may help us to respond to a variety of questions. I don't suppose that I have solved these questions; I do hope I have opened up fruitful ways of thinking about them. A book of this sort does not aim to represent the end of thought but to propose a way for thought to begin again.

For myself I can say that in the course of working my way out of this book I have also begun my work as a theologian. Yet it is certainly not a prolegomenon. It is rather more like an edited laboratory journal, a record of experiments in thought. In any case I do not believe that a prolegomenon or theological method or a fundamental theology can be constructed in advance of constructive and systematic theological work. Instead the work of a theological methodological reflection can only accompany the actual constructive work. That has been the 'place' of these reflections in my own work.

I have attempted to keep the line of argument as clear as possible without intruding a discussion of the literature into the main body of the text. I hope that the main text will be intelligible to readers without a specialized knowledge of the field. Thus the footnotes serve not only to supply warrants for some assertions but also to indicate the literature relevant to further exploration of these themes and to comment upon some of it. In addition, the notes develop implications of themes where such a discussion would unnecessarily interrupt the flow of argument.

This work could not have been undertaken at all had it not been for my wife's willingness to support her theologian house-husband. Only by thus being relieved of the routine duties of committee-work and pedagogical management so characteristic of contemporary educational institutions have I been able to find time to think about theology and my work as a theologian. Yet such reflection may well have proved barren had it not been for the opportunity to teach that was provided me by the Candler School of Theology and Emory University. Thus the reflection upon theology has been rhythmically related to the actual work of teaching theology.

Moreover my periodic visits to Emory have enabled me to continue my participation in that lively context of theological discussion so rarely found in contemporary universities. The character and quality of that discussion grew out of, and was provoked by, the presence and work of Thomas J. J. Altizer. Although Altizer is no longer at Emory, the habit of critical, dialectical, and radical reflection upon theology which discussion with him had fostered, continues to nurture those who remain. The reflections which prompt the writing and rewriting of this text have been nourished by this dialogue.

Whatever the inadequacies of the published form of this book they would have been far more serious had it not been for the penetrating critique of early versions offered by Hendrik W. Boers and Thomas J. J. Altizer. These critiques have served as provocation to more clearly articulate my theme. I and those who find this volume useful owe them a happy debt of gratitude. In company with them, Manfred Hoffmann, William Mallard and Theodore H. Runyon, Jr. are those to whom this work is dedicated in gratitude for their having enabled me to become a theologian.

Mexico City   T.W.J.
Advent 1984

Contents

**PART TWO   GOD AND THE LINGUISTICALITY
              OF EXPERIENCE**

Part One
The Problem of God

1

Introduction

Can we any longer speak meaningfully and responsibly of God? This question has become something of an obsession for academic theology in the last three decades. It has been the subject of scores of books and hundreds of essays. It has become virtually self-evident that upon this inquiry and its results depends the whole enterprise of theology.

Yet it is an odd question. At first glance it may even seem a silly one. For many millions of people it is quite self-evident that one can not only speak of God but also *to* God. Those who raise this question must therefore be afflicted with the curious incapacity to face the fact that such language is not only possible but actual. Or perhaps those who use this language will only attribute such an inquiry to a more fundamental incapacity—what the church has long identified as unbelief.

For another set of folk the problem is not so much silly or stupid as it is uninteresting. After all there are a number of folk for whom God is no longer of very much interest. It is a notion and a name which belongs to the now superseded childhood of the race. For this influential group of folk a preoccupation with such a question can only mean a nostalgia for the nursery tales of the human race.

It is an odd question—whether it is possible or meaningful to speak any longer of God. It is odd not only because it must seem irrelevant both to faith and to those who eschew faith. It is also odd historically. Over its long history Christian theology has occupied itself with rather a different set of questions: who is God, what is God like, how is God related to the world, and to us? Typically these issues have been addressed through the elaboration of doctrine with or without benefit of the close collaboration of philosophy. While these questions have continued to be the subject of theology, the last few centuries have witnessed several shifts in the way in which the problem of God has been formulated. In the late Middle Ages there is a noticeable shift from the *acts* of God to the *nature* of God as the focus of this question. More recently, in the modern era, the question of the *existence* of God became the more pivotal and "prestigious" question.

In the middle decades of this century a more radical question has assumed the place of previous ways of raising the issue, question or problem of God. It is the question whether we may speak of God at all. In some ways this is quite an old question. Theologians have always wrestled with what we would today call the oddity of god-language. Whether in the Greek theology of the Eastern churches with the question of the cataphatic or apophatic character of theology or in the latin theology of the Western churches with the questions of the priority of a *via negativa* or *via eminentia* or the discussion of *analogia* there has been a general and continuous awareness of the difficulties associated with speaking clearly and truly of God.

The contemporary question of god-language thus has a long and noble ancestry. But it is not merely the repetition of the problem which perplexed previous generations of theologians. It is, in a way, a mutation rather than a simple descendant of these earlier questions. It has become both more comprehensive and more radical. More comprehensive because it is a question asked not only of god-language but of language as a whole. More radical because it brings into question not only the coherence of theology but the reality of faith itself.

The contemporary debate about god-language (a curious locution which refers to all the ways in which the words, "god" or "God" appear in language) really asks two questions at once: a question about language and a question about experience. With respect to our experience the question is: is there any longer anything in our experience which corresponds to or gives point to our talking about God? Has not our experience become so secular, mundane, and "everyday" that god-talk no longer engages it, illumines it, arises from it? Whatever our experience, haven't the ways which we inherit for speaking about God become so empty, stifling, obtuse, and obscure as no longer to have any meaning for us? Has it not become for us a dead or at least a foreign language?

We could perhaps respond to this question with the observation that a great many people, some of them obviously intelligent, do continue to use this language very much as if they knew what they were talking about. This reply might suffice were it not for some peculiar features of our recent cultural and political history. We have been made to be suspicious of the ways in which people use language to describe experience. We have taken in some of the lessons of Marx who showed how even the most imposing intellectual systems could be ways of disguising reality, thus preventing us from recognizing and so from altering our true situation. These lessons have been brought nearer home by Freud's description of the way much of our rational or conscious life is but a rationalization of complex and hidden forces which determine our behavior, our thought, our feelings. The history of our century has been a vast and terrifying demonstration of the capacity of language to disguise, distort, and destroy human realities. "Freedom" is used to lure nations into slavery, "science" has been used to legitimate pogroms and the holocaust; "peace" to justify war. Even the parade of television advertising is a constant challenge to wariness with respect to language.

We have good reason to be suspicious of language, and with this suspicion has come the discovery of language itself. Language has become problematic. Of course since the time of Plato philosophers have puzzled about the relation between what we say and what there is. But now this puzzlement is joined to an active and fundamental suspicion. And this suspicion has itself given rise to a range of issues and inquiries which are extraordinary in scope and in complexity.

It is in this context that theology must come to terms with the peculiarities of its own use of language and with the question of the relation of that language to experience. Thus the question of God is raised as a question about language and experience. Whether its theme is God, or humanity, or world, theology has always the task of articulating faith in the contemporary idiom. Our way of speaking must take into account the particularities and peculiarities of our own culture, language, experience, and understanding. It is never possible or appropriate simply to reiterate the formulas of the tradition. This is so because of the very nature of the traditions of faith. The tradition of theology and faith does not consist of a series of simple reiterations, but of an organic, dynamic and diverse revision and re-interpretation. Paul did not speak of God in the same way as Jesus did. Aquinas' way of speaking of God is not a simple repetition of the language of Augustine. Insofar as faith is living, it requires new formulation, renewed expression, often startlingly revised articulation. Faith is not at home in a museum. Insofar as it comes to expression at all, it must do so within the language and horizon and in response to the problems and dilemmas of its own time. Thus, the contemporary problem of god-language must serve as our starting point if we are to make ourselves understood in this time and culture. (To say that we start here does not, of course, mean that this is where we must remain or conclude.)

Despite the radicality and the scope of the problem of language in general and of god-language in particular, there is no need to approach these issues with trepidation. For the very range and depth of these questions also presents an opportunity. Theology, as I have indicated, has long been engaged in the inquiry into the peculiar character of language when it is used to speak of God. It may well be that the new problem of language will prove to be particularly helpful in focussing this question and in providing new avenues for exploration. Thus what at first appeared as an assault upon the viability of theology may, in fact, provide a new and useful set of tools for our work. If so, it will certainly not be the first time that this has proved to be true.

Perhaps the most important consequence of taking this range of issues seriously is that it is an opportunity to reconsider what has become the virtually self-evident framework of the question—a framework provided by modern or enlightenment theism. For it is within this framework that the question of the meaningfulness of our god-language has been fought out for the past several decades. Indeed, the question of god-language is but the latest in a series of conundrums which have arisen within this framework and have exposed its fragility. The question of god-language opens up the question of the viability of theism as the form of our understanding of God. I believe that faith and theology have in fact been held captive to an essentially flawed and unsustainable understanding of God, and that the question of god-language provides us with the opportunity to liberate ourselves from its failing grasp.

This will at first seem an odd assertion for, as I have said, theism has succeeded in becoming the self-evident framework for our speaking about God. The rejection of theism seems to entail a rejection of all those ways of speaking about (or to, or for) God which characterize faith and theology. I wish to maintain however that it is possible to make sense of the language of faith and theology (including the god-language which occurs there) if we escape the confines of theistic conceptions.

To clarify this thesis it will be useful to review briefly the contemporary question of god-language as it has been addressed within Anglo-Saxon philosophy and theology. Fortunately this complex debate has been ably covered in a number of earlier treatments of this problem.[1] Accordingly we will content ourselves with a broad outline of the discussion.

It will become clear as we proceed that the question of god-language does open up the wider question of theism, and this will be the issue addressed in the next chapter. Theism itself arose as an apologetic strategy during the Enlightenment, and so a reconsideration of theism will lead to further reflection on the proper aims and necessary limits of such an apologetic enterprise.

As important as it is to become clear about the specific character and liabilities of theism as an apologetic maneuver, it is even more important to map our alternative responses to the range of issues which confront us under the rubric of god-language. As even the brief survey of this discussion will suggest, the problem of God in our time is a question both about language and about experience. With or without theism the way forward will lie then in a basic reconsideration both of our experience and of our language. Thus our survey of the twentieth century discussion of god-language not only exposes the weakness of theism, but also seeks to make clear the interdependence of the questions of experience and language which will occupy our attention in part two and part three of this essay.

In retrospect we may say that the new form of the question of god-language was launched by the appearance in 1936 of A.J Ayer's *Language, Truth and Logic.*[2] This essay proposed a verification principle which would enable its users to distinguish clearly between meaningful and meaningless assertions. To be meaningful a statement must be capable of being shown to be either true or false. There are two ways to determine truth or falsity and so there are two kinds of meaningful or sensible or intelligible statements. There are tautologies, $2 + 2 = 4$, and there are "synthetic" or empirical statements of fact, the cat is on the mat. In the case of tautologies we examine the rigor of the logic to make certain that the conclusions strictly follow from the premises. In such cases we may reach a verdict of 'necessary' truth or falsity. In the case of empirical statements we must turn to sense experience which enables us to reach a verdict of probable truth or falsity. Only statements which can be tested in one of these two ways are meaningful; all others are meaningless. Lest there be any doubt about the implications of this principle Ayer pointed out that all statements of a metaphysical, moral, or religious nature failed to meet this test and so were meaningless.

The discussion of this principle was largely deferred by the intervention of the Second World War. Ironically the war itself could be taken as either confuting or confirming the verification principle—by displaying the im-

portance of putatively meaningless moral judgments and by displaying the
catastrophic consequences of language used without regard to reason and
fact. With the end of the war and the publication of the second edition of
Ayer's book in 1946 the discussion was fully joined.

Although Ayer himself had shown that his principle made the assertions
of atheists, agnostics, and theists equally meaningless[3] the discussion quickly
took on the appearance of a struggle among these, typically, Anglo-Saxon,
opponents. In the course of this discussion the verification principle itself
had to be refined to take into account the character of the scientific and
mathematical assertions it was proposed to separate from the general confusion of moral and metaphysical discourse. The result of this process of
refinement was the insistence that to be meaningful an assertion must be
such that it would be possible to specify some state of affairs which count
against the assertion.[4]

One response to this reformulated principle of verifiability (or falsifiability)
has been to insist that religious language in general, and god-language in
particular, does meet the criterion. So, for example, it was proposed that
the assertions concerning the existence of God were 'verified' in the religious
experience of the believer, usually understood as specifically mystical experiences or as "encounters" under the analogy of encounters with another
person.[5] This approach came under withering attack from those who asked
in what way such 'experiences' could be distinguished from illusion (the
Joan of Arc controversy) or how talk of "personal encounter" could be
justified in connection with a 'person' represented as, among other things,
invisible, immaterial, and so on.[6] A further attempt to show that god-
language was related to possible experience was made by John Hick[7] who
has argued for 'eschatological verification', i.e., that we will see whether it
is true 'beyond the grave.' While this appears formally analogous to verifying
the existence of black holes in space by means not yet available in a far
distant future, it too has been criticized for begging the question by presupposing the meaningfulness of some religious assertions (eschatological
ones) and for positing a form of experience (non-corporeal) which is not
answerable to the demand for relevant sense experience. These debates can
not be regarded as finally closed but they have demonstrated the extreme
vulnerability of attempts to make god-language 'fit' the principle of verification.

A different approach has been taken by what now appears to be a majority
of respondents to the challenge of verificational analysis. This approach is
to dispute the principle's competence to determine the meaningfulness of
assertions. After all, one may ask, what is the status of the principle of
verification itself—is it a tautology, as in: all statements of type B are state-

ments of type B? Or is it to be understood as an empirical statement?[8] If the latter, then the fact that a great many people use language in a variety of ways not amenable to verificational language appears to tell against the principle.

It is this empirical question which opens up to view the immense variety of ways in which language is used and the corresponding dictum of Wittgenstein: the meaning of a word is its use.[9] Verificational analysis is replaced with functional analysis. The use of language is the empirical data to which our theories about language must correspond. Our attention is directed to ordinary language and its use.

Anticipating this development was the attempt to show the meaningfulness of religious language by associating it with moral language. Of course the initial view of the positivist was that moral and religious statements were to be linked together in that both were, from the standpoint of the principle of verification, meaningless. The identification of god-language and moral language has been a constant feature of modernity since the time of Immanuel Kant.[10] It therefore seemed a natural move to rehabilitate god-language by linking it with moral language and defending the latter against the onslaught of positivism. Braithwaite thus proposed that god-talk functioned to certify and promote a "way of life."[11] This proposal has been adopted and refined by other thinkers, most notably Paul Van Buren.[12] Yet this move has itself been beset by difficulties.[13] That religious language is related to moral language, that religious beliefs are usually held to entail certain ways of conducting oneself, is undeniable. But this connection is by no means an identity. For moral judgements are made and explained by persons with no religious beliefs. Moreover it is by no means clear that the whole meaning of certain religious assertions (God is good, God made heaven and earth, etc.) is reducible to ways of describing or commending a certain manner of life. This is all the more clear if we recall that quite different moral judgements are possible (and actual) on the basis of these religious beliefs: whether one should participate in the military, for example.

In spite of these difficulties the very attempt to link the meaning of god-language to the meaning of moral language suggests that the principle of verifiability does not adequately represent the variety of ways in which language may be used meaningfully. It was in the reflections of Wittgenstein that this possible expansion of kinds of meaning was given a new and fundamental basis.[14] Wittgenstein showed that language does not function merely to describe an empirical "state of affairs," is not a mere collection of labels to be assembled correctly so as to "mirror" or imitate the way things are. The failure of this view of language requires a new account of its function and meaning. With the aphorism: "the meaning of a word is its use in language"[14] the analysis of language was turned from verificational analysis (logical positivism) to functional analysis (ordinary language philosophy). This shift, introduced by one of the most prestigious of the early positivists, has succeeded in establishing itself as the basis of subsequent language philosophy.[15] This has had the result that the chief interest of a number of philosophical theologians lies in showing how the term 'god' functions within its own language: to insist upon the logical oddity of this term and to show how it nevertheless functions in accordance with certain rules. The insistence upon the oddity of god-language serves the purpose of distancing it from the critique of positivism, while the insistence upon the rule-governed character of this oddity makes clear that it involves no arbitrary or confused use of language but one which can be clearly understood as a discrete and legitimate (and so therefore meaningful) "language-game."

Yet in turning to an analysis of the 'logical oddity' of god-language, as undoubtedly essential and fruitful as it has been shown to be, there is a danger of forgetting one of the most important challenges of verificational analysis. That challenge is to show how this use of language is related to experience, most importantly, to the sort of experience which is available to us all (i.e., not just "mystical" experience). While it is no longer a question of verifying religious assertions by appealing to some generally available (through sense experience) state of affairs, it is still a question of the experiential relevance of religious language generally and god-talk in particular which is at issue here.

As we shall see in a subsequent chapter, the question of the experiential reference for god-language is a complex one. The developed consensus of those theologians who have made this problem a central concern is that it is quite impossible to advert here to a narrow understanding of 'religious' experience. Instead it is important to point to kinds of experience available to everyone regardless of religious or secular orientation. To this end it has become common to point to experiences of "transcendence and mystery" which are at least cognates of, if not identical to, what Christians and others have spoken of as experiences of God. The aim has been to discover embedded in the fabric of our ordinary, everyday life those intimations of transcendence which may provide a point of contact for the god-language of theism.

To this end a number of suggestive analyses of experience have been put forward.[16] They all depend to a greater or lesser degree upon three now classic attempts to root the language of faith in the structure of our experience. Schleiermacher's analysis, which opens the modern era of theology, derives the language of faith from the sense of absolute dependence that he takes to be the necessary concomitant of human experience as such.[17] Rudolf Otto located the experiential base of faith in the more specifically religious apprehension of the holy.[18] In his essay *The Meaning of God in Human Experience*, William Ernest Hocking sought to maintain that the sense of a single absolute person was the necessary concomitant to and basis for our interaction with other persons and the world. To these three classic studies which serve as the background for the contemporary discussion may also be added that of Paul Tillich, whose theology rests upon what he calls the "unconditional awareness of the absolute."[19]

These analyses have seemed vulnerable, however, to the contention that "modern secular" experience is less tinged with the sense of mystery and has less appetite for metaphysics than these analyses require in order to be plausible.[20] Accordingly a number of more recent analyses have sought to anchor god-talk in more clearly everyday and secular kinds of experience. What these analyses seek are clues to, or intimations of, transcendence and mystery rather than the thing itself. So, for example, Gordon Kaufman has suggested that the sense of *limit* is one which has cognates at every level of our experience yet, when properly understood, makes talk of god intelligible.[21] Schubert Ogden has put forward a claim for an underlying 'confidence in being' which can only be legitimated and explicated along theistic lines.[22] John Cobb has made a similar claim for the sense of being called or lured into the future, into greater levels of awareness and life.[23]

These analyses are like the earlier 'classical' ones in that they focus upon a single kind of experience as the legitimating basis of god-talk. To them we may contrast another sort of analysis which uncovers a plurality of such intimations of transcendence. Peter Berger's aptly titled essay *A Rumor of Angels* seeks to uncover a number of 'signals of transcendence' among which he lists the desire for order, the character of joyful play, the sense of hope, the sense of moral outrage, and the character of humour.[24] All of these are ordinary experiences that nevertheless transcend the ordinary. Langdon Gilkey's analysis, while indebted to Tillich's theology, also looks for a multiplicity of indicators for what he calls "the dimension of ultimacy in secular experience." Gilkey finds these indications both in our relation to the world (negatively in the sense of an absence of meaning; positively, though less directly, in the sense of joy, creativity, and courage) and in our relation to other persons (the sphere of freedom, guilt, acceptance).[25]

This brief survey of the contemporary discussion serves to indicate the range of issues which the following chapters will address. The aim of the present essay is to advance the discussion in several ways. I will attempt to relate the two sides of the contemporary discussion of God—the question of experience and the question of language. I will maintain that they are by no means so separate as is commonly supposed. This will mean that attention must be given to the linguisticality of our experience and to our experience of language. Working in this way will enable us to give a more careful and coherent account of the kinds of (linguistic) experience which may generate or provoke god-talk (part two). This will then affect our account of the oddity of god-talk, by allowing us to distinguish a multiplicity of structures of discourse within which the term 'god' has an important function (part three).

Before undertaking this discussion however it is important to get our bearings by attending to both the historical context and the theological aim of such an inquiry. The contemporary question of language and experience emerges from the relatively modern form of the doctrine of God *viz*. theism. Most responses to the question of god-language in the contemporary debate have aimed to reconstitute this, now badly eroded, theistic form of the doctrine of God. In this way these theologians hope to create a bridge between modern experience and language on the one hand, and Christian faith on the other. The reconstitution or revision of theism has been taken to be the essential middle term in the apologetic task. One of the characteristic features of my argument will be the claim that this middle term is extraneous and indeed fatally misleading. It is not necessary for the language of faith and it has destructive consequences for the plausibility of our analysis both of experience and of language. The following two chapters will attempt to clarify this contention. It will then be possible to undertake the analysis of experience and of language which constitute the bulk of this essay.

2

The Rise and Fall of Theism

The question of the meaningfulness of god-language has been widely perceived as a challenge to the possibility or at least plausibility of faith. Accordingly the response to this question from the side of faith has taken the form of a defense (apologetic) of the intelligibility and (sometimes) intellectual necessity of faith. In this instance faith has been taken to be a belief in God and an elaboration of that belief in terms of assertions about God.

The character of the contemporary dilemma regarding the use and reference of god-language in theology is attributable to the peculiar form which the doctrine of God has taken in modern times. In this chapter I will first trace two developments that have contributed to the shape of our dilemma: the decomposition of Trinitarian doctrine, and the concentration upon the doctrine of God. The erosion and decomposition of Trinitarian dogma tending towards a concentration upon the monotheism and monism from which it, in part, derived determines the modern form of the doctrine of God. The concentration of theology upon the doctrine of God to the exclusion of other loci brings the doctrine of God into greater public visibility while depriving it of a supportive context of meaning. Together, these two developments produce "theism." I will then show how theism has been exposed to a series of crises of which our contemporary dilemma is the last.

This historical perspective will lead to a suggestion for a reformulation of the task of apologetics.

I. The Trinitarian Form of the Doctrine of God

The doctrine of God in Christian theology has traditionally been Trinitarian in form. In order to see more clearly the direction in which subsequent reformulations have moved (culminating in "theism"), it is important to get some sense of the shape and function of Trinitarian doctrine.

In the modern era characterized by debates about theism and atheism it is difficult to remember that the distinctive character of Christianity's understanding of God is not the development of theism—or "monotheism." The initial problem for Christian theology was not to distinguish Christianity from sheer unbelief but from superstition. In this struggle the opponents did not believe that there was no God, but were all too sure that there was at least one and possibly several.

The distinctive character of Christianity then lay not in its assertion of the reality of the divine (more than granted by Hellenistic religions) nor the absolute unity of God as the first principle (already asserted in the philosophical schools) nor the existence and power of a single and personal God (something maintained in Judaism). In the context of these competing perspectives Christianity was compelled to articulate its own position with respect to God. This it did in the language and conceptuality of the time but in such a way as to distinguish itself from these competing perspectives. This was done by way of a doctrine of the Trinity. Whatever one may think of the intelligibility and usefulness of this doctrine (or complex of doctrines) for our own times, it is important to remember that it was in and through this formulation that the distinctive character of the Christian doctrine of God was expressed and maintained for well over a thousand years. The doctrine of the Trinity provides the framework for the classical formulations of the doctrine of God from Athanasius until the time of Aquinas.

We should briefly notice how this doctrine functioned. It emerged in the first place as an attempt to make sense of the event and experience of salvation through Christ. The attempt to speak clearly of this event and its meaning seemed to make questionable the unity of God. We see this most clearly in the "heresy" of Marcion which so stressed the person and work of God in Christ as to sever Christian faith from the God of the Old Testament and of creation. A way was needed to stress the togetherness and compatibility of the God of the Old Testament and of creation with the Word incarnate in Jesus Christ without surrendering the novelty and significance of the latter. The stress upon the unity of God would have the effect of diminishing the significance of that which had occurred in Jesus.

The doctrine of the Trinity then was a way of taking into account the important differences in the work of God in history while maintaining the unity of God. The language for such a formulation was, of course, that of Greek philosophical discourse.

The function of this Trinitarian formulation then is, in the first place, negative. That is, it proscribes those kinds of "one-sided" assertions which would vitiate the life and language of the community. The insistence upon the unity of the divine being prevents the dissolution of faith into superstitious polytheism. The insistence upon the difference in the "persons" prevents the dissolution of faith into philosophical monism, Judaistic monotheism (undermining the significance of Christ), or Gnosticism (repudiating God's lordship over the world).

Augustine notes that the Trinity is spoken of in order not to lapse entirely into silence.[1] But why not be silent? There is of course the essential character of faith to come to expression as a response to a "word." But beyond this is the controversial function of dogmatics—namely, to oppose heresy. Theology arises in concrete historical circumstances to serve the community of faith by opposing those formulations of faith which make faith itself superfluous, superstitious or unintelligible. Trinitarian language is thus corrective rather than constructive.[2]

It appears then that what is at stake in the refinement of Trinitarian language is the distinction between conceptual and figurative language. In general, what is opposed is drawing unwarranted ontological conclusions from the necessarily figurative (and thus, polysemous) language of faith.[3] Thus, in the language of preaching or of art it is appropriate and, indeed, necessary, to advert to "the crucified God." But an attempt to derive conceptual conclusions from this figurative language must subject itself to the Trinitarian formulation. Thus one is prevented from drawing the conclusion that there is no God from Good Friday until Easter or that because God is "immortal" the Crucifixion must have been apparent rather than real. Such conclusions render faith absurd or vitiate the assertions of salvation.

We could say then that dogma controls the passage from figurative to conceptual language. This is no heteronomous imposition. To the extent to which the conceptual language of theology intends itself as a reflection upon the figurative language of faith[4] it is appropriately guided by the Trinitarian formulations, though it proceeds within this framework in accordance with rational criteria. Similarly the Trinitarian dogma serves as a "grammar" of the language of faith but does not impose itself upon that language. The figurative language of faith is derived from and tested against the Christian mythos. Trinitarian language is a secondary explication of that mythos, and provides a grammatical rule[5] for subsequent elaborations of the figurative language of faith in theology's (and faith's) attempt to continue speaking appropriately of God.

Trinitarian language then serves as the form of the doctrine of God rather than as its content (the content is provided by Scripture, tradition, liturgy, etc.). It serves as a formal principle[6] for the elaboration of a Christian understanding of God.

II. The Decomposition of Trinitarian Doctrine

Most Christian communities continue to acknowledge the historical and liturgical significance of the Trinitarian doctrine, and some continue to give it a place of prominence. Yet it must be acknowledged that Trinitarian formulations no longer function as they did in the first half of the Christian era. The decomposition of Trinitarian dogma has played a major role in the emergence of the contemporary problematic of god-language.

The doctrine of the Trinity has always been somewhat unstable. In the West one feature of this instability has been the tendency toward a functional binitarian formulation (of "Father" and "Son") with a much less precise definition or rich elaboration of the doctrine of the Spirit. But for our purposes a yet more fateful instability needs to be noted. It is the tendency toward a unitarian formulation. The term "God" in Christianity usually refers either to the unity of the three persons or to the first of these persons (God as creator and preserver of the world). The weight of the philosophical tradition and of Jewish monotheism press in the direction of the focus upon God as Father or Creator, thus rendering the distinctive form of a Christian doctrine of God perennially unstable. It was this instability which Augustine attempted to correct by distinguishing clearly between "God" and the first person of the Trinity.[7]

This tendency toward instability is increased when the discussion "of the one God" is separated from the discussion "of the triune God" and priority of place and function given to the former. This fateful move is made by Thomas Aquinas in his *Summa Theologica*.[8] Karl Rahner points to this change of theological loci as the decisive moment in the isolation and subsequent sterilization of the doctrine of the Trinity.[9] In terms of our argument it is the decisive move in the decomposition of this doctrine—a decomposition which helps to set the stage for the modern form of the doctrine of God together with its ensuing crises.

Aquinas' reasons can be readily understood. The philosophical language which Thomas so brilliantly appropriated for Christian theology from the Aristotelian schools of Islam was itself principally concerned with questions of being and of causation. The apologetic situation in which Thomas found himself was occasioned by the mission to the Moors of Spain who had articulated their Islamic faith in the language of Aristotle. Thomas' task was to show the superior compatibility of "the philosopher" to Christian faith. The result was the *Summa Contra Gentiles*; its success as a mission tract is unattested by history, but its importance as a theological treatise cannot be overestimated. The latter and still more influential *Summa Theologica* also bears the stamp of this apologetic and even missional situation.[10]

The separation of Trinitarian doctrine from the discussion of the nature of God and the subordination of the former to the latter opens the way to the further collapse of Trinitarian discourse. This further collapse is propelled by the fact that discussions of the function of the first person of the Trinity (creation, providence) show an affinity for the same philosophical language employed to articulate the doctrine "of the one God" (the language of being and causation). The discussion of the being of God thus absorbs the discussion of the relation of God the Father to the world. The principal arguments for the existence of God adduced by Thomas are arguments that understand God as "cause" of the world and therefore as creator.[11] In this way the affinity of the language of causation for that of creation undoes Augustine's distinction between "God" and "Father." Thus theological energy is directed into the discussion of the being of God (as transcendent cause) and away from the still uncontested Trinitarian formulation.

Within this context of recasting the doctrine of God in the philosophical language of Aristotle one of the most striking features of scholastic theology appears. This is the unparalleled way in which the absoluteness of God comes into conceptual focus. The concentration upon the absoluteness of the being of God is the outcome of the struggle to maintain divine transcendence within a monistically oriented philosophical vocabulary.[12] Of course the theological tradition had always found ways to insist upon the radical difference between God and the world of which God was believed to be the creator. The language of stoicism (impassibility) and of Platonism (ideal perfection) had been likewise appropriated and refashioned to this purpose. The language of Aristotle posed its own peculiar problems and opportunities for this task, which gave the language of omnipotence and omniscience (for example) a very great importance. This together with the isolation of the discussion of the being (and attributes) of God from the discussion of the persons (and "operations" or "acts") of God produces an entire preoccupation with the absoluteness of the divine being and the attributes of this being.[13] Scholastic theology in the late Middle Ages was preoccupied with refining this absolutistic conception and with the diffi-culties this concept made for the interpretation of more directly religious language about God's relation to the world and to the believer.[14]

To summarize, the dissolution of the doctrine of the Trinity is accom-plished in three ways: (1) the isolation of the doctrine so that it becomes a doctrine alongside others rather than a "meta-doctrine" or grammar of doc-trine; (2) the subordination of Trinitarian language to preoccupation with the unitary being of God; and (3) the absorption of the first person of the Trinity (Father as creator) into the discussion of the being of God under pressure of the necessity of understanding this being as transcendent cause. Through all of these developments the doctrine of the Trinity remains uncontested as one of the principal "mysteries of faith." The dissolution is a dissolution of its function. It ceased to provide the context for a discussion of the doctrine of God and became instead one element in a discussion whose context was the being of God as Absolute.

III. The Concentration Upon God

Theism's development depended upon the collapse of the regulatory func-tion of Trinitarian doctrine. But a further development was necessary to produce theism as we know it in the modern period—the concentration of theological attention upon the doctrine of God as thus reconstituted. This concentration was stalled by the Reformation which shifted attention to other doctrines (justification, Christology, Sacramentology, etc.). But the Reformation did not achieve a restoration of Trinitarian language. The disinclination of the Reformation to do any such thing is typified by Me-lanchthon's early refusal even to discuss the doctrine of the Trinity in his *Loci Communes*, dismissing it as belonging to the province of scholastics whose "stupidity could be left unnoticed if those stupid discussions had not in the meantime covered up for us the gospel and benefits of Christ."[15] Of course there is some truth in Melanchthon's suspicion that discussion of the Trinity had become "vain disputation" since that doctrine no longer functioned to orient the whole of theology. However, the failure of the Reformation to recast and reconstitute this doctrine left theology in a vul-nerable position when the doctrine of God reasserted its primacy over the Reformation themes of sin and grace.

The renewed concentration upon the doctrine of God occurred in the course of that historical process and era known as the Enlightenment. This era may be understood as a response to the wars of religion that followed the upheaval of the Reformation. These wars were, for the most part, proto-nationalistic and economic in motive, but their rhetoric and legitimation came from confessional dispute. Weary with the civil and foreign wars that had decimated the population and vitiated the energies of Europe, people longed for the voice of reason and concord which would establish the basis for mutual toleration and social harmony. This coincided with the interest of the emerging bourgeoisie who required national and international peace for rapid and reliable economic expansion. Thus was the project of enlightenment launched.

An important element of this project was the search for a reasonable kernel of religious consensus which would make unnecessary the confessional strife so damaging to peace and stability.[16] The early formulations of this rational religion, or natural religion as it came to be called, included such elements as the divinity of Christ and the authenticity of the miracle stories.[17] But subsequent formulations increasingly focussed upon the existence of a "Supreme Being" and the "moral dignity of man" (sentimentalized in the late nineteenth century to the slogan of the "fatherhood of God and the brotherhood of man").

This concentration upon the doctrine of God occurred not only in Enlightenment philosophy but in theology as well. Theology's participation in this project was partly motivated by the recoil within Christianity itself from the bloody consequences of confessional dispute. But it occurred as well on apologetic grounds as theology sought to accomodate itself to the growing prestige of philosophy and the altered social circumstances in Europe. Thus theology had a major stake in elaborating and defending "essential Christianity" and coordinating it with "natural religion." The point of contact between theology and Enlightenment philosophy was theism—the belief in the existence of a supreme and beneficient Being.

The investment of Protestant (and later Catholic) theology in theism is quite understandable given its immediate historical context. But it must seem strange when we contrast theism to the Trinitarian language which it replaces. God has now become "a personal being" where before God was absolute Being (not *a* being) in three persons (not *a* person). The distinctive form of a Christian doctrine of God has been exchanged for the (presumably) universally acceptable form of theism.

The ensuing history of Protestant theology is very much bound up with the fortunes of this adopted form of the doctrine of God. If we understand this we will be able to understand the amount of energy that theology has invested in the defense of theism through the many vicissitudes which have befallen it. Indeed it has become almost self-evident that Christian theology stands or falls with theism.

As a consequence of the concentration of theological attention upon the doctrine of God as formulated in Enlightenment theism, proofs for the existence of God and the problem of theodicy assume great importance. The concern to establish proofs for the existence of God arises from the passion for certainty that gripped the Enlightenment following the collapse of traditional authorities. In this atmosphere of contending and discredited traditions, philosophy sought eagerly for that which, in Descartes' phrase, could not be doubted. In the eighteenth century, then, the attempt to prove the existence of God (and thus secure the basis of religious harmony) takes on immense importance. What had been almost incidental in Thomas' *Summa* became the major preoccupation of philosophers and theologians alike.

In the same way, the concentration upon a doctrine of God that identified God primarily as creator and providential lord of nature opened up the issue of theodicy in a way quite novel in the history of theology. The reduction of God to the role of creator/cause parallelled the fascination with the emerging physical sciences. Thus appears the intimate connection fostered by theism and by poetry between "nature and nature's God." But this connection was also to mean that apparent flaws in nature had to be explained or denied if theism was to be maintained.

IV. The Crises of Theism

In this way Christian theology was led into what has since appeared to be a trap. For the theism to which it tied itself was quickly exposed as vulnerable at those very points at which (philosophical certainty, scientific interest) it had first seemed strongest.

The proofs for the existence of God, far from insuring a theistic basis for European harmony and thus a secure apologetic foothold for theology, instead exposed it to a critical scrutiny it could not long endure. First by Hume then by Kant (himself a kind of theist) these "proofs" were, if not destroyed, then rendered positively questionable. Theism had been placed irrevocably on the defensive.

A second crisis even more far-reaching than the first is the apparently insoluble problem of theodicy. Having linked God to nature so inextricably, the defenders of theism found themselves having to answer for earthquakes! We have become so inured to the difficulties of the theodicy problem that it is difficult to see how traumatic the Lisbon earthquake was for the adherents of this emerging theism.[18] That event broke the spell of confidence in the binding force of theism. While natural catastrophe and social evil have been a constant factor in the human experience it is only in the eighteenth century that the problem of theodicy as we know it appeared. For this question to be raised in the way in which it has been for modern theology, the doctrine of God must be cast in a form which has God functioning only or primarily as creator and cause of what is. Beyond that, this God must be conceived as absolute in power admitting of neither rival nor limitation. Finally this God must be conceived of as beneficent in the sense of intending only good (or at least justice) for humanity.[19]

Now these conditions did not obtain before the emergence of modern theism (with the possible exception of stoicism).[20] The ancient gods, of course, did not have to justify themselves before the court of wounded human pride or sensibilities (or as we like to say: "before the court of reason"). But even more important differences separate theism from the Christian Trinitarian framework it replaced. Within that framework God is spoken of in other ways than creator (namely as saviour, liberator, comforter, etc.). Moreover this language about God retains many elements of struggle and pathos not compatible with an absolutistic framework for God-language. (Such an absolutistic framework is concomitant to the dissolution of Trinitarian discourse as we have already seen).

A clue to the importance of this difference can be found in the way in which the problem of unjust suffering is met in Christian communities not yet overtaken by theism. In the religious expressions which come to us from the experience of enslavement and oppression of black people in America we find scarcely a trace of what has now become the classic form of the theodicy question.[21] We find neither complaints against the injustice of God nor attempts to explain away the suffering or injustice. Instead we find a confidence in the justice of a God who befriends the lowly and delivers them from the hand of the oppressor (Pharaoh). Here there is little interest in God as creator but much in God as deliverer and comforter. The difference can be seen in the difference between two questions: Milton's "How to justify the ways of God to man?" and Luther's "How do I find a merciful God?" In the first it is a question of "saving" God; in the latter, of God's saving me. It is the latter question which provides the framework for dealing with suffering and evil in communities of faith not yet (or no longer?) dominated by the language of theism.

I am not suggesting that the religious response to suffering in these cases comes in Trinitarian formulas. The Trinitarian formulas functioned to preserve the integrity of the religious language of Christians—it was not itself that language. But the collapse of Trinitarian language leaves the figurative language of faith without adequate conceptual form. Thus in the mainstream of American Christianity it is not uncommon to find people who in adversity give the language of their faith the conceptual form of theism (why did God do this to me, God must have a purpose for this) while in fact wanting to ask a different question—who will deliver me?[22] What the "real" question is, is a matter for pastoral acumen to determine in any situation. It is striking however that it is precisely at the point of asserting God's real relation to human pain that Moltmann develops his case for the necessity of Trinitarian discourse.[23]

The controversy over the proofs for the existence of God and the problem of theodicy may have played some role in theism's shift to insisting upon God's relationship to cultural and moral values in the nineteenth century. Of course such a move was already implicit in the origins of theism as a response to and remedy for the devastation of culture during the religious wars of the seventeenth century. But it is in the nineteenth century that theism is openly and expressly identified with the values of an emerging middle-class culture. Kant, who had undermined confidence in traditional proofs for God's existence, led the way in transferring the function of God from that of a metaphysical principle to that of a moral postulate.[24] While this alliance took many forms (including that of "Throne and Altar") its consistent theme was that the values enshrined in "Western" culture and civilization were guaranteed by and derived from God. A caricature of this alliance lives on in the commonplace rhetorical question; who would want to live in a neighborhood without a church? The implication of the question is that, whether one is a believer or not, one has a stake in the presence of a church as a sort of talisman of the legitimacy and permanence of communal moral values. This alliance has not always been a caricature of itself, however. In Kant, Schleiermacher, and Hegel it has achieved a place of inestimable importance in our intellectual history.

This alliance between theism and cultural value continues more or less untroubled in American and British Christianity, but it received a series of catastrophic shocks in nineteenth- and twentieth-century Europe. The emergence of powerful critiques of the cultural values of modern and middle-class Europe meant that theism (having allied itself to these values) must inevitably be vulnerable to the same critiques. With Marx, Freud, and Nietzsche, theism found itself forced again to be on the defensive. Each of these thinkers in separate ways sought to expose contemporary cultural values as deceptions and hypocrisy. In their words one hears again echoes of prophetic rhetoric from forgotten centuries. Theology, however, could no longer afford to recognize its own claim to this prophetic heritage. Having linked itself to these cultural values for apologetic purposes, it could not extricate itself from them. Their vulnerability became the vulnerability of Christian theology as well. It is precisely "liberal" theology which has most strenuously sought to combat Marx, Freud and Nietzsche. The theological rapprochement with Marx, on the other hand, came in the context of vigorously Trinitarian, and therefore not specifically "theistic", theologies: those of Barth and Moltmann respectively. (A genuine theological rapprochement with Freud has not yet appeared.)

The crisis for theism occasioned by these assaults upon the cultural values of modern Europe only served to make the connection between theism and these values all the more unseverable. Having pledged itself to the defense of these values, theism was now forced to pay up and to deounce resoundingly the "godless" critics of bourgeois society. Unfortunately for theism and the culture to which it allied itself, however, the crisis of values could not be contained to the lecture halls and coffee houses. The outbreak of the First World War exposed to public view the hollowness and weakness of these values and the powerlessness of the defenders and representatives of these values. If we remember that theism originated as one element in a compromise formula for peace in Europe then we can understand how the outbreak of a world war could provoke profound disenchantment with the theism that had advertised itself as the bulwark of that concordat.[25] In any case the post-war period of disillusionment greatly eroded the position of theism (had not both the Germans and the English claimed God as guarantor of their respective nations' power and right?).

American and British Christianity were to a large degree spared the worst impact of this crisis of confidence. As a result theism has continued to be a major force in the Enlightenment ethos of Anglophone theology. Thus questions of God and also of the role of civil religion have a much greater place in the Anglo-Saxon theological discussion than in the European. Yet even here the power of theism to command consent and interpret existence has been seriously weakened. As a consequence English-speaking theologians have been obliged to invest most of their energies in defending theism to the exclusion of other theological concerns.

The history of theism as I have sketched it is a history of crises and gradual diminution of power. Because of its vulnerability on the counts of the proofs for the existence of God, and of theodicy and of its alliance to cultural values themselves badly eroded in power, it cannot serve as the assured basis or context for a theological discussion of the doctrine of God. What once served as an apologetic opportunity has become a major liability for the credibility of Christian theology.

V. The Context of Plausibility

As this brief sketch should make clear, the emergence of theism as the undisputed form of the doctrine of God did not occur in an historical vacuum. Its emergence depended not only upon the logic of the ideas involved but also upon its relation to a whole series of cultural, political, and economic developments associated with the rise of modernity: the rise of the middle class with its concern for commerce (and so for toleration), the preoccupation with nature and natural science, the appearance of cultural artifacts celebrating the human individual and the whole ethos of individualism and personalism institutionalized in capitalist and democratic movements. It was precisely in this cultural atmosphere that theism found its context of plausibility. Theism was plausible, indeed for many self-evident, because it resonated so richly with harmony of idea, experience and institution. Only in this way is it possible to understand how theism could so successfully establish itself as *the* form of the doctrine of God for which its antecedents were but preparation. 'Theism' is even now often used to describe *any* way of being concerned with God, however understood. That in my view this understanding vastly overstates the case and fatally misrepresents the facts should by now be clear.

But if theism's accession to this place of preeminence depended upon this context of plausibility[26] then its erosion is likewise related to the collapse of this context. It is not that all the elements and fruits of Enlightenment humanism and bourgeois culture have disappeared or are in disrepute. Far from it. It is rather than many of them are no longer self-evident or no longer have the ability to focus the dominating vision of Western culture.

In this connection we may notice first the growing awareness of cultures that enshrine values quite different from those of the modern Western world. Not even the ascendancy of Western commerce and technology has succeeded in eroding those other cultural values. The emergence of alternative and non-Western forms of Christian faith and theology in Latin America, Asia, and Africa is slowly penetrating Western consciousness and giving rise to the suspicion that no one form of Christian faith can claim to be definitive. With this recognition grows the sense of relativism and pluralism which ensures that no single world view can serve as an assured context of plausibility for theological formulation.

Beyond this phenomenon is a fundamental transmutation in Western culture and sensibility itself. In its youth the modern era could refer to itself as "the age of man." Such a designation no longer applies, not only because feminism has sensitized us to the sexism and, by extension, the multifaceted provincialism of this designation. A brief survey of the forms of our cultural expression bears witness to the disappearance of the human form from center stage. In its place we find an infinitely varied abstraction: of mass and energy in sculpture, of line and color in painting, of rhythm and force in music. The "story line" so crucial to the depiction of the human form in narrative and dramatic arts is effaced in favor of event, episode, and monologic reflection. Even the most popular movies of our time illustrate the suppression of dialogue in favor of photography, the subservience of plot to camera angle. I have no wish to evaluate this transformation—only to point to its multiple expressions and to its capacity to penetrate to the level of the artifacts of popular culture.

Associated with these developments has been the emergence of a quite different way of viewing ourselves. The "human sciences" concern themselves with roles, status, systems, institutions, and structures whether they concentrate upon the individual or the social manifestations of human "behavior" and "dynamics." History can no longer content itself with the saga of "great men" and their mighty or tragic deeds but must deal with economic structures and detailed observation of social systems. Our social and political experience is increasingly permeated with the awareness of bureaucratic structures, technological rationalization, the managerial ethos. The emergence of this as yet poorly defined culture has led Seidenberg[27] to speak of the end of history. More soberly we may agree with Michel Foucault[28] that we are witnessing the end of the "age of man." This is not to say that humanity no longer exists (though that existence is certainly more precarious than in previous eras). But it does mean that the notion of "personal being" so central to the emergence of theism no longer has the status of concentrating or focussing our experience.

Here then over and above all the vicissitudes of our recent history and indeed summarizing them is the gravest threat to the ascendancy of theism. With the collapse of the "age of man" and its leitmotif of personal being comes the collapse of theism's context of plausibility. The notion of "personal being" is no longer unproblematic, it is no longer mirrored in our social, political, and economic experience, it no longer guides our artistic and scientific endeavor. It is shorn of its previous stature. It no longer serves as the "root-metaphor" of our experience and thought.[29]

To be sure there are many indications of a corresponding reaction. The "culture of narcissism" with its quest for self-importance, self-acceptance, self-enhancement all too clearly demonstrates the existence of a quest for, and an attempt to reconstitute, the lost object of desire.[30] While we cannot yet say with any precision that will emerge as the root-metaphor of culture and so take shape as a new context of plausibility, we are entitled to doubt that this will occur in response to a nostalgia and a reaction which show no signs of having true culture-generating interests or capacities.

VI. The Revisions of Theism

Against this cultural backdrop it may be possible to gain some further clarity concerning what may be termed "post-theistic" developments in the form of the doctrine of God. Certainly the erosion of theism has not gone unnoticed in theology. While the reasons for this erosion and its implications are not always clearly understood, there has been an attempt on several fronts to offer alternatives to theism as the basic formulation of the doctrine of God. We will only indicate in broadest outline some of the salient features of these developments.[31]

Of course one way of responding to the crisis of theism is to attempt to reassert it in defiance of the liabilities which we have noted. It has been the task of 'personalism'—sometimes referred to as "Boston personalism" to attempt to make the presuppositions of personalism explicit and to construct a supporting "metaphysics of personhood."[32] This essentially American theological movement has given intellectual support to the common sense of American Christianity and so has been able to claim a wide influence. Certainly for those who find in the notion of personhood the root metaphor for thought and experience this school of thought has provided inestimable service. Yet it cannot be said that this approach has succeeded. On the one hand it always seems liable to collapse into the cliché's of American cultural Christianity while at the same time exposing itself to all the challenges to theism characteristic of late modernity. If it has failed to provide a persuasive rebuttal to these challenges this is not due to any lack of competence on the part of its proponents but more to the sense of its having become an artifact of a passing era. For reasons which we have indicated it has failed to capture the theological imagination. Whether fairly or not (history is not usually fair) it testifies to the truth of the observation that philosophical positions are not so much refuted as abandoned.

The diminished vigor that has characterized personalism has not meant the end of theism. Instead a fundamental revision of theism has been launched under the banner of "process thought" and the tutelage of Whitehead and

Charles Hartshorne. Also referring to itself as "panentheism" this revision of the doctrine of God has largely superceded the personalism from which it in part derived as the principal Anglo-Saxon expression of an apologetic, natural, or philosophical theology. As it bears upon the doctrine of God this school of theology, most ably represented by the work of John Cobb,[33] has undertaken a revision of the notion of the absoluteness of the divine being that was so important to medieval and early modern theology.[34] On the basis of this revision it has been possible to provide plausible responses to the theodicy problems[35] so troubling to theism and to reconnect the doctrine of God to the developments in natural science that are integrated into Whitehead's cosmology. Indeed it is precisely by way of its concern with question of cosmology, theodicy and, to a lesser degree, proofs for the existence of God,[36] that panentheism shows itself to be both successor to, and capable revision of, theism.

Yet many difficulties still stand in the way of this attempt to reformulate the doctrine of God. The internal consistency of the cosmological scheme remains in doubt, ironically precisely at the point of its account of the person-like being of God.[37] It has not yet succeeded in coming to terms with the effect on theism of the erosion of "liberal" values under the banners of Marx, Freud and Nietzsche.[38] It has, finally, not yet demonstrated that capacity to give adequate expression to a whole range of Christian doctrine from Christology to eschatology[39] which would enable it to consider itself a theological movement of broad significance. It should not be thought that these difficulties make process theology impossible. But they are obstacles that still stand in the way of its attempt to command consent as the reformulation of the doctrine of God.[40]

In some ways a far more radical revision of theism is represented by a movement which I will call "ontologism." While personalism and panentheism have been largely confined to the English-speaking world, where the ethos of Enlightenment modernism has not yet fully succumbed to the shocks characteristic of European thought and experience, 'ontologism' has grown out of the European and especially the Germanic context. Drawing nourishment from the heritage of romanticism (itself always suspicious of modernity) it is characterized by the rejection of the category of "person" and the elaboration of the category of being.[41] With respect to the form of the doctrine of God the most notable representatives of this perspective are Tillich and Macquarrie[42] although we could include a number of "Heideggerians" in this list.

The strength of this position has lain in renouncing reliance upon the category of personhood as the basis for its formulation of the doctrine of

God. In this way it has been able to circumvent many of the crises of theism. It has been able to absorb many of the perspectives of Marxist criticism and of psychoanalysis and to accomodate many of the characteristics of late-modern culture. Yet precisely at the point of its formulation of the doctrine of God it has seemed vulnerable. The notion of God as ground of being, the god beyond god, or being itself, despite its links with ancient, especially Platonic, forms of theology and its avoidance of the pitfalls so characteristic of the theism it seeks to replace, has not yet "caught on." Indeed it is noteworthy that even Tillich, after a quarter century of immersion in the American ethos, moved toward an accomodation with panentheism even at the cost of marring the internal coherence of his *Systematic Theology*. It was perhaps not to be expected that so radical a post-theistic perspective would find hospitable soil in which to flourish in the American theological landscape, but it remains clear that the influence of Tillich's theology has been largely confined to the areas of the dialogue between theology and culture. It is in the work of John Macquarrie and, less directly, that of Langdon Gilkey that we find the most concerted effort to correlate this form of the doctrine of God to the contemporary issues of language and experience.

Without seeking to evaluate the work of these theologians in detail it is possible to suggest one of the reasons the attempt to reformulate the doctrine of God in terms of "Being-itself" has not yet succeeded. It is that the notion of 'being' is no more a central root-metaphor than is the notion of 'person'. It lacks a context of plausibility. Certainly as articulated by Heidegger and Tillich, and perhaps less obviously by Macquarrie, it has about it the inevitable aura of mysticism and of metaphysics—the twin ogres of late-modern, secular, pluralistic sensibility. This view is by no means without importance or without a future. Clearly it has great importance in a number of areas. But it lacks the present persuasiveness which would enable it to supplant theism as the primary form of the doctrine of God.

Looking at the matter in this way brings the question of the apologetic task into view. This task has been at the forefront of the emergence of theism and the revisions of theism. It is certainly a question which is sharply focussed by the problem of the relation of God to our language and experience. It is to the question of the apologetic task, therefore, that we now turn.

3

Apologetics after Theism

The history of the rise and decline of theism is inextricably bound up with the apologetic task. From its inception theism has functioned as a middle term between the language of faith and the cultural context within which that language must come to expression. Already in the work of Thomas Aquinas, which prepared the way for theism, we have seen the apologetic motive at work—the attempt to show Christian faith as intelligible within the context of a philosophical discourse initially perceived as alien and superior to received modes of doctrinal formulation. Theism proper developed in the context of an attempt to reconcile Christian belief to the thought world of the early modern period, the interests of the commercial and managerial classes, the themes of the Enlightenment. Its greatest traumas have been associated with crises which shook the plausibility of modernity's thought world itself, and the defense of theism has entailed the defense of the world view to which it had accomodated itself. It is within this context of crisis that the question of god-language must be understood. Many of the responses to the questions of linguistic analysis have taken the form of attempts to defend theism.[1]

The response to the question of god-language must take into account the factors leading both to the rise and to the decline of theism if it is to make a cogent response to this last crisis of theism. In so doing, theology is driven once again to ask the question of the aim and procedure with which it approaches the apologetic task. Above all it is necessary to recognize that theism can no longer serve as the middle term in building an apologetic bridge between Christian faith and contemporary culture. It cannot so serve because it has lost its context of plausibility. Thus the apologetic task must be prosecuted, if it is to be prosecuted at all, without the dubious aid of theistic conceptions. To make this point clearly it is necessary to examine some of the attempts to carry forward the work of theology in the presence of this apologetic crisis.

I. Apologetics

Since the time of "Gentile mission," associated in our minds most closely with the Apostle Paul, Christianity has been in the position of having to persuade a "religious" people, who had some predisposition to believe in the power of a divine and transcendent reality, that their religiousness was a distorted or imperfect or dim reflection of a light which has been made fully manifest in the revelation of God in Christ. One paradigm of this procedure is to be found in the speech which the author of Luke-Acts attributes to Paul in Athens.[2] However little or much this sermon may tell us about Paul's actual homiletical procedure, it does represent one way in which the task of Christian apologetics has always been prosecuted. The religion of the hearer serves as the "point of contact" for the gospel which renames and thus replaces the unknown (or misidentified) god with the name of the one who raised Jesus from the dead.

Now the specific character of this religious point of contact has been quite varied. Often it has been a polytheistic or animistic religion of nature (as among the Germanic peoples of Europe or many of the peoples of Africa and America). Sometimes it has been a heavily speculative and humanistic philosophy (as in Greece or India). On occasion it has been the monotheism of Judaism or Islam. Or the religion may take the form of a cult of redemption as in the Hellenistic mystery religions.

In each case we can see the way in which Christian theology has struggled fruitfully to confront an indigenous religion or world view with its own peculiar gospel and faith. This situation has always been fraught with danger and difficulty as well as opportunity. There has always been the danger of a simple cultural imperialism that imposes a given form of Christian belief and practice upon a people of quite different culture, confusing the essentials of the Gospel with accidental cultural accretion. Perhaps the first example of this danger is encountered in the "Judaizers" against whom Paul argues in Galatians. There has also been the danger of simply giving a nominal Christian identity to a religious perspective that remains basically alien—a difficulty already experienced in the early church's struggle with Gnosticism, and perhaps by Paul in his struggle against his own converts in Corinth.

In the face of such dangers, however, theology has proceeded to wrestle with the apologetic task, and in the process has greatly enriched the vocabulary and conceptuality of Christian faith. Much of the language of Paul and of John appears to be appropriated from mystery and Gnostic religious vocabularies. The language of theology has long echoed with the genius for abstraction and precision of Greece and Rome, the concreteness and profundity of Germanic tongues. And we have good reason to hope that further enrichment will come through the confrontation of Christian faith with the peoples, cultures, and religious traditions of the third world.

The difficulty which now presses upon us, however, is that we can no longer count upon the "religious connection" as the basis for theology's apologetic task. Much of the world within which faith must come to speech appears to be post-Christian rather than pre-Christian, secular rather than religious, atheistic rather than theistic.

II. Reverse Apologetics

In the face of such a situation it has seemed to a good many theologians that the most urgent task is to reconstitute the point of contact in culture for Christianity. For reasons we have already indicated, this "point of contact" is taken to be the credibility of the idea of God as a supreme and beneficent being. In this struggle theology has had recourse to one of its oldest opponents—and allies—philosophy. Any philosopher who will say a kind word for Being or God is seized upon as the source for a credible theism.

This situation results in some extraordinary moves on the part of contemporary theologians, moves which may be characterized as "reverse" apologetic. John Macquarrie, for example, argues that the traditional language about God has become so obscure as to require a new (and presumably less obscure) language. Macquarrie then offers a revision of Heideggerian language as showing "the connection between theological discourse and everyday discourse."[3] This results in the proposed translation of god-language into language about Being whose essence is "the dynamic of letting be."[4] As intriguing and provocative as this proposal undoubtedly is, it must be doubted whether it contributes anything to solving the dilemma that gave rise to it. It is unclear how language about "Being which lets be" is more intelligible to modern ears or closer to "everyday language" than is language about God as a "heavenly father" who "loves his children." If theological language has become obscure and unintelligible to many people in technological societies (a claim I do not dispute), it is not obvious that an effective remedy is to translate this language into the, if possible, more arcane vocabulary of Heideggerian ontology. This move must surely be made in response to a very different question, namely, how can our god-language be fruitfully connected to the philosophical language of Heidegger? As an apologetic strategem this would aim at the "conversion" of Heidegger and Heideggerians—not serve as a way of making theological language intelligible to "non-Heideggerians." To accomplish the latter task a further move is required—namely, persuading people to become Heideggerians—surely an awkward detour for apologetics.

Something very similar happens when the machinery of process philosophy is summoned to the aid of theology in its current discomfiture. Here again we are met with an appraisal of our situation—namely that theological language has grown cold, barren, or obscure to many intelligent persons. To their aid, and that of theology, comes the analysis of metaphysical notions which are presumably more intelligible to such individuals. Despite the obvious intellectual achievement of process philosophy, especially as represented by Whitehead's *Process and Reality*, a problem similar to the one noted in the case of Macquarrie arises. The translation of theological categories into the categories of process thought is persuasive and apologetically effective only to the extent to which there is a prior commitment to the persuasiveness of this philosophical system. Otherwise a whole series of other moves must be undertaken—in this case to persuade people to become Whiteheadians. Once again the apologetic task of translating the language of faith into a contemporary idiom is deflected in favor of the new necessity (the reverse apologetic) to propogate process philosophy as an antecedent basis for rendering faith intelligible. The difficulty is increased by an antimetaphysical bias which is at least as characteristic of modernity or a scientific world view as is the loss of credibility or intelligibility of theological language itself.

Now what is odd about all these attempts is that rather than seeking to engage the actual "religious situation" and confront that situation with the Gospel, Christian theologians have increasingly assumed responsibility for developing or sustaining the religious situation itself (or a surrogate metaphysical system) leaving little or no time and energy for the task of interpreting and applying the distinctive perspectives and faith of Christianity. It is as if we were puzzled to discover in our new "Hellenistic world" no mystery religions with which to dialogue and concluded that our first task must be to constitute and defend a mystery religion in order to dialogue with it. One imagines Paul going in disguise to the Areopagus, setting up an altar to an unknown God, then persuading all the secular Athenians that this altar really belonged there, really was an integral part of their tradition. All this in order "someday" to return as an apostle to unmask the unknown God as none other than the one who raised Jesus from the dead.

III. The Double Reverse Apologetic

The awkwardness of this apologetic situation has led some theologians (especially Karl Barth) to conclude that the project ought to be abandoned altogether. Barth's distinction between religion and faith serves as a warning and a reminder that the task of the theologian is to articulate Christian faith—not first to convert folk to paganism in order someday to convert them to the Gospel.[5]

The making of such a distinction has made it possible for theologians to begin to entertain the possibility that it is the "secularity" or "nonreligiousness" of modern culture which properly serves as the point of contact for a new apologetic situation. Following Bonhoeffer,[6] some theologians have renounced the awkward task of trying to persuade people to be theists or "religious" as a precondition for Christian faith and have sought instead to accept the worldliness or maturity or secularity of those moderns as the situation in which the Gospel must be announced.[7]

There is much to commend this position, I think, but it has also led to rather extreme calculations or miscalculations concerning the secularity or nonreligiousness of modernity. The danger, in addition to those always attendant upon the apologetic task, is that this secular apologetic may be led to mimic the "reverse religious apologetic" to which it seeks to provide an alternative. In this case theologians must first persuade people to be, in some preconceived manner, secular or nonreligious. It is possible to become so involved in this task as to postpone the apologetic task itself while cultivating the appropriate nonreligious soil in which to plant the Gospel.

In the process of developing such a "double reverse apologetic" one notices an over-selling of secularity. This over-selling is a result of confusion about the task. One gains the impression that some theologians conceive their first task to be to serve as apologists for secularity. One of the most extreme examples is to be found in Conrad Simonson's *In Search of God*.[8] There we are told, with great assurance, that post-Copernican 'man' cannot believe in any absolute, any transcendence, etc. Unfortunately for his thesis, however, it is clear that since the time of Copernicus more Christians of rather an old-fashioned sort have lived than before the time of Copernicus. Moreover, there has been a rush of contending absolutes and new and old religions of transcendence. That the thesis, in the form in which it is presented, is false should be apparent. But how do such silly notions achieve a hold upon otherwise intelligent students and practitioners of theology? In part the answer may lie in the confusion about the apologetic task.

Despite the occasional excesses of this attempt to relate a secular or nonreligious perspective to the Gospel, it may present the advantage of seeing more soberly the situation within which the articulation of the Gospel must "make sense." Of course it has this advantage only so long as it does not fall into the trap of having first to persuade readers, against their own self-understanding, that they are really secular, as the precondition for understanding the Gospel. The character of apologetics is that it articulates the Gospel in the actual (religious or otherwise) situation of the hearer. It is always a confusion to suppose that some one form of religiousness or nonreligiousness is the necessary context within which this task must be pursued.

Now this consideration of the apologetic situation provides one perspective on the difficulty of developing a doctrine of God or making sense of our "god-language." It has been possible, in the past, to make sense of Christian god-language by appropriating and reinterpreting the philosophical absolute of philosophy or the monotheism of Israel or Islam. Another way in which it has been possible to make sense of god-language is to appropriate and reinterpret indigenous religious (polytheistic, or animistic) language. In modern industrialized anti-metaphysical and "secular" societies such ways of making sense of our god-language to others are cut off. Neither theism nor religion any longer characterizes the situation within which faith must articulate itself. But if this is so, how are we to make sense of what we mean by God? If our society has become so pluralistic as to be neither religious nor reliably unreligious, what point of contact is there that can facilitate the translation of God-talk?

IV. The Abandonment of Apologetics

It is a possible and, I believe, a legitimate theological move to conclude that theology should simply renounce the apologetic task altogether (and therewith the labors of "natural" theology) and confine itself to elaborating the language of faith. This I take to be the proposal of Barth and of the "neo-orthodox" theologians who follow him.[9] Such a renunciation of the apologetic task extricates theology from the rather plodding comedy of "reverse apologetic." It also enables theology to concentrate its energies on clarifying the language of faith within the community of faith without endlessly dispersing theological energy in "preliminary" and "methodological" discussions. Finally, it extricates theology from the necessity of defending a cultural status quo in order to defend itself. Thus theology is freed to criticize this religious and cultural status quo.[10]

Despite the attractiveness and legitimacy of such a "dogmatic" option it involves serious liabilities as well. The questionableness of god-language has become too significant a point of controversy to be simply dismissed as impertinent or immaterial. If such language has become unintelligible or seriously misleading, it is the responsibility of theology to make clear its own way of using this language and to demonstrate its appropriateness. The issue here is not one of establishing some "point of contact" for the Gospel. It is rather one of establishing a "point of contact" for the *language* within which that gospel is formulated. This latter task is one which theology can avoid only at the cost of refusing to serve that Gospel in its intention to reach all hearers.

We do not fully grasp the magnitude of the problem of having to speak of God in our changed situation if we suppose that this change of situation concerns only those who are not yet or who are no longer Christian. The difficulty of speaking of God lies not only in the apologetic context but in the confessional context as well. The questions to which we will address ourselves here are not simply the questions of unbelievers but also are raised most urgently from the side of contemporary faith.

That this is so can be seen from the emergence of a large body of literature within theology which characterizes our time as a time of the silence of God, the absence of God, the death of God—or a time which has been abandoned by God. Whether from Buber[11] or Altizer[12] or Ellul[13] these descriptions of our time are not concessions of faith to unfaith (we will quit speaking about God so that you will not be offended by what we say), but testimonies of contemporary faith, which seek to confess faith without "theism."

It is undoubtedly true that the main work of theology is the clarification of doctrine for the community of faith and that this task must not be circumvented by the tortuous and self-defeating process of "reverse apologetics." Yet the language of faith must be rendered intelligible both to those within and those outside the community of faith. This is as true for "god-talk" as for "sin-talk." An appropriately carried out dogmatic theology will therefore inevitably intersect the concerns of apologetic theology.

V. Apologetics Without God

A very different proposal has been made by theologians like Gabriel Vehanian[14] and (in quite another sense) Paul Van Buren[15] in suggesting that we attempt to "do" theology without recourse to god-language. Again such a proposal seems to me to be both possible and at least provisionally legitimate. Our survey of the rise and decline of theism shows the way in which the question of god-language, which has been inextricably tied to theism, demands so much theological attention, it obscures all other issues of theological importance. This is implicit in the move toward a concentration upon the doctrine of God which gives rise to theism. Moreover, the use of god-language does seem to involve inevitable misunderstanding and, indeed, idolatry (Vahanian). Our desperate attempt to give this language *some* meaning only increases the danger that we will give it a meaning that distorts our theological tradition and the faith which is articulated and analyzed in that tradition. Thus the name "God" may be applied to apparently overwhelming and "primary" phenomena—thereby legitimating them (as in the case of Nazism). Or we may give it content according to our various antipathies (God against "them") or loyalties (God with us). Finally it may be argued (with the "secular" theologians) that our god-language derives from a world view that in important respects no longer obtains for many persons today—both inside and outside the church.[16] Precisely in order to render the language of Christian faith intelligible today it must be interpreted without adverting to "god-language."

Now these arguments are weighty ones and ought not to be lightly dismissed. Still it is not obvious that a refusal of god-language (or of an analysis of that language) is required by our situation.

That I am sympathetic with the proposals discussed above should already indicate that I do not believe a consideration of the doctrine of God to be the whole of theology and therefore do not agree with those who maintain that theology stands or falls altogether upon its capacity to assert persuasively the cogency and intelligibility of its god-language.[17] The history of the form and function of the doctrine of God which we sketched in the preceding chapter should suggest to us that this concentration upon God is a vestige of theism. Theology, as I have argued in another context, is reflection upon the Christian mythos. To isolate only one term from the rich and varied vocabulary of that mythos and to make it "the" content or even the "litmus test" of theology must be arbitrary. It is by no means apparent that "god-talk" is more likely to be misunderstood in our day than, for example, are assertions about "total depravity," "justification by grace," or the relation of "law and Gospel." Surely it is at the heart of Protestant theology to assert the fundamental importance of these sorts of doctrines—if need be—at the expense of considerations of the doctrine of God. Those who argue that theology cavalierly disregard the problems of theism (Barth) or not use god-language at all (Vahanian or Van Buren) cannot be entirely wrong. Nor can those who assert the absolute centrality of the "God-problem" be confirmed in their reduction of theology to the defense or revision of theism. It is ironic that the charge of reductionism is frequently hurled against those who would eliminate god-language by those who bid fair to eliminate everything else.

Still there is a certain relative importance to an analysis and even "defense" of the use of god-language. Here we must distinguish two contexts of discussion: the apologetic and the confessional. In the latter the language of proclamation, prayer, and praise makes regular and unavoidable use of god-language. Some account of the way this language is employed in these settings is a necessary part (though only a part) of dogmatic theology. Moreover, in proclamation, god-language has a rather peculiar character in that it both proclaims and indicates the foundation of the proclamation itself. Similarly, in prayer and praise, god-language serves to indicate the aim or goal of that speaking. An analysis of god-language is thus an unavoidable part of the task of clarifying the languages of faith within which it is embedded. (Lest this be misunderstood it must be remembered that this is analogous to the way in which "sin-language" functions crucially in these same linguistic contexts: to designate the ones addressed by proclamation and the ones addressing in doxological language.)

Precisely to that extent to which the analysis of god-language is necessitated by the confessional situation, it also becomes necessary for the apologetic situation (apologetics follows dogmatics). Since the language of the Christian community inevitably involves god-language it is important to indicate those points of contact with that language that would facilitate its comprehension by others to whom it is also addressed, i.e., those outside the church. The point here is not to engage in a "bold apologetic" which will seek to persuade people that rationality requires belief in God or at least a use of god-language consistent with such belief. Rather the aim should be more modest: namely to indicate how some uses of god-language even in a non-Christian or non-religious context have points of contact with the god-language of the Christian tradition. Thus an apologetic involving an analysis of god-language would aim at rendering intelligible some point of contact between a non-religious or non-Christian use of such language and the Christian use or uses of such language. The "defense" of such language involves no more than demonstrating its *intelligibility, not its necessity.* The necessity of undertaking such an apologetic is entirely "situational". If this is the language we are asked to clarify then we must attempt a cogent response.

VI. The Way Forward

A major point of those who propose the elimination of god-language from theology is that theism, as normally construed or as revised, is not tenable as a presupposition of theological reflection, nor can it be fruitfully and securely established as a position from which to develop a theology. I agree with these positions to the extent that I believe it to be possible and important to develop meaningful theological alternatives to theism. But this need not entail suspension of all reference to God.

Nor need it mean, as those who reject the apologetic task propose, the abandonment of the attempt to give a generally intelligible account of the use of "God" in theological discourse. In short we may undertake that modest apologetic which seeks to prove not the necessary and universal truth of theological assertions but rather their coherence and intelligibility.

The way forward here will lie, if I am not much mistaken, in an investigation of the relationship of language to experience. In this way we will be able to take up the challenge posed in the first chapter by the questions of language analysis and to make good the suggestions and intimations contained in the earlier attempts to discover elements of "transcendence and mystery" in the universal experience of humanity.

This means that we must undertake two kinds of investigation, which we will expect to converge. The first is an analysis of experience, which will seek to determine whether in our "experience with language" we may discover a point of contact with theological discourse. That investigation, carried out in part two will suggest that in a "word-event" (Ebeling) there is a cognate to a particular use of "God," namely an expletive use which signals the rupture of the structures of our language and thus of our experience.

This description of a "word-event" then requires that we undertake an investigation of this as an experience in language and therefore of the relation, at least at this point, of theological discourse to the articulation of experience. On the basis of that analysis we will be able to describe the principal characteristics of an experience which may be termed "word-like". I will then propose that the use of "god" to name these qualities be understood as predicative in character. This will then open the way to a more concrete analysis in the following chapters of experiences that meet the criteria we have developed for the non-religious use of god-talk.

In this way we will be able to avoid the difficulties of theism. We will be seeking not to establish the credibility of theism but the pertinence of a particular use of "god" to indicate certain features of our experience. A "point of contact" is, of course, not yet a "bridge." The argument of part three will be concerned with a kind of "architectural sketch" of such a bridge. At no point, however, will it be necessary to invoke the cumbersome machinery of theism in order to pass from an analysis of our experience and language to the particular features of a confessional and theological use of language that prominently displays a variety of kinds of discourse which employ the term 'god'.

It must be stressed again that the bridge we seek to build here does not abrogate the gulf which separates the discourse of faith from the non-religious language and experience of our world. The apologetic bridge is intended not to compel assent but to convey intelligibility. Assent is not won by apologetic design but by what has long been known as conversion, a fundamental reorientation of perspective, attitude, and behavior. Apologetics has nothing to do with the latter. Apologetics must content itself with a less ambitious task—to defend the intelligibility of the articulation of faith.

Part Two
God and the Linguisticality of Experience

4

The Experience of Language

The preceding chapters have shown us that the question of the relation of God to language and experience has far-reaching implications for the form of a doctrine of God and for the apologetic tasks of theology. What is involved here is an attempt to move beyond the now badly weakened structure of modern theism in an effort to reformulate the pertinence and intelligibility of Christian talk about God. In order to do this it will be necessary to inquire into the character of our language and our experience, not in order to find proto-demonstrations of 'the existence of God', but in order to find cognates and connections to Christian (and perhaps other) talk of God.

In part two of our investigation we will undertake one part of this inquiry, *viz* the relation of god-talk to our experience. This is a question concerning the pertinence of theological language. Here we will be attempting to identify aspects of our experience that give rise to some ordinary and extraordinary uses of the term 'god'.

This chapter will explore a provisional model for the relation of 'god-talk' to our linguistic experience. The next chapter will explore some of the methodological issues raised by this model, and the three subsequent chapters will apply this model to our experience. A chapter on the relation of the results obtained to the question of religious experience and to linguisticality will conclude part two.

I. The Question of Experience

We now turn to the question of the experiential referent of god-talk. In certain ways this is a rather old question. Certainly there is ample evidence of attention to the "experience of salvation" in the early Christian community. Yet this kind of focus upon experience is rather different from the contemporary problematic. Theology has always understood the importance of experience for an understanding of the anthropological and soteriological doctrines that form the core of Christian teaching. But not until the modern period did an appeal to experience serve an important function in establishing the doctrine of God. This is not say that "natural theology" previously played no role, quite the contrary. But it functioned typically through an appeal to reason and to reason's discernment of order in the cosmos.

The turn to experience was the result of a two-fold assault upon this traditional form of natural theology. From the side of Christian faith a growing sense that the God of cosmic order bore little resemblance to the God of salvation provoked, in the Reformation, a turn toward experience. As we have already seen, this turn was initially accompanied by a turn away from concentrating upon the doctrine of God and toward the soteriological doctrines of sin and salvation. Even so to the extent that consideration of the doctrine of God continued, it was now linked inextricably to the question of the experience of faith. Luther's famous dicta: "that upon which your heart depends, that is your God" and "faith alone creates both God and idol"[1] may serve as the watchwords of modern theology in its turn to the experience of the individual as the new correlate of a doctrine of God.[2]

But the medieval form of natural theology suffered another blow as well from the attempts of philosophy and science to establish their own autonomy and thus the autonomy of the "natural order" from the domain of theology. The shift from "natural law" to the "law of nature" is emblematic of this move. Of course this change did not mean that the cosmological form of natural theology was entirely abandoned. But alongside and eventually overwhelming it was a new form of natural theology, which appealed not to the rational order of the universe but to the religious, moral, or aesthetic experience of the individual. Thus was launched in modern thought what Kant termed (referring to his own philosophy) the second Copernican revolution. The modern period then is distinguished from the medieval period by this turn to the individual as the subject of experience; it is in this altered context that the question of the relation of talk about God to our experience has taken on such importance.

Talk of God has become problematic for modern theology partly because it has been noticed that the ways of talking about God that were hammered out in the speculative theology of the Middle Ages and of periods of orthodoxy no longer decisively engage or interpret our own experience. That what is said about God by theology *must* decisively engage our experience is the radical proposal of the Reformation. Whatever may have been the case for those who created them, the formulas for speaking of God as impassible, omnipotent, omniscient, and absolute no longer seem able decisively to illuminate our actual and concrete and everyday existence. At least since the time of Luther, however, it has become the almost unvarying presupposition of theology that talk of God must somehow be directly related to the way in which we experience ourselves in the world.

It has been precisely because of this presupposition that talk about God has become problematic. To what in our experience as a culture, as a people in the world, does our speaking about God refer? To raise that question is to raise the possibility that it refers to nothing in our experience. The question of the nature of contemporary theology is therefore implicitly the question of contemporary experience.

This question is of paramount importance for faith. When faith no longer recognizes itself in its own language—no longer finds itself illuminated by the use of god-language, then we must ask whether faith any longer continues at all.

That talk of God must engage experience is thus one of the most striking characteristics of modern theology. But which experience? One possibility is to isolate kinds of experience which are specific to faith or religion. From post-Reformation pietism to contemporary evangelical and charismatic movements, the stress upon inwardness, feeling, and 'experience' has assumed institutional form of considerable power and effectiveness. These movements of a kind of 'folk-mysticism' have, in varying degrees, opposed the rationalism and rationalization characteristic of industrial and postindustrial bureaucratic societies. While these movements have kept alive the demand that theology relate itself to experience, they have not themselves been particularly fruitful theologically (owing, in part to their suspicion of rationalism and rationality). In theology itself the concern for 'experiential' grounding of both natural (apologetic) and doctrinal theology has been taken up in a variety of ways: Schleiermacher and Otto, Kierkegaard and Bultmann, Buber and Hocking may serve as examples (chapter one).

This turn to experience however encounters two fundamental difficulties. The first owes to the as yet imperfectly assimilated consequence of Kant's second Copernican revolution. We may call it the loss or renunciation of the object. The turn from an analysis of the world to an analysis of consciousness produces a phenomenology that focuses upon the construction of experience by the implicit categories of reason and judgment. No longer is the mind a kind of mirror of the world or a tablet upon which the world of things inscribes itself through sense 'impression'. Instead the mind is active in molding and predetermining its own experience. This need not mean that 'the object' entirely disappears but it 'appears' or is apparent only on the conditions predetermined by the operation of consciousness. It is of consciousness, its contents, and of the determinative categories that shape those contents that we can have 'knowledge'. Thus for Kant God is not an object of experience but the presupposition of a certain kind of experience (moral experience). God is a necessary postulate of practical reason.[3] For Schleiermacher God may also be understood 'categorically' as the 'whence' of the sense of absolute dependence constitutive of our selfhood.[4] Even for Kierkegaard, God appears not as an object of experience but as the categorical impetus for self-determination (the eternal in time).[5] The well-known translation of theological and cosmological assertions into anthropological ones in Bultmann is but the self-evident extension of this concentration upon the categories that constitute consciousness. The shift then is that 'god' is not related to experience as one object among others which we may 'perceive', but instead becomes a category constitutive of some other mode of consciousness. This does not mean that discrete experience becomes irrelevant to the notion of God, but rather that the experience which is relevant must be understood as generic. The analysis of experience does not provide us with the discrete perception of an object (called God) but rather with an understanding of the fundamental conditions of experience. To relate 'god' to experience is then to relate 'god' to some universal or fundamental aspect of experience.[6] We will return to this in the next chapter.

A further complication of the turn to experience is the recognition that experience itself is mediated and reconstructed by language. Language does not simply mirror, name, or 'tag' our experience; it structures that experience, even may be said to 'produce' it. This recognition, which we are tempted to call a third Copernican revolution, arises in a variety of contexts which may be conveniently summarized with the following names: Wittgenstein (functional analysis), Heidegger (the linguisticality of existence), Saussure (structural linguistics), to which we may also add the project of a hermeneutical phenomenology (Ricoeur), and a sociology of knowledge (Berger). More recently the work of Foucault (archaeology, genealogy) and of Derrida (grammatology, dissemination) has reshaped our understanding of linguisticality and thought. What unites these exceedingly diverse projects and perspectives is the critique of the notion that language simply 'reflects' either objects or phenomena of consciousness and the insistence that language is instead irreducibly constitutive of our experience and thought.[7]

This third Copernican revolution has the effect of rendering the notion of 'experience' itself somewhat problematic. The modern notion of experience is correlated to the modern notion of the person or subject. Thus many of the ways of speaking of experience in theology are correlated to the emergence of theism, or at least to the context of plausibility within which theism has existed. The question of linguisticality is therefore, in a certain sense, a post-modern framework for the question of experience. This has the result that any appeal to experience must be an appeal to that which is already structured by and articulated within our linguisticality.

The consequence of this view (which will be elaborated in the course of our subsequent discussion) is that to speak of experience is to speak of experience as shaped or formed (or distorted) by language. What is of crucial importance then is to bring into sharper focus our experience of language and the linguisticality of our experience. It is in the terms of this problematic that our discussion of the relation of 'god' to experience must take place.

II. The Experience of Language

To see the implications more clearly of an insistence upon the relation of god-talk to our experience it will be important to understand more precisely the complex relationship between experience and language generally. This will assist us in "locating" god-talk more carefully in relation both to language and to experience.

The first thing to be emphasized about language is the way in which it pervades human activity and experience. This is, in a way, a quantitative fact about language. Human beings have been defined as *rational* beings by philosophers, but as "rational" is ordinarily understood it designates a very narrow range of human activity and experience. We might rather call ourselves *speaking* beings. While we may sometimes be rational, it seems we are always talking, hearing, participating in language. Our world is a world of language.

We may illustrate this by a look at our contemporary society. There is a revolution in language as a system of communication.[8] A veritable avalanche of words is spewed out by printing presses and computers. Radios and televisions issue steady streams of simultaneous "programming." We are inundated by language. Our minds keep up a continous chatter, sorting, naming, expressing, evoking. When we sleep our unconscious insists upon sending messages—an unconscious that Freud has described as structured like a language.[9]

To see how dependent upon language our existence is we need only try to get by in a strange country where a language is spoken which we do not know. Or try thinking without words. If the final switch is pulled—the unconscious turned off—we have nothing left of experience, nothing recognizably human about existence.

The second thing that I want to emphasize about language is its power. Robert Funk rightly maintains that what we say presides over and determines what we can see.[10] Our language structures reality. Language is introduced into the whirling confusion of passing sense experience to "sort things out." It is by language that order is summoned out of chaos, that trees stand out of forests, that blue is distinguished from green, that the child distinguishes Mother from other adults and Father from Mother. In the beginning is language. Through language the worlds of nature and history are born into consciousness.[11] The world of things must fall into line with the world of language.

The sorts of illustrations of this point are virtually endless. I will indicate only a few.

(a)   The word creates an institution.[12] At the altar the man and woman say "I do" and it is done. The word alone has performed, has created, a socially, legally, even psychologically, binding institution.

(b)   The word creates a view of reality. Some biblical scholars attribute great importance to the difference between Hebrew and Greek—between a language built up of verbs and one built up of nouns. The world looks quite different if all is seen as an action rather than as a thing. That is why it is so difficult for an adult to learn a new language—it involves a new way of structuring and apprehending the reality in which one lives.

(c)   The poet by a combination of images creates a new perception, like the fog that comes in on cat's feet, or the marching of mountains across the horizon, or life as a "poor player who struts and frets his hour upon the stage . . ." The poet takes a new line of sight upon the familiar things of life and thus enables us to see as if for the first time. A new perception and thus a new reality is evoked by the image.

Thus far, in indicating the pervasiveness and power of language I have pointed to language as though it were something that we use. We, however, are not usually, if ever, the masters of language. Rather, language is our master. So enmeshed is our perception in the webs of language as to render us its servant. Language determines our destiny. When the child enters the realm of language he or she enters into a structure which the child has had no part in creating. Language is a law to which one must conform oneself and one's experience. This structure sets the categories by which one will be known as just or felon, as 'normal' or insane, as faithful or faithless, as traitor or patriot. Once this structure is entered into the categories that determine the character of one's life and world are given and one can do little to change them.[13] By language we have created our world and by language we have been made human.

We have been looking at the character of language as a fundamental structure and structuring of existence and our world. I want to suggest now something of our predicament as a speaking animal.

This predicament has been suggested by Fritz Buri and Rudolf Bultmann among others—it has to do with the way in which language is "objectifying," while existence is "subjective." In coming to speech the subjectivity of existence is alienated from itself in the objectivity of language. There is no 'subjective' language—no language commensurate with the subjectivity of existence.[14] All language involves objectification, "thingification," even of that which is not itself truly an object, a thing. Yet it is not possible for existence to remain silent, for to exist is to stand out, to press out, to give ex-pression to itself. Without that *ex*-pression there is no *ex*-istence. Our existence is made present to us only in its expression; but to come to expression in the language of objectification means that the subject becomes an object. Yet there is no other language.

Speaking occurs between subjects—yet how may one subject truly address another? If we recognize that another, a friend or lover, has bestowed upon us a new sense of being, has awakened within us a new life, we feel a compelling need to address ourselves to the other, to express to the other our being. Yet it is impossible. How, for example, can one speak any more of love when the words have all grown cheap and common, have been used for lies, to manipulate and deceive? How is it possible to trust one's being to those words—to cast one's life into the wind of speech? For there is no other language with which to reveal ourselves than that in which we ordinarily conceal ourselves. No other language with which to approach the other than that with which we coerce the other. No other language to speak the truth than that which deceives. The same words that make up the idle chatter of our days are the only ones available to utter the meaning of our lives. The hollow sounds of silence—how may they become the fertile womb of the Word?

I have not exaggerated our predicament. It is the impasse in which we live as ones whose destiny is entangled in the destiny of language. Silence is impossible. Speaking is equally impossible. We must speak because that is the character of our existence; we cannot speak because it is the alienation of our existence. We only notice this impasse when there is something of importance to say, something fundamental.

This impasse leads to a distinction—not one that eliminates the problem but one which may help to clarify it. It is the distinction between *Language and Word*. Language is that to which I have referred when I have said: we have only one language. The Word is that to which I have referred when I have spoken of that which must yet cannot be said, of that which brings existence to expression. The Word is not identical with the words by which it is said (they belong to Language) yet apart from these words there is no Word.

Where is the Word? It is there when in the objectifying web of Language the subjectivity of the speaker comes to expression. It is there when despite the brokenness of Language our Word is heard by the other as one which addresses her. It is there when the trivial words of love convey, despite their triviality, love. It is there when in the stuttering or glibness of another's speech we hear her speaking. The Word is not outside of or 'behind' the Language. It is there in the Language—not apart from it.

How does it happen that Word echoes in Language? One cannot determine its occurrence. With the best of intentions (if there ever are any such things) one has only the one Language at one's disposal, one does not have the Word at one's disposal.

The Word happens, the Word in which existence comes to expression, the Word in which life is shared with the other. But it may pass unnoticed. Language closes in again—was there all the time—and talk rules over address, *Gerede* over *Rede*, *parole vide* over *parole pleine*, Language over Word.[15] It is possible to forget in the pervasiveness of Language that there is a Word to be spoken. It is possible to suppose, given the power of Language that the Word may be manipulated. It is possible to despair of the Word amidst the clangor of the empty sounds of Language. The mystery of the Word may disappear in the sophistication of our much speaking.

Thus far our reflection has specificied a dilemma. On the one hand our experience is structured and controlled by our language. On the other hand we are able to experience and name a discontinuity between our experience and the linguistic structure that articulates (or distorts it). This experience of discontinuity does not lie outside language—it is what we may call the experience of the Word (its absence or presence in and through Language).

Before proceeding further to clarify the relationship between "Word" and "Language" it may be useful briefly to review a theological tradition that converges upon this same relation and distinction. It will then be possible to say precisely what bearing this convergence has upon the task of clarifying god-language.

III. "God" and "Word"

It cannot be unimportant for an account of god-language that the Judeo-Christian traditions have pointed consistently to the peculiar tie between "God" and "Word." The identification of God and Word is made most throughly by Karl Barth and most nearly approaches our analysis of the relation between Language and Word in the suggestive work of Gerhard Ebeling. In this section therefore I will indicate some of the principal features of contemporary attempts to clarify and intensify this relationship.

Barth's theology is essentially a theology of the Word, of God's Word as God's self-disclosure to us. It is clear that for Barth there is no God apart from God as Word.[16] That is why he is accused of Christological Monism—for in traditional theology the Word is associated with the second person of the Trinity. But for Barth the Word is the beginning of all theology. Apart from the doctrine of the Word there is no doctrine of God. The doctrine of God is but a special category of the doctrine of the Word.

The thrust of Barth's argument is that God is as God reveals himself. This stands against the view of general revelation which natural theology took as its starting point.[17] The emphasis upon the Word as God's self-revelation means that the focus is shifted away from the being of God to the act (speaking) of God; away from God as such and in isolation to God as present in the Word.

Barth's emphasis upon the Word takes the form of a denial that God 'says' anything in the Word apart from himself. The Word then is not a word *about* God or humanity, or the world or history. The Word is God present in God's speaking. This Word conveys no information. God does not say something else by means of the Word. Word is the very reality, being, presence of God. God *is* Word.

A second theologian who has been much concerned with determining the way in which God is to be understood as Word is Ferdinand Ebner.[18] Ebner stands over against the idealistic tradition inherited from Hegel. From Hegel, at least, the notion of the Word had achieved great importance in philosophy. But the Logos that is there elevated to Absolute Spirit is the Logos of dialectical and "abstract" reason. The subject of such a Logos is the isolated and autonomous *cogito*. Ebner maintained that this violated both the nature of the subject and the nature of Logos. Any understanding of the subject of the Logos must take its bearing from the concrete situation in which speech occurs, that is, in spoken dialogue.

The core of Ebner's position is that we are human only in relation to the other and that the bearer of this relation is the word. Ebner's position, especially in his emphasis upon the I and Thou, bears some similarity to that of his better-known contemporary Martin Buber. But in his insistence upon the word of address and response as the actual bearer of relationality he overcomes much of what in Buber seems to verge upon an uncritical mysticism.[19]

The primary thing about the word is that it is addressed by one subject to another. It is a word of address. The word "I am," which is in a sense the primary word, is itself a word of address—it introduces the subject— not to itself (as in Descartes' *cogito ergo sum*) but to the other before whom the speaker stands.[20] But, as his analysis probes deeper, Ebner shows that this first word must itself be a response. One must initially be addressed, for it is only in relation to a thou that one is constituted a subject.[21] Of course the same must be true of the other as well. Without the relation there is no subject, without the word there is no relation.[22] Without being addressed there is no response.

That it is in the Word that one is summoned into being a and thus into 'response' means that the only meaning of word is Love.[23] The Word (in contrast to chatter) is opening toward the other. The content of the Word is being toward and for the other. The language of indifference, of distance, of withdrawal, of deception is a fundamental perversion of the Word. It is the Word inverted and subverted—in Ebner's terms it is madness.[24] The bearer of the relationship between I and Thou is the Word and that which is thus borne is Love.

In contrast to Buber, who speaks of God as the 'eternal Thou,' Ebner speaks of God as the one by whom we are addressed and thus as the primordial I or subject of address. It is by virtue of the address of this I that one is summoned into being, into speech; into relation. Thus "God" names that which is the basis of our existence as relational and thus also our existence as linguistic.

With the work of Gerhard Ebeling we reach a new level in this intensification of the relationship between God and Word. The decisive point is this: that the Word which is God's Word and thus God himself is an *event*, a "word-event." The eventful character of this "Word" follows from its concreteness. Concretely a word is spoken and this speaking is not a permanent state of affairs but an event (or perhaps, a sequence of events). By thus focusing upon "word-event" as the paradigm for Word of God and thus for God as Word, Ebeling overcomes the tendency in Barth's theology toward a static and thus abstract use of "Word." By focusing here upon word-event it becomes clear that there is no Word apart from its concrete and actual occurrence as word.[24] But since God is identical with (or at least inseparable from) Word then it follows that the reality of God is also eventful in character. "God" therefore designates in the first instance not a perduring subject, but an occurrence, an event, a word-event.[25]

But what sort of event is this that we call 'a' or 'the' word-event? Ebeling rejects the bifurcation of word into human word and "Word of God," a bifurcation which he takes to be present in the theology of Barth and Brunner. "Word," whether of God or of humanity, must finally designate the same thing.[26] What is spoken of as God's Word therefore must be "word that as far as its word-character is concerned is completely normal, let us not hesitate to say: natural, oral word taking place between man and man."[27]

But this "normal word" stands in contrast to much human use of language. Ebeling is aware of language that distorts and is misused to conceal, benumb, or even destroy the other. Here we have no life-giving occurrence of "normal word" but an abnormal and deadening use of language.[28] The word-event that is identical with "God's Word" and with a "normal word" is, for Ebeling, an illumination rather than an obscuration of existence, a self-manifesting rather than a self-concealing, a future opening rather than a future closing occurrence.[29]

Thus from a direction quite different from the one we were earlier pursuing we come to a dilemma in the heart of language itself. The dilemma is that the words which deaden and distort our reality are also the locus of the Word which expresses and creates our reality. To this dilemma we have added the suggestion from dogmatics that the occurrence of a true word is the occurrence to which god-talk refers. How this directs our quest for an understanding of such talk must be our next concern.

IV. Language and Word

The convergence of an analysis of the relation of language to experience and of God to Word upon the notion of a "word-event" must serve as our starting point for an analysis of the meaning of god-language. Put briefly my thesis is that god-talk signals the irruption of a wordlike-event within the structure of language. This thesis depends upon a distinction-in-relationship between "language" and "word." The clarification of the thesis and of its basis is the task of this section.

The distinction between language and word is founded upon the observation of structural linguistics that language may be looked at as a complex structure which can be analyzed as a set of contrasts and identities.[30] On this view, which is crucial for an understanding of the relationships within and between language, a particular element in language (a sound or a word) may be understood through an analysis of its relations to other elements of the same type. The meaning of an element of language then is not so much a datum to which it points outside of language but instead is its 'location' within the structure of language itself.

It is not possible or appropriate at this point to indulge in a lengthy discussion of structural linguistics but an analogy may be useful. There are in our language a whole series of conventions for expressing gratitude to a host (or love to a friend, or antipathy for an enemy). Thanks to these conventions it is possible for us to 'speak' our gratitude (or whatever). Whether I use or violate these conventions, my speech-act is dependent upon them. If I violate the conventions I may either be churlish or a poet but which of these I am will have to be determined, especially if I keep a "straight-face," (that is an unspeaking face) by comparison with other things I say (that is, by attempting to discover the 'location' of this speech-act vis-a-vis other speech-acts). The meaning of what I say is determined by its 'place' in language as conventionally used in society or as determined through comparison with my (only partly) idiosyncratic conventions. In any case this speech-act is governed by the conventions or 'surface structure' of language.

A more fundamental level of the 'structure' of language appears if we remember that the structure of language organizes our perception of and participation in reality at the price of conventionalizing this perception and participation. This is what lies at the heart of the protest against the objectifying character of language which has become a prominent theme in theological and philosophical discourse since the work of Bultmann and Heidegger. The paradox is that subjective expression can occur only within (though also "against") the objectifying structure of language, which itself exists as a deposit of such speaking. At this point a fundamental tension between a speech-act and the regulatory structure of language appears.

The tension between language and word is further intensified by the observations of Jacques Lacan who points to the way in which the structure of language is tied to the structure of the unconscious in such a way that it virtually guarantees the disappearance of "truth," "disclosure," or the *"parole pleine."* The speaking of a true or honest word within the structure of self-deceit which language is, constitutes a fundamental rupture of language as *"parole vide."*

Both the protest against objectifying language (Heidegger) and the suspicion of the regulation of discourse by the dynamics of desire (Lacan) make for a distinction between word on the one hand and language (and discourse) on the other. Both the structure of language (*Langue*) and the exemplification of that structure in discourse (*Parole*) become the objects of a radical suspicion. The occurrence of 'word' or 'word-event' stands in contrast to discourse and its structure. In this context "Word" as the word of address (Ebner), as nonobjectifying speech, as normal word (Ebeling), as *parole pleine* (Lacan) contrasts with 'mere talk', *parole vide*, or objectifying language.

We may now draw together the threads of our discussion. We have noticed, following structuralist linguistics, that language is a structure. This structure may be observed both at superficial levels (the grammatical and lexical "rules" or conventions of a language) and at more fundamental levels, as in the objectifying character of language generally (Heidegger, Bultmann, Buri) or in the subversion of language by the dialectic of unconscious desire (Lacan, Derrida). As a structure, language stands in contrast to acts of speech. This contrast may be only superficial or it may be quite radical. There is in the first case the superficial contrast between an abiding structure and the events or acts which are governed by that structure. A more radical contrast emerges when the speech-act occurs in such a way as to overcome the objectifying or deceiving 'depth' structure of language. It is this last sort of speech-act that is meant when Ebeling speaks of a word-event or Lacan speaks of a *"parole pleine."* It is this that we mean when we speak of the occurrence of word, or of the 'rupture in the structure of language.' Such a rupture can only occur within language at the same time that it is 'over-against language.' Thus it is relative to language and depends upon language. On the other hand language depends upon such word-events in the sense that, this is what language intends or "pre-tends" itself to be.

This leads to the identification of 'word' as a rupture or interruption of the structure of language. To the extent to which an act of speaking actually occurs in such a way as to reveal human reality it is an abrogation of the structures of language. In abrogating these structures it throws them into question—thereby throwing into question our habitual and conventional ways of perceiving, patterning, and participating in 'reality' through language. Such a rupture, to the extent to which it actually happens, could only have the consequence, like Ebeling's "word-event," of rendering everything radically questionable. [31] The fissure in language opened up by the occurrence of 'word' renders the structure of language suspect and problematic. Now this would only be true of rare speech-acts—most speech-acts only exemplify both the superficial and the fundamental structures of language. Only where a rupture of the fundamental structures of language occurred would we be justified in speaking of a "word-event."

But, of course, such a fissure or interruption can only occur within language itself. Where and how else could it occur? This means that the occurrence of the word is dependent upon the medium of language—one can only break what is already there.

If we follow up the decisive clue provided by Ebeling we are led to say that 'god' designates and names this occurrence of 'word' within the structure of language. This would mean that the term 'god' may name the quality or character of an event or occurrence within the structure of language. It may name the peculiar character of a word-event which destructures and re-structures, ruptures and founds language.

As such, the term 'god' would designate a 'gap' in language which resists assimilation to the structure of language. This would correspond to the insistence in Judaism that the name of God must not be 'pronounced'. Such an assimilation of God (YHWH) to language fundamentally distorts the function of such a name since it names that which ruptures as well as founds language. The avoidance of pronouncing it (through the use of a substitute or circumlocution) serves to indicate its peculiar status within and over against language. That a substitute or circumlocution is necessary (that is, that silence is not an option) shows that this radical rupture in language nevertheless happens in and through language and indeed is the point of the discourse in question.

But does this not mean that contrary to expectation 'God' cannot come to expression in our language at all? Are we, after all, left with silence? Does not the radical distinction between word-event and language return us to the situation of the mystic? Or does the 'anti-language' of the word-event come to be articulated with language, and if so, how? And, finally, what has become of the notion of experience with which we began these reflections?

V. The Linguisticality of Experience

Any appeal to experience must take into account what we have termed the linguisticality of experience. That is, we must be clear that any experience we have is shaped, molded, indeed even generated by the linguistic world in which we dwell. We are not plants or stones or beasts but (for better or for worse) human beings caught up within the web of signs and meanings which are most clearly visible in our use of language. So pervasive is this linguisticality that the workings of our unconscious or the posture of our bodies may be understood as articulating a system of signs—a kind of language.

But we are also aware that the ordinary and everyday character of language is somehow unsatisfactory. Whether we speak of objectifying language or of mere talk or of the structure of desire and deceit we know that language also betrays us. The 'other' of language is not 'experience' however. That is, there is no stable and enduring subjectivity or interiority to which we may appeal 'outside' of language; or rather, outside our linguisticality. Even experiences difficult to "put into words" have a linguistic character and may even be generated by language. One may be 'told' both by words and deeds of rejection that one is unworthy. One may 'internalize' this as a pervasive sense of guilt. One may find it exceedingly difficult to articulate this pervasive sense. But it is not 'outside' of language. It is produced within language and may even be exorcized by analytic or therapeutic strategies known, significantly, as "talk-therapy."

Thus experience is not the 'other' of language. The 'other' of language is 'Word' in the special sense of the event or occurrence of 'true word' that we have found described in a variety of ways by thinkers as diverse as Heidegger, Lacan, and Ebeling. It is the occurrence of such a word that renders language questionable for us, and which we hope to hear within language.

Accordingly the 'experience' with which we are concerned in these pages is an 'experience event' which 'breaks through' the typical and everyday ways of experiencing. It is the word/experience-event which ruptures the structure of everyday language/experience which is of concern for us in attempting to make sense of 'god-talk'.

In the following chapters we will concern ourselves with the question of the character of such events and with ways of speaking of God that correspond to these events. But throughout it will be important to bear in mind that the experience of which we speak is always experience of a 'linguistic' character.

It may be useful to conclude this chapter with a few summary propositions and definitions. *Language* refers to the structural character of our common linguisticality. *Linguisticality* refers to all human activity which may be understood as analogous to language. *Discourse*, speech, talk are used to designate the acts which instantiate Language and corresponds to '*parole*'. *Word-event* is used here not to designate a lexical item but to indicate the rupture in the structure of language. "Word-like" will refer to any event with the characteristics of a word-event. The more cumbersome term "experience-event" will have the same use.

5

Methodological Issues

Thus far we have seen that our experience of language opens to our view a tension between language as the structure of our discourse and those occurrences within the domain of this discourse which may be understood as rupturing that structure. We have seen that the description of this linguistic experience converges upon the results of the contemporary theological stress upon the connection between God and Word which culminates in Ebeling's identification of God with a "word-event." The more sharply we draw the distinction between "word-event" and language structure the more elusive the former becomes until it becomes un-utterable. Yet we have also seen that there is a relationship not only of opposition but also of mutual implication between word-event and language structure. If this is so, then we must be able to discern, within the domain of our discourse, traces of the rupture of its structure. I will contend that these traces may be found and described within ordinary language.

One way of establishing this contention is to demonstrate its results in practice through an analysis of actual experience. That will be the work of the next three chapters, which will be concerned with the practical application of the model that has been proposed in chapter four. It is also important, however, to draw out some of the theoretical and methodological implications of the model so that it will be clear why this application functions in the way it does. It is to these theoretical and methodological questions that we turn in this chapter. Some readers may find it more profitable to come back to this discussion after considering the application of chapters six through eight.

The methodological problem of our inquiry may be simply stated: it is to discover in the domain of our discourse traces of that which eludes and ruptures the structure of that discourse. The sort of traces for which we are to look are those that indicate the occurrence of a word-like event. We need to know the implications of our model to isolate and evaluate these traces. Our reflections on the nonpronouncability of YHWH should warn us not to expect to find direct linguistic representations of the occurrence of the "word-event." It is therefore necessary to speak here of 'traces' of such an event, traces in our discourse of that which contests or ruptures the structure of that discourse.

Clearly our procedure must be indirect. But what instruments will enable us to proceed with confidence in this investigation? I will propose three related sets of implications of our model for its application. I will first identify those uses of the term 'god' which are most closely related to the occurrence of a word-event: the expletive and predicative uses. I will then indicate criteria for their use in relation to this sort of occurrence. Finally, I will suggest a broadly phenomenological method for describing the experience events thus isolated.

I. Uses of 'god'

We are concerned here with two ways of using 'god' in our discourse, both of which bear the imprint of the radical event of the occurrence of word. These two ways are the expletive and the predicative uses of 'god' in language. These two forms of god-talk most nearly approximate the rupture in the structure of language that Ebeling has called a "word-event."

The Expletive Use of 'god-talk'
Ian Ramsey has remarked upon the striking similarity in character between swearing or profanity on the one hand and religious language on the other.[1] He supposes that it is just on account of this similarity that the users of religious language prohibit the use of profanity. I propose that we follow up this clue.

What is the relation between profanity and god-talk? Of course it is quite misleading to suppose on the basis of the prohibition against taking the name of YHWH in vain of Exodus 20:7 that the religious use of god-talk excludes all use of what a modern (and still partly Victorian) temper excludes as "swearing." The biblical prohibition has a far more restricted meaning. The Old Testament prohibition only refers to the use of the names (or circum-locutions for the name) of God to legitimate *false* statements, promises, or testimony. What is excluded is the use of god-talk in connection with falsehood. Interestingly, this prohibition occurs in the same tradition that subsequently prohibits the use of the proper name of God in ordinary discourse.[2]

In the New Testament this prohibition is expanded to include all uses of God's name to legitimate or to authorize vows *regardless* of the truth or falsity of the vow.[3] What is opposed here is a *solemn* use of god-talk to authorize or legitimate or certify assertions. What is forbidden is not "pro-fanity" but the solemn "swearing" which we associate with a court of law, a pledge of allegiance, a vow of fidelity, etc. It is, in our terms, the use of 'god' to vouch for the veracity of discourse governed by the structure of language that is prohibited. Oddly, the Victorian temperament accepts this use of god-talk while excluding "swearing." We have turned the prohibition on its head!

In stark contrast to the use of 'god' to certify the veracity or legitimacy of our language is another use, also called "swearing" or "profanity." This is the use of 'god' to express the rupture of language and so of discourse. This is what I will call the 'expletive' use of 'god'. The rupture of language by a "word-event" is marked by the explosion of an epithet, an expletive. This explosion typically makes use of those words of our discourse that are charged with positive or negative force. Indeed only words that have a taboo-like character and so are "fenced-off" from ordinary discourse exercise this func-tion effectively. The classes of words available here are typically scatological, erotic, and "religious" (God, Christ, hell, damn, the devil, etc.)[4]

Now, of course, not all uses of expletives can be understood as signifying a radical rupture in the structure of our discourse. Expletives can be used simply to "decorate" this discourse, to make it lively or colorful or to sub-stitute for its articulation. Nevertheless the expletive use of god-talk is nearest in character to the "word-event" which ruptures language. Even when expletives are used only decoratively, moreover, their very use points to the inadequacy of language and so to its vulnerability to the rupture of its structure.

The "word-event" may be simply a gasp and a gap, a caesura in language. It does not directly enter into language but rather ruptures it. Yet it remains relative to language. Even if it is "silent" it is a "speaking silence," a silence located within the language it ruptures. It is an anti-language that language is compelled to acknowledge in the explosion of the expletive.

The Predicative Use of 'god'

Closely related and dependent upon the expletive use of god-talk yet still distinct from it is the predicative use of god-talk. If the expletive is like a wound in language, then the predicative use of 'god' is like a scar, which covers the wound yet testifies to its presence. The rupture of language signalled by the expletive is not permanent; it is, after all, an event. The gap is assimilated, swallowed up again in discourse through the naming of that gap, the description of the event. The scar (predicative god-talk) is the recovery of language—a recovery that for a longer or shorter duration bears the mark of the rupture it names.

The predicative use of god-talk is the use of 'god' to name the quality, the how, of the word-event. It stands in contrast to the 'nominative' use of god-talk to objectify that which, by hypothesis, is the source, cause or agent of the word-event. The nominative use is endemic to theism. By contrast the predicative use of 'god' is more modest. It does not refer to that which 'stands behind' the event but draws attention to the specific character of the event itself.

The predicative use of 'god' has been quite widespread. It may lie behind "primitive" or "animistic" religions. It was characteristic of certain strands of popular Greek tradition, as suggested by the saying: "it is a god when friends meet."[5] But it is not only an ancient usage. Indeed, the reflections of Ebeling at which we have looked point in this direction: 'god' names an event, a word-event.[6] Herbert Braun has suggested that the teaching of Jesus concerning love may be understood in this way. In effect he proposes that the occurrence of love *is* God.[7] When one commits oneself unreservedly to the welfare of the neighbor—'God' occurs or happens. 'God' then designates an event.

But not just any event. The predicative use of 'god' in such a case functions as a kind of "italics," underscoring the importance of the event. The event is thereby certified as one that decisively qualifies or determines the existence of the one who experiences it. Beyond registering the importance of the event, the predicative use of 'god' also expresses astonishment. This astonishment, awe, or wonder results from the rupture of the structures of our discourse. We may say that the rupture itself "takes one's breath away" or "leaves one speechless." The predicative use of god-language is the residue in discourse of a language shattering word-like-event.

Before exploring the characteristics of such a predicative use of god-language, it is necessary to remind ourselves of the difference between such a usage and the nominative usage to which we are accustomed. However odd it may seem it is actually far closer to our experience than the more familiar nominative use. We are used to using 'god' as a noun, most often as a proper noun. We use it most often as if it named a being—perhaps an odd sort of person. Less commonly perhaps it is used to name a class of beings. In this usage we normally think of "imaginary" beings (the gods of the Greeks, or the Goths, or whomever). In a still less customary usage 'god' is used to refer to 'being itself', that is to name the hidden power or structure common to all that is. All of these usages of 'god' employ it as a *noun*. It names something that is 'there', external to us, independent of our experience. The predicative use of 'god', on the other hand, names the quality of an experience that we have or imagine ourselves having. It describes an occurrence rather than naming a thing. It works like an adverb (quickly, devastatingly, ponderously) rather than a noun (Joe, Frodo, Unicorns).

The predicative use of 'god' is far better suited than the nominative use to meet our concern for an experiential referent for our use of 'god'. The nominative use of 'god' tends to sever god-talk from our experience; to focus attention away from the concreteness of experience and toward an inferred agent or source. As a consequence, the experience itself is taken to be 'less real' than that which, by inference, stands behind it. The hypostasizing and objectifying character of this nominative use of 'god' then all too readily becomes open to Feuerbach's charge that 'god' is simply a projection and form of self-alienation. Of course as long as the root metaphor of person holds firm, this critique may not seem plausible. But once this metaphor declines in explanatory power (and with it the theism which is fashioned upon it) the critique gains in plausibility. For this reason the attempt to experiment with a post-theistic account of god-talk must focus upon the predicative rather than the nominative use of god-talk. This does not mean that we will simply ignore a nominative use of 'god'. Rather we will attempt to understand it (in part three) on the basis of a better understanding of the predicative use of 'god'.

The predicative use is both distinct from and inseparably related to the expletive use of 'god' which we discussed previously. The expletive use is clearly more primitive, more closely associated with the "word-event" that ruptures the structure of our discourse. But we have also seen that the mere presence of an expletive does not necessarily indicate the kind of rupture in our language which characterizes a "word-event." As we have noted, expletives may be only decorative. But where they are not merely decorative, where they do indicate a rupture in language, there we may find the predicative use of 'god' serving as a kind of description of the rupture. Thus the predicative use of 'god' ('god' as the quality or how of an event) is derived from the expletive use of 'god' ('god' as the ex-pression, the explosion of that rupture); the use of 'god' as a predicate tends to confirm the use of 'god' as an expletive. We may express the relation in this way: 'god' as an expletive is an immediate but ambiguous sign of rupture; god as predicate is an 'after the fact' certification that what *seemed* to be such a rupture actually *was* one. Although the predicative use of 'god' is more reliable than the expletive as an attestation of the occurence of a "word-event" it too has a kind of ambiguity. It is much more securely embedded in the structure of discourse than is the expletive: it is more like 'language' than like 'word'. Thus it is farther removed than the expletive from the word-event.

Taken together, the expletive and the predicative uses of 'god' constitute a "line of sight" along which we may direct our attention toward our experience to discover in the linguisticality of our experience the word-event that ruptures the structure of our discourse. Neither alone can provide this line of sight. But together they may direct our aim to this necessarily elusive target. Necessarily elusive, let us remind ourselves, because it stands both within and over against language.

II. Criteria

We have now acquired some of the tools that will enable us to determine the relation of our experience to at least some uses of 'god'. We have been guided by the distinction between Word and Language which derives from Ebeling's description of a word-event and by the notion of language as a structure derived from developments in structuralist thought from de Saussure to Lacan. So far we have simply posited such a distinction and have shown that there are two ways of using 'god' which would be indicative within language of a word-event that stands over-against language. The expletive and predicative uses of god, taken together provide a 'line of sight' within language to that "word-event" which ruptures and so eludes language.

If we are to make appropriate use of this 'line of sight' it is necessary to give some closer attention to the implications of such a trajectory for an understanding of our experience. If we are to relate our experience to a predicative-expletive use of 'god' then we must be able to say which kind of experience gives rise to, or is referred to by, such usage. Our aim then is to clearly identify features of experience that appropriately give rise to expletive and predicative uses of 'god'. If the criteria for such identification are not to be arbitrary they must derive from our concentration upon human experience and from the model of that experience provided by our discussion of word and language. If they are carefully derived, these criteria will enable us to know what we are doing when we use the term 'god' to name the quality of some of our experiences.

In general terms we may say that *we are concerned to identify those kinds of experience which are "word-like" in character.* This means that these experiences must be understood on the model of the word-event (Ebeling) which ruptures the structure of our discourse to produce the kinds of traces in that discourse identifiable as expletive and predicative uses of 'god'. *The phrase "word-like" will be employed here in the sense of the radical distinction (and dialectical relation) between word-event and language.*

The terms most often employed to describe the sort of experience that gives rise to or is referred to by 'god' are transcendence, mystery, the supernatural, extraordinary, numinous, etc. These terms are deeply ambiguous. They are heavily freighted with the traditions of theological and philosophical discourse. Moreover they are often enough also used in trivial contexts. Despite this ambiguity there is no real alternative to using them or some of them in our discussion. In order to make the least confusing use of these terms it is important to see how their use may be related to our discussion of word/language. This will also give us a preliminary list of criteria that experience must meet in order to qualify as generative of the uses of 'god' in which we are interested.

The Criterion of Transcendence
The decisive contribution of Jewish, Christian, and Islamic philosophical theology to the philosophical discourse inherited from Greece resulted from the concern of these theologies to articulate and refine a category of transcendence originally alien to philosophical (monistic) discourse.[8] The residue of this medieval tradition is the universal insistence upon some element of transcendence in our discourse. It is necessary to attain some clarity about the meaning that transcendence can have for our discussion of word and language.

In terms of our present discussion we may say that the criterion of transcendence points to a quality of experience. Talk of transcendence (or its many cognates: mystery, the astonishing, etc.) must not deflect our gaze away from experience but rather advert to the experience itself, to its specific character. We may see how this can be so if we look at the way in which transcendence is an element of *all* of our experience. When we experience, perceive or "prehend," one element or feature of this experiencing is the sense that it "comes to us," "befalls us," "impinges upon us—"in short that in experience we are confronted, encountered, or acted upon. We experience x as if x is not ourselves. This is the "felt" quality of our experience, even when we believe that we have ourselves produced the experience as in dreams, fantasies, and so on. Husserl has described this feature of experience as the "intentional" character of experience—experience is always 'experience of'.[9] In a different way Whitehead has analyzed this character of experience as the "vector" quality of experience—experience as bearing with it a felt sense of its coming to us from outside of us.[10] In this context we would use 'transcendence' to identify this characteristic feature of our experience—that however much it is *our* experience it nevertheless *comes from beyond us.*

Now this ordinary sense of transcendence provides us with an analogue to more radical uses of this category. In traditional philosophical theology the category of transcendence was used to distinguish between the natural order of the world and that which stands outside, apart from and in a kind of opposition to that order. We may appropriate some elements of this tradition for our own discussion of word-event in relation to language. Here we must recall aspects of our previous discussion. 'Language' is being used here to designate the structure of our discourse. We are accepting the attitude, represented by Heidegger and Lacan, which regards this structure with some suspicion as intrinsically falsifying of our experience. In contrast to this structure and the discourse that exemplifies it is what, following Ebeling, we have termed a "word-event"—the rupture of the structure of our discourse. This event "transcends" language. That is, it stands outside and over-against the structure of our discourse. Yet it is nonetheless a "word-event," that is, it occurs within the domain of language, it befalls language, it comes to language. It transcends language in a way which is pertinent to language. It is not merely "something else"; it is the eruption or explosion of that something else within the ordered domain of language. The traces of this transcendence are to be discovered precisely in language itself, namely in the expletive and predicative uses of 'god'. Such uses of 'god' are indicators within discourse of the eruption within language of that which transcends language.

Now analogies can be drawn between this use of transcendence and the traditional use of the category in distinguishing God and the world. Unlike that traditional usage, however, we are here concerned with a feature of our linguistic experience. We are not concerned with that which eludes our experience but with that in our experience which eludes our Language. Moreover we are not interested in developing a theory about what lies behind the experience but in the experience itself. Thus with respect to such an experience-event some might argue that what really stands behind the experience is the interference of a supernatural being or, alternatively, the dynamics of unconscious desire. Both of these moves deflect attention away from the experience and reify a theoretical construction about the experience. Both operate in accordance with the nature-supernature distinction; one by affirming, the other by denying, its pertinence as explanatory of the experience. In terms of that traditional distinction we are satisfied to remain on the end of the "natural." Conversely in terms of our distinction between word-event and language we would maintain that talk both of the natural and the supernatural remain within the domain of language and so miss the essential character of transcendence.

On the basis of this discussion of the category of transcendence we may appropriate some of those terms that have served as cognates to transcendence, giving them now specific meaning within the relation of word-event and language. Closely associated with talk of transcendence is talk of mystery. The categories of transcendence and mystery enter the contemporary discussion of the experiential basis of 'god-talk' together, as we have seen. Originally talk of transcendence was more at home in philosophical discourse, while mystery was more at home in religious discourse. The talk of mystery is more akin to experience, while the talk of transcendence had a more speculative intention. Since we are concerned here with an understanding (theory) of experience they come together in our discussion.

To speak of 'mystery' in connection with a word-like experience is to draw attention to the way in which such a word event eludes or baffles the ordering capacities of language. This bafflement is not the temporary and corrigible bafflement of not knowing how to express ourselves properly in the face of an unfamiliar experience. It is rather the incorrigible bafflement that arises from the permanent incapacity of language to capture, domesticate, and order experience. In the terms of the theological tradition, we are confronted here with the *totaliter aliter*, and so with the *mysterium tremendum*. But we must beware of importing specifically religious criteria into our discussion of experience. The mystery here is one that is specific to the linguisticality of our experience. It is precisely in this linguisticality that we are confronted with that which ruptures the structures determinative of our discourse. The notion of mystery points to the way in which the word-event resists articulation.

To this we may add the notion of the astonishing. The word-event transcends the structure of language not only in that it stands over against it and eludes it but also in the sense that it "abolishes" it. Within the structure of our discourse we are confronted with that which leaves us speechless— which takes our breath away. Because it transcends the structure of discourse it calls this structure into question, it constitutes an assault upon the structure, a violation of it. It is this assault, this abolition which constitutes astonishment. Of course the abolition is only episodic. Language closes in again. But precisely here in the closing over of this gap or rupture we may still discern the traces of the astonishment that is the trauma inflicted upon Language by a word-like-event.

The Criterion of Importance

If we are to identify properly the kind of experience event which gives rise to expletive and predicative uses of 'god' then the criterion of transcendence needs to be supplemented with a discussion of a criterion of 'importance'. By this criterion of importance is meant simply that the rupture of the structure of our discourse by a 'word-event' is not to be regarded as trivial or as of only relative importance if it is to establish the uses of 'god' in which we are here interested.

In the tradition of philosophical theology a similar move has been made by way of the *via affirmativa*. The way (via) of speaking about God properly proposed by this method is to transform positive attributes of being (power, knowledge, etc.) into metaphysical superlatives—a procedure which Whitehead has called paying "metaphysical compliments to God." In any case it is a characteristic of the function of god-talk that it employs a 'logic of perfection' (Hartshorne) to construct pertinent attributes of God, including, in the ontological argument, the "attribute of existence." Most often in theism this procedure is indicated by the criterion of "worthy to be worshipped."

The tradition of philosophical theology has been concerned with the characteristics of the 'being' of God. But we are bracketing out the question of being. We are concerned with characteristics of our experience. We want to know which kinds of experience may appropriately give rise to or be referred to by an expletive or a predicative (rather than a nominative) use of 'god'. Accordingly the 'criterion of importance' while carrying forward some of the concerns of traditional philosophical theology modifies them in accordance with the contemporary problematic. Thus we are not asking whether we experience "perfection" or whether our experience legitimates worship but rather whether our experience is such that it has moments of importance of a kind to give rise to an expletive and/or predicative use of 'god'.

Thus we would agree with the philosophical-theological tradition that 'god' ought not to be applied to that which is trivial or only of marginal importance. This term is properly reserved for that which is taken to be of fundamental or of radical importance. In terms of our discussion of a 'word-event' in relation to language the 'word-like' experience must be such that it is taken to be of fundamental or radical importance for the structure of our linguisticality.

Of course 'importance' may be either positive or negative. That which overthrows a structure is 'important' for that structure just as that which founds or grounds the structure is important for it. When we want to stress the importance of something we say that it is 'a matter of life and death', showing thereby that importance is both positive and negative.

The 'word-event' has just this sort of importance for us as linguistic beings and for our linguistic engagement in and ordering of our world. As we have seen, it is a crisis for language. It transcends language but not in such a way as to be irrelevant to or unimportant for language.

It is easiest to see this importance negatively. The 'word-event' ruptures the structure of language and so brings it into question. Because our existence is linguistic in character, the 'word-event' similarly ruptures our existence, and brings *it* into question. Because our world is structured by language, the word-event that ruptures language similarly brings into question the ordered world which we 'have' in and through our use of language.

Yet the word-event has not only a negative but also a positive importance for language. Without the rupture of the structure of language we would not truly 'have' language. The rupture which makes language vulnerable also makes it visible and valuable. But even beyond this the word-event may also be taken to be what language is "about." The reflections of Jacques Lacan remind us that the *parole pleine* is precisely what the *parole vide* pretends to be.[12] The "word-event" is the *raison d'etre* of Language.

Both the positive and the negative importance of the 'word-like' experience is attested to by the expletive and predicative uses of 'god'. When the expletive is not merely decorative it signals the occurrence of that which is of radical importance. With the predicative expression "it is a god when friends meet" or "love is god," what is stressed is the importance of encounter for one's existence.

The criterion of importance suggests then that in our investigation of experience we will need to look for those kinds of experiences which are appropriately described as having radical or fundamental importance for the way in which we exist in the world through the structure of our discourse. Thus the quality of experience that will give rise to expletive and predicative uses of 'god' will be such that the word-like experience will call into question the structure of our discourse. It will be describable either as making discourse impossible or, alternatively, as that without which discourse is impossible. The word-event is the end of language, in the sense of being either the catastrophe of language or its consummation.

The Criterion of the Generic

The criteria of transcendence and importance must not be understood in such a way as to focus upon specifically "religious" or "metaphysical" kinds of experience available only adventitiously to a few specially equipped persons. No special prerequisite of faith or religious inclination may be introduced here. We are interested only in the sort of experience that is possible for us by virtue of our participation in language.

Of course there have been attempts to legitimate talk of God by means of some reference to 'religious' experience. I believe this procedure to be mistaken. It cannot in any case serve the exigencies of the apologetic task since it cannot serve as a bridge connecting the non-religious to the religious or the non-Christian to the Christian. It may, of course, be employed to attempt to persuade people that they really are tacitly religious but, as we have seen, this leads to the awkward procedure of the "reverse apologetic" and so is self-defeating. Experiences are not religious—people and their world views may be. "Religious" properly designates the sort of attitude one takes toward (among other things) some of one's experiences and, especially, the form of life organization one takes as following from them. Thus one meaning of the criterion of the generic is that we prescind from the dichotomy religious-secular. Our task after all is not to promote religion but to show how one element of Christian discourse functions in relation to human experience.

Our model of the relation of word-event and language makes evident that the only prerequisite for a word-like experience is that we participate in Language. This will mean that our investigation of experience will seek to discover those kinds of experience which are both transcendent of and consequent upon our linguisticality. The linguisticality of our experience, let us recall, is the specifically and generically human aspect of our experience. It is thus with the experience available to us by virtue of our humanity that we are here concerned.

Of course to say that such experience is possible for us because we are human does not mean that we necessarily have such an experience. It is possible, for example, for us to live entirely within the domain of Language never being made aware of its rupture, or for such ruptures as they occur to be trivialized or made to seem unimportant (Language closes over the wound without visible traces), or for us to forget having such experiences. To make our analysis of experience plausible, however, it will be necessary to show that we are capable of these experiences. It will, of course, help if these experiences can be described in such a way that they "ring a bell," that is, recall to mind having had such an experience.

One major difficulty here is that there are different languages. French is different from English, both are even further distinct from Basque and so on. Each of these languages contends with a cultural-historical sphere quite different from that contended with by the language of the Pygmies of the rain forest or the Tasaday of the Phillipines. These different languages embody importantly different ways of naming and structuring existence in the world. In each of them what we have called the linguisticality of our existence takes on a different form—the degree of difference being indicated by the difficulty of translation. In order to describe our experience we employ not Language but a language. Presumably any language has the character of Language and thus the word-event stands in a similar relation to different languages. But clearly the ways of naming and describing a word-event will vary, as will the indicators within a language of the rupture occasioned by a word-event.

The description of our experience that will follow, as well as the analysis which has brought us to this point, necessarily transpires within a language (in this case English). We may assume that there would be significant differences in description in a different language (one for example which has no word for love.) But the elusive goal of our description is the kind of experience that is possible for us not because we speak English but because we speak.

III. The Description of Experience

Thus far our discussion has provided us with a variety of instruments for the interrogation of our experience. We have been developing a model based upon our experience of language which distinguishes and relates 'word-event' and language. On the basis of this model we have discriminated expletive and predicative uses of 'god' as indicators within discourse of the rupture of the structure of that discourse and have developed criteria for their appropriate relation to experience. These instruments, used in conjunction, will enable us to detect the kinds of experience that are related to at least some uses of 'god'. Yet with detection must also go description if we are to actually deal with and recognize the experience. The method of description that we will be employing is a broadly phenomenological one and this must now be briefly explained.

The Regions

The most obvious feature of the phenomenological approach used in these pages is that we concentrate upon the way we experience and the content of our experience rather than upon that which, by hypothesis, stands behind or causes these experiences. We are concerned with phenomena of awareness or experience rather than with the 'noumena', with the 'reality' that lies beyond experience. This is necessarily so because our question is whether ways of using 'god' may be reliably related to our experience. We bracket the question of the being or attributes of God in order to ask about our experience.

But where in our experience do we look? How shall we begin or proceed? Is there any way to order or to organize our investigation of experience? Must we contend with a "blooming buzzing confusion of experience" (James) or are some areas of our experience more promising than others? We begin with an ordering of our experience. Any such ordering is necessarily somewhat provisional. But without it we can neither begin nor proceed. The 'ordering' that will be employed here is one of regionalization. That is, we will divide experience into regions (areas, spheres etc.) This will entail a kind of map of our experience, of the kinds of experience we have by virtue of our existence as human beings.

But in accordance with what principle will we divide the field of experience into regions? We are concerned with the relation of god-talk to experience. Accordingly we will be guided by the way in which this god-talk has been employed. To what kinds of experiences, for what clusters of such kinds of experience has this terminology been applied? It is by way of this sort of question that the three regions named here have been initially descried: The ontological, the aesthetic, the historical. These regions are a kind of heuristic device. They provide us with a way of dividing, ordering, organizing experience for our investigation. [13]

These regions have several important characteristics. First they are treated here as relatively autonomous. It is often the case that philosophical theology attempts to isolate some one most basic experience, whether it be Schleiermacher's sense of absolute dependence or Kaufman's sense of limit. But a quick review of religious literature discloses a wide and apparently irreducible variety of experiences associated with the use of 'god'. The variety is best taken into account, I believe, not by an attempt to reduce these to a single kind of experience but by a kind of grouping in accordance with 'family resemblances'. Such a process of grouping does produce the first intimations of a 'region'.

But the regions are regions of generically human experience. There is here no 'religious' region. Rather the regions are determined by ways of human experiencing fundamental to such human enterprises as philosophy and science, art and culture, ethics and society, etc. The character of the region will be explicated partly in terms of the human endeavors that grow out of or together constitute this region.

But this alone would by no means establish the coherence of a region. To this end, I will attempt to show the fundamental categories in terms of which our experience is articulated in each of these regions, and to show that these categories in fact belong together in such a way as to constitute a unified field of discourse.

Feeling and Metaphor

Within each of the regions it will be necessary to describe the sorts of experience characteristic of the region which meet the criteria for expletive and predicative uses of 'god'. But how will these experiences be described? Any description must occur within language, yet the experiences themselves, if they are 'word-like', rupture and transcend language. Once again we find ourselves functioning within language to describe that which ruptures language.

Our description then will necessarily be indirect. The function of such description cannot be to capture the experience-event or to possess it in language but to turn our attention in a particular direction. Descriptions are directions. For our description we will use two sorts of 'debris,' debris that is cast off by the rupture of discourse: descriptions of feeling states and descriptions of fundamental metaphors. These correspond to the subjective (*my* experience of) and objective (my experience *of*) poles of experience. These must be briefly explained.

An experience is always someone's experience. It is this subjective aspect of experience that is articulated in the language of feeling states. A particular difficulty, which has been encountered at every turn in this generally phenomenological inquiry, is the disorderly state of our ways of naming this aspect of our experience—especially with respect to the sorts of experience in view here. Not infrequently, for example, terms like dread, despair, and terror are used interchangeably. At other times, however, they are quite sharply distinguished or applied in divergent ways. This is partly due to the lack of serious attention to these and other feeling states. This lack of attention collaborates in debasing the linguistic currency that names them. I have had no recourse but to attempt to make clear what meanings I intend and what discriminations these meanings entail. There are points at which this may seem arbitrary but I can only hope that the present analysis will provoke other analyses still more precise and persuasive.

One way of overcoming this disarray in the ways of naming feeling states is to attend to the ways in which the objective side of the experience (experience *of*) comes to expression in fundamental metaphors. Such fundamental metaphors as light, dark, order and chaos, ground and abyss have the advantage of being the common property of both religious and non-religious discourse, yet are also typically invoked to designate the content of experiences with the requisite characteristics of transcendence and importance. To make it clear that such fundamental metaphors also meet the criterion of the generically human, it will be important to show that they occur in both secular and religious contexts and in a variety of each. The use of such fundamental metaphors in this connection follows up on the suggestions of Paul Ricoeur concerning a hermeneutical phenomenology.[14] In combination then, the discrimination of feeling states and the clarification of fundamental metaphors will point us more accurately to the sorts of experience-events which are 'word-like' (i.e., have the characteristics of a 'word-event') in character. I do not intend to take sides in the quarrel as to whether the image or the feeling state is the more original. They are presented together as indispensable for the description of the experience and so are dealt with as correlative.

Any phenomenology is experimental in character. It is an attempt to direct our attention to our experience. If the directions supplied are too vague or are imprecise, we will miss the experience. On the other hand if the instruments and directions are not employed—if the reader does not look in the direction indicated—it is not to be expected that the description will be recognized. It is clearly an experiment that can go wrong in a variety of ways. But it is one that must be attempted if we are to determine whether there are in our experience (understood in terms of the linguisticality of experience) those moments or occasions which may be plausibly connected to an expletive or predicative use of 'god'. The answer to such a question cannot be determined a priori but only by a disciplined attention to experience and language. I have sought to indicate the necessary instruments for this disciplined attention.

IV. The Application of the Model

We turn now to the application of the model of 'word-event' to our experience. We will consider in turn three fundamental regions of our experience within which we have reason to believe that we may find the kinds of radical experience-events which correspond to the model of a word-event. In each case our discussion will include

(1) a general characterization of the region as a whole;

(2) an analysis of the fundamental categories which together constitute its most basic structure;

(3) the isolation of those experience-events which may be understood to rupture the structure constituted by the basic categories;

(4) a description of these 'word-like' events in terms of feeling states and the basic root-metaphors corresponding to those feeling states;

(5) an evaluation of these 'events' in terms of our criteria.

Taken together these steps will be held to show that uses of 'god' derived from the discussion of 'word-event' function appropriately to name aspects of our experience that are available to us with no other precondition than our common participation in the linguisticality of our experience. It may be helpful to summarize briefly in advance the line of our argument.

The first region to be discussed is the ontological region of experience. This region is defined by the contrast 'whole and part' (or by similar contrasts of Being and beings, universal and particular, infinite and finite, etc.). Within this region there are two ways of experiencing the whole, totality or 'all' which meet our criteria for an expletive use of god-talk. These are the experience of the whole as ground (the feeling of peace) and the experience of the whole as abyss (the feeling of despair).

The second region (chapter seven) to be discussed is the aesthetic region. This is defined by the interplay of energy and order. Aesthetic structures are interrupted by the word-like experiences of awe, joy, wonder, and terror.

The third region (chapter eight) to be discussed is the historico-ethical region. This region is defined by relationships in time and thus by temporality and relationality. The structure of temporality is interrupted by the 'word-like' experience of the future as annihilation (dread) and of the future as advent (hope). The structure of relationality is interrupted by the word-like experience of the other as alien (abandonment) and as 'Thou' (love).

6

The Ontological Region

Much of our lives is spent attending to a seemingly endless succession of details. At home it may be taking the dog out, putting the kids to bed, washing the dishes, shopping for groceries. At work, whether working on an assembly line or in a hospital, a church or a classroom, our days are devoted to a series of routine tasks. Often the accomplishment of the routine may seem sufficiently rewarding—sometimes it does not.

Upon occasion we may feel the need to get some perspective, to assure ourselves that there is a pattern of significance, a thread of meaning in all of these brief encounters, these repetitive chores. Upon such occasions we may sit back and ask ourselves: what is it all about anyway? The question may seem urgent or ironic, desperate or a pastime but most of us do ask that question and in so doing we catch sight of or have already caught sight of that field of human experience which I want to call the ontological region.

On such occasions we are not, I think, asking for just any kind of 'meaning' covering this or that activity but for a particular kind of meaning—namely the most general possible meaning.

Another example: I come home from a long day at work; someone has set before me a good meal. I smile at my spouse—and feel that somehow *all* is well. Of course I couldn't mean by that—if I were to try to sort it out—that every detail of my life is in order, that my wife is perfect, or my students perceptive, or my colleagues appreciative, or my dog obedient. But neither do I really mean that all it takes to satisfy me is a good meal and a friendly grin from my wife. Many are the days those things cannot even penetrate the gloom or anxiety with which I have cloaked myself. Rather, in and with this food, wine, and smile I have had a quite different sort of perception—namely that *everything* is well, not in particular but in general or at heart, or at bottom. Indeed there are times when the food is awful and my wife agitated and yet the same feeling may creep over me.

Another example: this time from Peter Berger:[1] A young child awakens in the night crying out against some nameless terror of the dark. The father (or mother) comes into the room and laying a hand on the brow of the child says: it's okay. *Everything* is all right. What sort of assurance is this? Is the parent lying to the child, or saying something true in some odd way?

Or take the case of the young suicide who leaves a note: I can't go on; *nothing* makes any sense any more. Again we have an assertion that attempts to cover everything—that is a statement about the whole. This time the whole is represented as nothing, as an abyss.

Now these examples all point to some perception or experience of the whole or the totality of things. They illustrate what I will be calling the "ontological region" of human experience. We must first give some attention to the character of this region and then determine whether it includes experiences which may give rise to expletive or predicative uses of 'god'.

I. Definition of the Ontological Region

The ontological region may be defined as that region of experience which adverts to the whole, the totality, the all. It embraces a basic contrast— namely that between the one and the many, Being and beings, the whole and the part, all (or none) and some, the infinite and the finite, the universal and the particular. Each of these ways of articulating the basic contrast opens into an entire range of philosophical disputes and syntheses. Our concern here is not with the philosophical structures that articulate this contrast, but with the sorts of experience which give rise to (among other things) philosophical or ontological reflection.

This is the first place to look for experiences that may give rise to god-language, since it is the region most often adverted to in discussions of the religious sense. Friedrich Schleiermacher, for one, has asserted that the specific character of religious sensibility is rooted in the intuition or feeling for the relationship of the individual to the whole, the totality.[2] Of course any such 'intuition of the whole' must depend upon the contrast between whole and part, the one and the many. By beginning at this point we link up with the Western philosophical tradition and with ways in which that tradition has permeated modern theology from Schleiermacher to Tillich.

In order to advance our discussion it is important to give some attention to the basic contrast which, by hypothesis, defines or delimits this 'ontological region' of experience. This contrast may best be understood if we concentrate upon the notion of 'the whole' or the 'totality' in a variety of contexts.

The first thing to notice about the category of the whole is the way in which it tends to designate 'more' than, or something 'other' than, a simple sum of parts. A 'sum' or 'collection' of parts is a notion clearly dependent on parts or 'particulars' and thus provides no basic contrast to the notion of part. A couple of illustrations of this may be useful here.

Many of us know the frustrating and/or intriguing experience of having to take apart some domestic contraption (my more ambitious friends do this with automobiles) to discover what ails it or what makes it 'tick'. There comes that moment when all is disassembled. No parts have been lost. But the sum of them is rather different from the whole that they once constituted (and will, hopefully, constitute again). The whole of the machine is different from (perhaps we would also say more than) the sum of its parts. If we concentrate upon a particular element in this 'whole' we see that its meaning is dependent upon the whole of which it is a part. This or that 'gizmo' is intelligible only in relation to its place (or function) within the whole of which it is a part. On the other hand if we misplace one or more of the parts we will be unable to organize the remaining ones into the whole. Thus the whole is dependent upon the part just as the part is dependent upon the whole, but neither is reducible to the other.

What is true of a machine may be all the more true of an organism (whether an amoeba or a frog or a human being). In biology an organic structure is a totality which, while immanent in the parts is not simply derivable from them individually or together. This "organizing" principle is that which gives the living being its identity and its integrity. Yet it is not another part (as a 'soul' or 'life') but the unifying structure: a unity which is other than the parts but inseparable from them.

These rather naive examples may serve at least to open up the question of the relation of whole and part. Among the issues raised by these examples are: is the whole simply the assembly of the parts or is it the principle by which the parts are assembled? In the case of the machine the 'whole' appears at first to be simply the clock or automobile as assembled. We would thus distinguish between an aggregate of the 'parts' spread out in the garage and the 'ensemble', the parts as assembled into a coherent (and functioning) whole. The move from aggregate to ensemble is, in this case, made by way of an 'idea' or 'vision' of the ensemble: a knowledge of the principle (chronometric or automotive) that determines the relation of the parts on the basis of the function of the ensemble. In the case of the machine this 'organizing principle' is separable from any particular aggregate or ensemble of parts. Thus 'parts' can be interchangeable between 'wholes' (I can replace a faulty carburetor) and some parts are not even specific to this particular kind of whole (nuts and bolts). In the case of nuts and bolts we might at first doubt that the part actually is dependent upon the whole. This would be a mistake. While such parts are not specific either to this whole (my Honda) or even to this kind of whole (automobiles) they are specific to a broader range of wholes (machines and structures that can be assembled and disassembled).

From these reflections come the following results. (1) The notions of part and whole are correlative, even though some parts may be independent of particular ensembles (interchangeable, etc.).

(2) We have found it necessary to distinguish, at least provisionally, between aggregate, ensemble and principle. In the case of a living organism the notion of an aggregate is an abstraction from the whole. That is, we don't 'have' an aggregate but only an ensemble. (The development of techniques of organ transplant, however, demonstrates the utility of looking at an organism as if it were composed of 'interchangeable parts,' while the resistance of organisms to such procedures demonstrates that we are dealing with wholes of greater integrity and coherence than the model of a machine would suggest.) In the case of organisms the distinction between the ensemble and the principle can be made in at least three ways: (1) taxonomically— what sort of whole (species) is this? (2) functionally—what is the function of the organism as a whole? (The theory of natural selection focuses upon successful reproduction: can it survive in order to reproduce, reproduce in order to survive?) (3) The organism is the coherent *integration* of its cells, systems, etc. In all of these ways the organism is 'more' than the ensemble, the whole is more than the sum or the unity of the parts.

We are entitled to wonder whether we are to understand the 'principle' as immanent in or as separable from the whole ensemble. In the case of the organism the integral coherence of the organism is immanent, the aim is extrinsic (propagation) to the individual organism but (perhaps) inseparable from 'life'. In the case of the machine or artifact, the principle is extrinsic to the particular machine. Let us call the derivation of the ensemble from the principle 'idealism', and the derivation of the (immanent) principle from the ensemble 'naturalism'. Biological models may be slanted in the direction of materialism, naturalism, realism (Aristotle, Feuerbach, Marx), while mechanical and cultural models may be slanted toward idealism (Plato, Kant, Fichte).

At this point a further issue develops. In both of our examples the 'whole' is also a 'part'. The automobile, for example, must be understood in terms of its integration into a whole system of transportation, a system itself productive of such cultural-economic phenomena as the development of suburbia, the cult of speed, the quest for autonomy, the disintegration of urban centers, and the energy crisis. The case of an organism, an amoeba, a bee, a tiger is similar. They cannot be properly understood save as parts of a wider, ecological whole to which they are adapted (or maladapted). Indeed looking at the matter in this way opens up a new perspective on the organism itself, which can be understood as an ecosystem harboring a number of quasi-autonomous organisms. Finally, the whole of 'technological culture' and the whole of natural ecology interact with one another in complex ways constituting reciprocal (and often antagonistic) parts of a further 'whole'. But what 'whole' is that?

This last reflection points us to the question of an "all-encompassing" whole, that is of a whole which is not itself a part. We certainly use a variety of terms for such an all-encompassing whole: world, reality, universe, being, even nature or history. We may, however, take an alternative step, and deny the appropriateness of the category of an all-encompassing whole. That is, we may seek to content ourselves with a series of expanding and contracting 'contexts' or 'horizons' in which units are always analysable into constituent parts themselves capable of further analysis, while wholes must always be understood as parts of still larger wholes and so on indefinitely. Developments in subatomic physics, in astrophysics, in microbiology and in the understanding of ecosystems may be used to illustrate this tendency (and the resistance to it)—the tendency to conceive of an open-ended series of transformations from whole to part. But this is only an apparent alternative. What is this open-ended series? By virtue of what is it a 'series'? Of what is it a series? The question of an all-encompassing whole persists. It can be displaced, it can be ignored. It cannot be silenced. Depending upon the way in which this question is raised and answered we may have to do with metaphysics, cosmology, ontology, or a meta-epistemology.

The distinction between physics and metaphysics, between science and philosophy, is thus determined at least in part by the oddity of the notion of an "all-encompassing whole." We may become clearer about this if we focus upon one aspect of this oddity, namely that the 'whole' to which ontology adverts is a whole of which the inquiring subject (like everything else) is a part. One way in which this oddity has been expressed is in the distinction between perception and intuition (or feeling) as modes of awareness. We would have to say that the whole of which one is a part is apprehended only through 'feeling' or intuition and not by 'perception'. We are using 'perception' here in a broad sense to indicate both conceptual (ideational) and sensual (sense perceptional) ways of relating a subject and an object. In either of these modes the character of perception is movement toward the isolation of the object from other objects and the distancing of that object from the subject of perception. For me to 'see' something I must isolate it from the field of other things by which it is surrounded and with which it might be confused; and I must disentangle it from myself: objectify it.

The situation is very different, however, when it is a matter of apprehending a whole or totality of which I take myself to be a part. As my way of being aware of the whole can only be 'participatory' rather than 'objectifying', so in a case in which that to which the subject is related is that within which the subject stands, there can be no question of 'perception' through distancing or separation. Here there can only be the intuition of the encompassing whole. It is in this connection that Tillich speaks of the unconditional awareness of the absolute or Schleiermacher of the sense of absolute dependence. What these have in common is the intuitional character of the epistemological relationship between the knowing (intuiting) subject and the whole or "All" of which it is a part.

An analogue to this distinction between perception and intuition can be found in Kant's distinction between the perception of the phenomena and the "thematic apperception" of the perceiving subject. The knowledge of the whole is like the knowledge of the subject: both cases involve a mode of epistemological relationship quite different from, even if dependent upon, the epistemological relation between a subject and an object. It was the recognition of this similarity between the sense of the whole and the sense of the subject which led German idealism (especially in Fichte) to conclude that they were identical. The subject and the all or absolute were identified as the absolute subject. Such an identification is thoroughly anticipated and elaborated in, for example, the Upanishads in which the self (atman) and the whole (Brahman) are religiously identified.

At this point it is necessary to recall the distinction, which we have temporarily suppressed, between the whole as ensemble and the whole as the principle of unity by virtue of which the ensemble is a (coherent, integral) whole. In the case of 'Brahman' we have to do neither with an incoherent aggregate nor with the assembly of parts into a whole (ensemble) but with that by virtue of which there is a whole. So strong is this distinction that it is possible to claim that the whole as ensemble is unreal, in comparison to the principle from which it is derived. In Schleiermacher we may notice a certain wavering between these two notions of the whole. The sense of absolute dependence is correlative to the whole but apparently not simply to the whole as ensemble (as some pantheists, possibly including Spinoza, might suggest) but to the whole as 'god', i.e. as that by virtue of which the ensemble is constituted as a whole.[4] Or in Tillich's case the distinction, perhaps not always carefully observed, between being (as generic all-encompassing whole) and the Ground of Being (that by virtue of which there is such a whole) may serve to illustrate this issue.[5]

This issue is complicated by the possibilities of considering this principle as intrinsic or extrinsic, as immanent (Greek metaphysics) or transcendent (medieval metaphysics).

This brief discussion indicates something of the character of the ontological questions that arise from the complex interrelationship of whole and part. But these questions are not solely abstract and theoretical. They are not only conceptual but also in some sense experiential.[6] We have already indicated one of the ways in which the subject is implicated in questions concerning the whole but this must now be expanded upon.

For the most part I think, we simply presuppose that there is a whole of which we are a part. This presupposition is at least a crucial element of what we refer to when we say 'life has meaning'. We simply presuppose the whole as an ensemble rather than as a mere aggregate. This presupposition can become problematic in the face of a sense of the contingency or questionableness of some part. After all, the part has meaning by virtue of its integration into a whole. But the disintegration of this connection may bring into question the 'meaning' of the whole.

The best way to elucidate this notion is perhaps in reference to Tillich's talk of "ontological shock."[7] This shock occurs with the recognition that this or that part of our world far from being "self-evident" and to that extent "necessary" might just as easily not be there at all—that it has come into existence and will pass away. One may experience this in relation to oneself—as in the recognition that one will die (mortality) or the recognition that one might not have been born (contingency). Now one may attempt to mend this rupture in the self-evident surface of things on the same level of self-evidence; one distracts one's attention from the rupture by pointing to something else on the level of the part. In terms of the illustration with which this chapter began, the mother distracts the child from the nightmare by producing a rattle. But when reassurance on the level of the part (distraction) does not work, the result may be a radical crisis in awareness. It is not that this or that seems arbitrary, contingent, mortal. The rupture in the surface means the questionableness of "everything." We may then ask "why is there something, anything, rather than nothing?" The experience of the contingency of existence raises the question of being-as-such. The experience of the contingency or arbitrary character of the part raises the question of the whole.

We have thus far identified the ontological region of experience as one that is defined by polarities such as Being and beings, whole and part, infinite and finite. We have focused upon the whole—part polarity as being most susceptible to intelligible analysis. We have seen that the apprehension of the whole is necessarily different in character than the apprehension of the part and that the 'intuition' or 'feeling' of the whole arises through experiencing the part as contingent, arbitrary, or questionable. When this way of experiencing the part is not eliminated by distraction on the level of the part, the question of the whole as such arises.

II. The Question of the Whole

Having described the ontological region of experience we are now in a position to attempt to identify more precisely the sorts of experiences-events within this region that might appropriately give rise to an expletive and predicative use of the term 'god'. I will argue that there are two basic and generic modes of apprehending the 'whole' which appropriately give rise to god-talk. We have seen that a description of such experiences will need to identify them in terms both of feeling states and of basic metaphors. Accordingly I will describe the first of these as the experience of the whole as 'Ground' or as 'Being'. This experience we can label 'peace' or 'ontological confidence'. The second will be described as the experience of the whole as 'Abyss' or 'Nothingness', which corresponds to feeling states that we can label 'despair' or 'ontological vertigo'.

Peace (Confidence) and Ground

The first of these kinds of experiences is at the heart of Tillich's theology and we can use elements of his thought to elaborate our analysis of it. In Tillich's thought the event of ontological shock directs the subject to a depth below the now shattered surface of things (what we have termed the ensemble). This penetration to the depth aims at the 'Ground of Being', participation in which gives the experiencing subject the "courage to be" in the face of the threat of non-being.[8] This participation in the ground of being, which Tillich also terms "the unconditional awareness of the absolute," or ecstatic reason, or 'essentialization', is a way of apprehending the whole that lies behind or beneath the surface structure of parts. The whole (Being) is experienced positively as grounding or rooting the parts (beings). This experience is necessarily episodic or eventful for Tillich since no *complete* overcoming of the split between Being and beings, essence and existence is possible.[9] Existence means to 'stand out' of Being into the threat of non-being. But the eventful experience of participation in Being-itself can provide the existing subject with the necessary courage to exist in the face of threat.[10]

A different analysis of this type of experience is provided by Schubert Ogden in *The Reality of God*. Here, following Toulmin and others, Ogden argues for the "reality of faith," understood as a universal "confidence in the final worth of our existence." Ogden argues that such a basic or onto-logical confidence is not only possible for all persons but is a necessary condition for human existence. In terms of our discussion we would say that such a confidence is rooted in the apprehension of the whole of which we are a part, as assuring or 'grounding' the meaning, worth, or importance of our existence. Such a confidence cannot be directed simply to another in a series of 'parts' but instead is directed toward 'the whole'.[11]

The designation that I believe may best describe that feeling of the whole which Tillich has called courage and Ogden has called confidence may be the term "peace" as used by Whitehead. In Whitehead's use, the term peace designates the sense that each part (actual occasion) contributes importantly to the meaning and value of the whole. It does so by way of its objective immortality—its being 'remembered' by God (the principle by virtue of which the ensemble is constituted as a whole) in such a way as to be 'available' for the further enriching of the experience of subsequent actual entities and thus of the world.[12]

The apprehension of the whole as 'ground' of the parts and their ensemble may be what lies behind the assertion of the mother to the crying child that "everything is all right." The effect of this 'ontological assurance', whether at the level of childhood reassurance or philosophic contemplation, is dif-ferent from the anesthetizing effect of an insistence upon preoccupation with the parts. In the latter case ontological shock (the nightmare) is displaced by a distraction which may either be soporific (a bottle, television) or frenetic (a rattle, consumerism) or some combination of these. In this way the rupture in the structure of self-evidence characterizing our "everydayness" is erased, elided, or ignored. In such a case no expletive use of god-talk properly arises.

Despair and Abyss

The second generic way of experiencing the whole is as abyss or void felt as ontological despair. Here the "ontological shock" that shatters the self-evidence of the level of the part does not "touch bottom" with a feeling of being grounded but instead opens into a sense of vertigo and bottomlessness. Instead of existence (at the level of the part) finding an anchor of security in Being (the whole) it is cut adrift. Beneath (or above) the level of beings there is Non-Being.

Ontological despair is therefore to be clearly distinguished from disillusionment, frustration, or disappointment at the level of the part or the finite. Despair is not a quality of the perception of the part but a quality of the intuition of the whole. Here, however, the whole is not "more than" but "less than," and devouring of, the part and the "sum of the parts." Despair is not relative but "absolute." It too is an "unconditioned awareness of the absolute" but here the absolute is "not-being" or "Non-Being." By contrast, disillusionment or disappointment are clearly "relative" and partial. They may be localized or "contained" without radically rupturing the structure of experience and language. But with despair our language halts and the structure of experience disintegrates.

Ontological despair constitutes a qualitative rupture in the structure of experience and discourse, and we are therefore obliged to say that the expletive use of god-talk is as justified here as in the case of ontological confidence or peace. Both stand in radical contrast to the surface structure of self-evidence which characterizes our everydayness.

This contention that despair is as "ultimate" as "peace" entails a rejection of the Western philosophic bias that insists upon the primacy of Being over Non-Being. This primacy is regularly assumed in contemporary discussions of the experience of "transcendence and mystery" (for example by Ogden). Tillich also argues for this primacy of the metaphysical level, maintaining that Non-Being can only be privative of, and thus derivative from, Being.[12]

Actually both Being and Non-Being may be understood as logically derivative in the sense that both depend upon the rejection of naive confidence in 'the way things are'. Both categories entail a suspension of the level of parts and their ensemble. Each constitutes a 'threat' to the superficial confidence in the interconnectedness of the parts. This is why some mystical traditions can be quite cavalier as to whether we designate god as Ground or Abyss, or that which is most real as Being or Non-Being. Of course semantically 'non-being' is derivative from 'being' but this doesn't take us very far. It may be clearer if we speak of peace and despair. Both depend upon (and challenge) the level of superficial confidence. We cannot argue that peace depends upon despair without confusing despair with the ontological shock upon which both despair and peace depend.

In contrast to Tillich, Langdon Gilkey does seem to recognize the radicality of the experience of the void[13] though he (wrongly in my view) equates this with the expression of Fate[14] and associates it with "contingency" rather than "ultimacy." This equates "ontological shock" with "despair," whereas I am suggesting that ontological shock is a transition from the level of the part to the question of the whole not yet an apprehension of the whole. The whole as Abyss and the whole as Ground are equally the 'aim' or the 'end' of ontological shock.

That the experience of the whole as abyss does give rise to god-language is seen in the mystical traditions of East and West, in poetic discourse and in the traditions of Buddhism. A variety of complex symbolic structures attempt to articulate the relation of Abyss and Ground, of Being and Non-Being. Some mystical traditions symbolize these as coincident, thereby stressing their common 'distance' from the levels of beings, particulars or existence. Metaphors of divinity such as 'conflagration', 'tiger' or 'storm' give expression to the negative apprehension of the whole. The symbols of the wrath or judgment of God also express the ultimacy of the intuition of ultimate or total negativity. In Buddhism the contemplation of non-being yields nirvana, a cessation of experience, existence, selfhood and language; this cessation is itself liberation or salvation from the level of participation in the finite and temporal.[15] In other traditions, the symbolic representations of radical negativity are separated and rigorously segregated from the symbolic representations of radical assurance. In this case an ontological or radical dualism may appear, as in the contest between God and Satan, Ahura Mazda with Angra Mainja, light and dark. Finally, the experience of the void may be figured forth as the necessary path to the experience of the plenum or Ground. Thus despair is a way-station on the road to faith (Kierkegaard, Tillich); the dark night of the soul the necessary path to the vision of God.

Thus we see that a variety of religious and poetic traditions confirm the assertion which I have made on phenomenological grounds, namely that an experience-event qualified by ontological despair is as clearly transcendent as is an experience-event qualified by ontological reassurance. Both legitimately give rise to the predicative and expletive uses of god-talk.

III. The Ontological Region and Linguisticality

Thus far our discussion of the ontological region has proceeded on the level of phenomenological description. We have described this region in terms of the question of the whole or totality and have indicated the feeling 'states' and the basic metaphors associated with the opening up of this question. We are now in a position to relate the ontological region more precisely to the 'criteria' that we postulated for the correct application of the notion of a word-event. These criteria—the generically human, transcendence and importance—will now be briefly reviewed and applied to this region.

The Generic

On what grounds can we maintain that the apprehension of the whole (felt as peace or despair) meets the criterion of the generically human? We have seen that these apprehensions receive a variety of expressions both religious and secular, and that they do not appear to be culturally provincial. Thus they are neither specifically religious nor specific to a particular cultural or religious tradition. Is it possible to go further than this, to claim that these apprehensions are not only widely distributed and independent of a particular world view but are also actually endemic to the human situation? I believe so.

That they are endemic to the human situation may be shown by relating them to what we have termed the linguisticality of human existence. It appears that the ontological region must be understood as an irreducible feature of our linguisticality. The interplay of part and whole is embedded in the character of language, composed as it is of parts (phonemes, graphemes, etc.) that combine to produce words, sentences, discourses. If these elements could not enter into combination (be parts of wholes) and be discriminated through a system of differentiation, there would be no articulation, no discourse.[16] The complex dialectic of part and whole is necessary to the existence of language and to the linguisticality of our existence.

In this connection we may recall the words of the 'Stranger' in Plato's the Sophist: "to rob us of discourse would be to rob us of philosophy."[17] What is at stake here is not only the existence of discourse as the medium of philosophy but discourse as the basis of philosophy. Indeed in this dialogue what threatens both discourse and philosophy is the misunderstanding of differentiation and distinction on the one hand[18] and of combination and relation on the other.[19] These are what structural linguistics has taught us to recognize as the most fundamental characteristics of language. Without detailed discussion of this point here we may nevertheless be struck by the association of philosophy with discourse and grammar at the origin of our philosophical tradition—a connection newly apprehended and radicalized in the work of Jacques Derrida.[20] To this we need only add the well-known tradition that philosophy begins in speechless wonder, subsequently articulated as the question: 'why is there something rather than nothing?', in order to confirm that what we have termed the ontological region is embedded in the fundamental character of our linguisticality.

But to exist linguistically, in this structure of relationships between parts and wholes, is to be exposed to the threat that the dissolution of the 'part' may call into question the whole, that is, expose us to 'ontological shock'. Precisely this is illustrated dramatically, or perhaps melodramatically, in the question of suicide, which Camus called the only metaphysical question. From the outside, suicide appears as simply a failure of nerve, a confusion of the part with the whole, an egocentric globalization of an only partial collapse. But where else than at the level of the 'part' can the collapse of the whole occur? It is precisely the disintegration of the part (systematically integrated let us recall in the ensemble) that is capable of raising the question of the whole, of producing ontological shock, of confronting us with despair—or its opposite. The interrelation of the parts constitutive of our linguisticality makes it possible for a partial disintegration to become global, for the structure of our linguisticality to be ruptured and for this rupture to be subsequently and partially appropriated into discourse through speech of ground or abyss, as ontological peace or despair.

It is important to be clear, however, that demonstrating that these experiences are implicated in the character of linguisticality and so are 'generically human' by no means establishes the necessity either of theism or of expletive or predicative uses of 'god'. In the first place we have not said that all persons must necessarily have some acquaintance with the rupture of this structure, and so apprehend the whole as ground or abyss, as peace or despair. In the illustrations with which this chapter began we noted that the question of the whole may be 'deradicalized' or deflected. We have simply maintained that these experiences are *available* to anyone on the basis of our common linguisticality—not that all persons actually have such experiences. Even if persons do have such experiences and are inclined to relate them to uses of the term 'god' (something by no means to be assumed) then our argument only goes so far as to warrant the expletive and predicative uses of 'god' in connection with these experiences—if the next two criteria are met.

Transcendence

The kinds of experience isolated in the discussion of the ontological region are determined by a rupture in the self-evident fabric of our language and experience. The structure of language and so of experience depends upon the interrelation of whole and part. But, as we have seen, the occurrence of 'ontological shock' disintegrates this interrelation and so ruptures this structure. It is in this way that we can maintain that these events transcend language. They plunge language into a crisis.

The fact that these events nonetheless do enter into and are 'domesticated' by language is not a cogent objection to this position. If these experiences did not enter language we would have no way of speaking of them, of drawing attention to them, of 'experiencing' them. Language is not silent about that which concerns it, about that which threatens or disrupts it. If the events to which we are drawing attention were outside language in the sense of being irrelevant to it, we should expect only silence here. But by naming these events as 'word-events' we have drawn attention to the way in which ontological shock concerns or bears upon and so affects language. They are, if our analysis is correct, symptoms of the trauma inflicted upon language by the dissolution of the self-evident interrelation of whole and part. In the face of this crisis language either speaks of the whole which exceeds (and thus relativizes) the ensemble of discourse or speaks of the dissolution of discourse in the anti-whole of the abyss. Both transcend and thus pose a crisis for language.

Importance

A word-event here is that which stands against language, that which is the 'other' of language. Yet it is the character of language that it exists to conquer this otherness, to suppress it, to bring it to expression. Language is the articulation of our desire for global mastery. It is the way in which we structure, appropriate, and seek to master all that confronts us. To the extent to which this is true, then, we can also say that language has as its true content and raison d'etre that which eludes language. This alterity is that which engenders and motivates language. It is that which, in transcending language, founds it. The renunciation of concern with this alterity condemns discourse to becoming "mere talk." "Mere talk" is discourse deprived of an object, it is the surface chatter that is the background static of our everyday life.

This can be expressed a bit more concretely. In chapter four I spoke of the relation between that which cannot be said and that which must be said. I indicated that the dilemma of language is that these converge upon the same 'that'. It is when something is of most importance to us that we discover this convergence. To avoid this dilemma is to renounce 'importance' in favor of the relatively safe, the self-evident, the superficial. Yet even this everyday 'talkativeness' is sustained only by the pretension that it speaks of something important. It is precisely in the piercing of this pretension that the structure of language is ruptured. The non-important becomes nonsense. Discourse crumbles. And from this silence, in confidence or despair, discourse begins again in poetry, philosophy, myth, or theory.

The word-event that ruptures the structure of the ontological region gives to this region its specific character. From that which ruptures this region comes the ontology of being, or of nothingness. Both contradict the surface structure of the relation of whole to part. Both arise from the collapse of this surface. Both seek to unveil the fundamental character of this surface. Despite the permanent crisis for language constituted by the apprehension of the whole as Ground or Abyss, as Being or Void, such experiences cannot remain outside the language that they call into question. Whether in metaphysics or poetry or a suicide note they come to expression in language and thereby alter, disarrange, and rearrange its structure.

7
The Aesthetic Region

In this chapter we turn to that dimension of our experience most overlooked by Protestant theologians in the discussion of the character of religious language and, especially, of god-language.[1] Whatever the reasons for this avoidance on the level of dogmatic or speculative theology, our phenomenological approach cannot stop short of an analysis of this sphere of human experience and expression in our search for word-events that rupture and found structures of our experience and so give rise to a predicative use of god-language.

Obviously the aesthetic region of experience includes all that we call "the arts," as well as our response to works of art. But beyond this we must also include here much that we call culture: the individual and social organization and expression of experience. More precisely, this region is constituted by the interplay of dynamic and form, of energy and order, an interplay that when maximized instantiates 'beauty' but which more modestly and typically is articulated within the polarity of the pleasing or displeasing, the arresting or the merely jarring. It will be necessary to characterize this region more specifically before moving on to an investigation of the 'experience-events' that rupture and found this region and which may give rise to a predicative use of god-language.

I. Discrimination of the Aesthetic Region

The 'aesthetic' is probably usually linked in our minds to the sensations evoked in us by great beauty or ugliness. Without asking, in the first instance, what is the beautiful or the ugly, it may be helpful to attend briefly to the sensations themselves. While there are no doubt many degrees and even kinds of aesthetic feeling we may provisionally indicate two types of aesthetic response.

We may remember that we have thrilled to a dappled landscape, a nobly aging face, a spirited animal, a graceful gesture. In contrast we may also remember that we have flinched or shuddered at jarring discord, a deformed hand, a vicious beast, a stumbling ballerina.

Is there in and behind these sensations that which has concern for us, which defines or constitutes our existence? Or are they merely the unimportant conventionalized twitches of the sensorium?

To be sure, our responses *are* often conventional, but this may simply mean that our thrills and shudders are patterned in conventional ways. But *that* we thrill and shudder—what is this?—what is the basis of this way of experiencing our world?

I believe that these naive aesthetic responses are, in varying ways, connected to the balance or imbalance of form and energy, of order and vitality. The coincidence of these contraries may produce aesthetic pleasure. Their separation (and the loss of one) may produce rudimentary aesthetic revulsion—the shudder. The development of these responses, the tutoring or altering of them—is often the work of the artist, and of the art critic.

With the help of the reflections of Paul Tillich we may more clearly define the aesthetic region as that region constituted by the problem of meaning and the problem of vitality.[2] In Tillich's language the problem of meaninglessness corresponds to the category of form, pattern, and order, the problem of "emptiness" corresponds to the category of dynamic, energy, and vitality.

The question of 'meaning' is the question of pattern, relationship, or structure. Thus the question of the meaning of this or that event is a question of how it 'fits' into a pattern with other events. If my friend scowls I may wonder, what does it mean? An answer to this question may be sought by inquiring, what is this scowl connected to?—is it for example connected to (caused by, referring to, commenting upon) his indigestion, my behavior, that of the dog, etc.? When we discover its 'place' and its primary 'relations' or connections, it is brought into a pattern: meaning.[3] The question of meaning may thus be understood as a question about order, pattern, and structure. Even questions of fundamental meaning may be seen in this light. Thus the naive forms of the question of the meaning of human life are "where do I come from, where am I going, what am I here for, what is my place (or importance) in the 'scheme of things?" These are all questions of order.

When this sort of question is pushed radically it becomes a question of order or pattern as such. Does anything make sense? Is there a pattern, is there any form at all or only chaos?

Linked to but not simply identical to the question of meaning is the problem of 'emptiness' (Tillich). Emptiness as an existential condition is to be understood as the felt absence of vitality, novelty,[4] or possibility. In confronting emptiness we are confronting the question of vitality. Is there energy, force, power, or possibility for and in me. To feel 'empty' is to feel drained, without possibility, without power, without spontaneity.

This may be the essence of boredom—the sense that everything is the same—nothing is new—and the frantic quest for novelty and sensation is but the reflex of this fear of and flight from boredom, repetition, the reiteration of the same, which admits of no spark or flash of possibility, of novelty, of surprise, of joy.

Meaning and vitality are closely linked to one another. When one says "I just can't go on" this is often linked to "there just doesn't seem to be any point" (meaning). Thus apathy (the lack of vitality) and anomie (the lack of form) interact and complement one another to produce what may be the characteristic malady of our age.

We may now return to our initial description of the aesthetic region. How are the thrill and shudder of naive and immediate aesthetic apprehension related to the questions of meaning and vitality at which we have been looking? Is it not the case that the sense of aesthetic pleasure sometimes evoked in us is evoked by precisely those things in nature or culture which present us immediately with an embodiment of form and vitality? And do not these things at an unreflective and spontaneous level embody or portray meaning and vitality, in union, not discursively but with a kind of presentational intermediacy?[5] And on the other hand can we not recognize in that which causes us to shudder a break in form or energy which opens up at our feet the gaping maw of emptiness and meaninglessness?

Between the level of immediate aesthetic apprehension and the more discursive and reflective level indicated by the question of meaning and vitality (and the corresponding anxiety about meaninglessness and emptiness) is the level of our everyday experience of this aesthetic region. It is on this level that we participate in the aesthetic as 'culture'. Culture is scarcely a discrete phenomenon and cannot be readily defined. Provisionally, however, we may say that 'culture' designates the constitution and ordering of the human life-world. This purposive organization may be expressed in a variety of ways, but perhaps most instructive for us is the way in which it is 'represented' in the creation of 'works' which command and focus our attention as 'works of art'.[6] These in turn may open up to view the typical ordering and rhythms of social organization which together constitute the culture of a particular group or epoch.

Whether at the level of immediate aesthetic apprehension or at the social level of "culture" the questions of energy and form, order and vitality, emptiness and meaninglessness belong inevitably together. For purposes of our present analysis, however, we may separate the issues of order (pattern) from those of dynamic (rhythm) in order to inquire how the questions of meaning and of "emptiness" arise within our aesthetic-cultural experience.

II. The Question of Order

The question of meaning (which, I contend, is a question of order and form) arises in the breakdown of the regular patterns of life and experience. We are all acquainted with the ways in which the interruption or disintegration of social structures may occasion an all too marked attempt to enforce such structures, to maintain them, and to impose them upon a social experience to which they no longer correspond. The emergence of totalitarian regimes in our recent history answers the hunger for the appearance of order that characterizes newly urbanized and industrialized people cut off from the traditional patterns of social organization.[7] Yet this apparent order all too quickly unmasks itself as a relentless nihilism crushing all orderliness and imposing the rule of arbitrary and relentless force for that of law and reliable structure.[8]

The question of order and thus of meaning may also be deflected into the struggle for technological mastery of events and world. But this too is readily unmasked as a consuming and ungovernable process destructive of unselfconscious and therefore reliable patterns and structures.[9]

These examples are only illustrations of the way in which the quest for reliable order may arise in our epoch. It certainly arises or has arisen in very different ways in other societies and epochs; for example, under the impact of cultural and religious pluralism in the Hellenistic world, or of political pluralism in ancient Greece.

The question of form and order may be deflected into other regions of experience; by abstracting from the reality of the concrete and particular into the ontological region of the 'all', or by displacing it into the historical region of the other and the future. In the first case—the deflection of aesthetic shock into the ontological region, the question of order is rendered superfluous by the abrogation of the reality of the particulars in favor of a totality or all. This Parmedian or mystical totality renders the question of order entirely illusory—for that which is to be thus ordered is taken to be "mere" appearance.

In the second case the question of order may be dropped in favor of some interrogation of the 'other'. This may take the form of a concentration upon the sphere of the intimate[11] (as in romantic love as the guarantor also of 'meaning'). Or, in the face of the incomprehensibility of events, this task of comprehension may be assigned to a 'wholly other' in whom is reposed confidence in the ultimate meaningfulness of existence and world.

In these cases historical and ontological reassurances are found for an aesthetic issue. When the question of meaning as the question of order is not deflected, however, it plunges into the radical interrogation of all structure to inquire whether if all structure only disguises a chaotic darkness or if there is instead an order which shapes, governs, and illumines.

Terror and Chaos

The radical questioning of order and pattern may disclose the negation of all order in the face of a primitive or chthonic *chaos*. This absence of order is not merely privation or absence but indicates the presence of a raging and ungovernable dynamic. However it is 'figured', this obliteration of order is felt as *terror*. Terror may be understood as the affect corresponding to dissolution, the feeling or sense of being overwhelmed.

The feeling of terror in the face of unchecked and all-consuming power is not an uncommon theme in religious history. While it does not seem possible to reduce all religion to an attempt to cope with terror, as Max Muller thought,[12] it is nevertheless clear that traces of this affection may be found in virtually all religious traditions. This is by no means restricted to the "primitive" religious sense of 'mana'[13] or to the special connection between the sacred and the obliteration of reliable structure in storm and natural catastrophe. In the religious traditions of ancient Israel traces of this terror in the face of chaotic power may be observed in the highly charged exclusion of sea, of wilderness, and of the realm of the dead. But even in this tradition, aspects of a chaotic and consuming dynamic may be appropriated into the character of the deity. So for example, Israel's God is not only the one who separates the land from the sea but also the one who obliterates the land, as in the flood narrative.

In the religious and post-religious traditions of ancient and classical Greece we also catch glimpses of a primeval chaos in the figures of the Medusa and the Furies. These appear as figurations of primitive chaos which lurks upon the margins of cultural and psychic order. When this ungovernable and order-destroying power is introduced into the midst of culture (as in parricide or incest) it must be appeased lest it engulf all stability.[14] Elements of this terror in the face of an all consuming power may also be found in the Indian figures of Kali and Shiva.

In our own more recent cultural history we may note the fascination of the romantic movement with the appearance of an unbridled dynamic that engulfs all order and pattern. In its extreme form this was welcomed or feared as the eruption of anarchic power and revolutionary nihilism. Rauschning has proposed that Nazism in particular and fascism in general should be understood in terms of this fascination with an all-encompassing nihilism.[15] One of the finest expressions and analyses of this terror in modern literature is to be found in Jean-Paul Sartre's depiction of the fallen chestnut tree in *Nausea*. The depiction of the terror of modern warfare is most striking in Picasso's "Guernica."

However figured, the experience of a radical or primitive terror in the face of an order-destroying power has the marks of a 'word-event'. It corresponds to the questionableness of order, pattern and regularity in such a way as to transcend all language-like cultural and psychic patterning. Despite this it is implicit in the patterned character of our experience and so is generic in character.

Adoration and Light (Doxa, Logos)

The radical questioning of order may, however, be encountered with a different word-like event, an epiphany of order as *Logos* or form, which tames chaos. Alternatively the epiphany of order may be figured as '*doxa*', the inbreaking of radiance, light, illumination. The connection of light and form is primitive rather than synthetic—for it is light that brings order out of the chaos of the night.[17]

The epiphany of order may be *felt* as *adoration*, a sort of wonder and astonishment and delight in the presence of unanticipated form. The faint echo of this feeling of adoration and wonder is experienced quite often in the moment of insight or illumination when unexpectedly some group of ideas or thoughts come together or fit.

The theme of the epiphany of order as light awakening or evoking adoration in the beholder is a common one in religious history. In our own Western tradition the cult of Apollo is a particularly striking example, to which we might also add the religious aspects of the Pythagoreans. The account in Genesis of the controlling of chaos through the word that creates light is but the most striking of the examples which could be cited from Judaism. The paralleling of light and Logos in John's Gospel takes up and develops this connection. Once again, however, this is not an experience that is only thematized in religion. It is also the governing image of that historical era which called itself, significantly, the Enlightenment.

The experience of adoration in the presence of the appearance of form as illumination has the character of a word-event. It too corresponds to the questionableness of pattern and is not reducible to any merely given or domesticated pattern and regularity. Indeed it is often said in the religious tradition that the appearance of 'transcendent light' is blinding, which suggests the impossibility of reducing this adoration to any simple reliance upon the self-evident patterns of culture. Plato's allegory of the cave aptly depicts the transcendence of illumined order to the everydayness of 'mere appearance'. Yet this everyday patterning itself 'intends' the fundamental order of which it is but the reflection. Thus the experience of adoration in the epiphany of logos/doxa transcends the distinction between secular and sacred, religious and profane.

The collapse of normally self-evident patterns and structures under the weight of the fundamental question of order produces a global crisis for the aesthetic mode of experience. Whether this collapse issues in the apprehension of order as demolished by an uncontrolled dynamic chaos (felt as terror) or as the epiphany of doxa/Logos (felt as adoration), the experience will resist assimilation into the everyday and self-evident patterning of experience. In either case the rhythms and routines of customary articulation are brought to a standstill in the face of that which cannot be simply appropriated by them. We know all too well the extreme difficulty imposed upon even poetic discourse by the challenge of effectively evoking such experiences.

Although the experiences of terror and of adoration transcend and rupture the patterning capacities of language they nevertheless are presupposed by this same capacity. We have seen that these experiences are not restricted to particular religious or cultural traditions but appear to be more or less universally distributed. This distribution is not merely fortuitous; it is produced by the universal human preoccupation with the ordering of the life-world through the use of language.[18] As we have seen, the question of meaning is a question of relation. Structural linguistics has shown that the capacity of sounds (phonemes) to become bearers of meaning (language) depends upon a system of differentiations. These differentiations (the difference, for example between a long and a short 'a') enable us to pattern sound in order to speak. Similarly the meaning of a word is determined by its location within a set of differentiations. Thus we may define a word by listing its synonyms and antonyms. It is a common feature of our experience with words that we may render them meaningless by repeating them rapidly. Try repeating the word "meaningful" aloud for perhaps two minutes! The repetition deprives the term of its context, its location within language, and it becomes mere sound. Our linguisticality, then, is deeply embedded in the activity of patterning and ordering. That this patterning and ordering may break down both within language (aphasia) and in the experience ordered or patterned by language is what makes possible the kind of aesthetic shock that takes the form of the questionableness of order as such. This is possible for us simply because of our linguisticality.

It is therefore appropriate to speak of the occurrence of the radical question of order with the corresponding experiences of terror and adoration as word-event, which appropriately gives rise to expletive and predicative uses of 'god'.

III. The Question of Energy

We have been describing the ways in which 'aesthetic shock' may produce the radical question of order, a question to which may correspond the apprehension of the absence of order or pattern in an uncontrolled and unilluminable chaos or, contrarily, in the apprehension of light and logos. Aesthetic shock however may be given expression in a different question, the question of energy, dynamics and power. We may sense our existence as a wearying repetition of "the same," in which the proverb 'the more things change the more they remain the same' becomes the threat of emptiness and impossibility. The echo of this question is regularly experienced in our day to day existence as "the-can't-help-its" or the "blahs." When it becomes more pervasive, we call this, significantly enough, "depression." In either case it is the experience of apathy, of helplessness and impotence.

This experience may lead to the radical questioning of force, energy, or possibility. When this occurs it no longer suffices to distract attention from the question of energy by pointing to limited accomplishment or movement on the level of the everyday rhythms of culture and language, for it becomes the question of a vitality which is really superior to or finally triumphant against the stifling entrapment of the repeated and the same. Aesthetic shock thus is the radical rupture of the language-like rhythms and regulated transformations on the level of cultural experience.

Awe and Law

The question of energy and of possibility behind the facade of only apparent change and of standardized movement corresponds to the possibility of a negative response—the apprehension of a mute and implacable *law*. This is order without energy, form without dynamic. It is the immutable. It is law as iron necessity, unyielding decree. It is order apprehended not as 'light' but as *law*.

These are all ways of figuring the experience of the cessation of possibility and movement. Perhaps the best way of saying how this is 'felt' is to speak here of breathlessness and of emptiness or, more traditionally, of *awe*. The term 'awe' is often used of religious feeling generally but it is here used in the much narrower sense still dimly conveyed by the adjectival forms 'awful' or 'awesome'. This sense or feeling was the subject of a good deal of eighteenth-century poetic meditation upon the implacable immensity of the Alps, and of the implacable law of nature reigning through the infinity of space. In 'religious' figuration this sentiment is allied with the majesty of God which grinds opposition to powder, the inscrutable but irrevocable will which determines destiny or, in Greek thought, with the irresistible decree of fate (Ananke). Unlike the form that is light, to which we have earlier referred, this form is "hidden in darkness," inscrutable, devoid of illumination. Together the imagery of the irresistible, the irrevocable, the unvarying and inscrutable point to the end, the final absence of energy, vitality, and possibility.

The sense of awe is word-like in character. It stands opposed to the language-like structure of *regularity* in that it utterly resists being articulated into a system. It is massive and unitary in contrast to the variety and complexity of system and structure. It is as different from structure as a block of adamant is different from a computer.

Yet this aweful apprehension of the negations of life and energy is latent in the cultural rhythms and action that operate on the level of language. It is latent in the character of our experience of variation as limited or regulated variation.

Joy and Spirit

The question of energy and possibility may also be aroused by the epiphany of power as *inspiriting* or making vital. Instead of being figured as *chaos*, energy or dynamic is figured as *Spirit* which makes alive, as the dynamic overflow of being that charges form with exuberant energy. This apprehension of dynamic as Spirit is felt as *joy*, as *joie de vivre*.

This experience-event is by no means restricted to the traditional religious and metaphysical contexts. We may detect a reflection of it in our ordinary way of speaking. For example we speak of a "spirited" horse, or say of some individuals that they "have spirit." We are speaking here, I think, of manifestations of force or energy that 'take us by surprise'. The mere sight of such surprising energy evokes from us an irrepressible smile or grin—the trace of joy. The ordinary and everyday, always threatening to become fixed, routine, and humdrum, is suddenly charged with energy and exuberance.

This experience in its most radical form is found expressed in different ways in various religious traditions. The Dionysian and Bacchanalian traditions of ancient Greece, for example, concentrate on this sort of experience in much the same way that the Appollonian traditions focus upon the perception of order as illuminating Logos. [19] In the Judeo-Christian tradition this kind of experience is focused in the language of the Spirit of God, which surges like the wind (Ruah) through the person of the prophet and issues in ecstatic utterance. In later Judaism this energizing Spirit is that which mobilizes "all flesh" (Joel 2:28). It is this Spirit whose fruit is joy according to Paul (Gal. 5:22).

The apprehension of life-giving power enters into the philosophical tradition of the West in the quasi-romantic philosophies of a life-force (Bergson) and contribute, under the heading of "creativity," to the cosmological system of Whitehead. It is especially interesting to note that Charles Hartshorne develops his *apologia* for 'process' philosophy against a backdrop of a critique of the concept of God as absolute. This 'absolute' is depicted by Hartshorne in terms reminiscent of our preceding description of the absence of energy in the awesome epiphany of order as immutable and adamantine law. [20]

In the aesthetic shock occasioned by the experience of change as the dreary repetition of the same, the radical question of energy, life, novelty is raised. Insofar as this questioning of energy or dynamic receives a positive response it is in the experience-event of joy in the surge of an energizing and exuberant spirit. This experience meets the criteria for a 'word-event'. It is generic in that no particular religious disposition is required—only the experience and question of change, movement or dynamic. Yet it transcends the language-like regulation of this change and dynamic in terms of rhythmic alternation or predictable alteration. It resists assimilation to language and culture, while at the same time engendering many of their most notable accomplishments.

The question of vitality is like that of meaning in that its radical formulation produces an aesthetic shock which is global in character. To be sure, this question can be localized so as to prevent its shock from becoming global, as it can also be deflected to some other, more secure, region of experience. For the most part these strategies will be successful. Where they are not, however, aesthetic shock occurs in such a way as to obliterate the self-evident rhythms of our lives. Whether in the joy that reduces them to triviality or in the awe that views them as illusory, these rhythms of our everyday life are ruptured and immobilized.

The rhythms of our life in the world can by no means absorb the apprehension either of the presence of vitality as Spirit or of its absence as Law. Yet these apprehensions and the radical question that engenders them are fundamental to life's becoming conscious of itself. Nothing more is required for this aesthetic shock than that life come to expression and thus to consciousness as rhythm. This it does most immediately in the speaking voice, its pitch and tone, its timbre and timing, to which our attention is most insistently drawn by the poetic devices of meter and rhyme. Our life awakens to speech in the songs sung over our cradle and in the sing-song melodies we utter long before we learn to speak. The final silence is surrounded by the ululation of lament and the litany of consolation. Perhaps even before it is speech and grammar language is melody and rhythm.[21] To voice or to hear this rhythm is to expose ourselves to its questionableness—to become vulnerable (even if we do not succumb) to the aesthetic shock of the radical question both of vitality and of meaning.

The question of energy is immanent in the rhythmic patterning of our life not only as the threat of its immobilization but also as the aim of its mobility. Whether to forestall the awe-ful apprehension of life-destroying Law or to celebrate the joy-ful apprehension of surging Life, speech is set in motion, in rhyme and rhythm. Though these rhythms become again the routine structures of our everyday they have their end and their beginning in the occurrence of word-events of joy and awe.

Here again we have discovered events which appropriately issue in expletive and predicative uses of 'god'. The expletive use marks the explosion into the rhythms of speech of the awe or joy which founds and confounds those rhythms. The predicative use of 'god' functions to certify the 'how' of this experience (transcendence, importance, immanence), indicating that the expletive is not merely decorative but the enunciation of a radical crisis in speech.

IV. Conclusion

The relations among the four kinds of aesthetic experience we have been describing are complex. My procedure has been to take in turn the question of meaning and the question of vitality. It is possible to arrive at the same results by asking—what is the radical character of order (resulting in the pairing of awe and adoration) and what is the radical character of energy (resulting in the pairing of terror and joy).

A different pairing of the same elements is also possible on the basis of the distinction employed by Kant[22] between the beautiful and the sublime. The translation of our analysis into these Kantian terms would lead us to say that beauty is constituted by the positive apprehension of form and dynamic (adoration, joy), while the sublime is constituted by what I have described as the negative apprehension of form and dynamic (terror and awe). Kant makes a further distinction between the qualatively sublime and the quantitatively sublime. Despite Kant's connecting the latter to the sense of the immense (a common theme of eighteenth- and nineteenth-century aesthetics), the distinction corresponds tolerably well to the distinction between terror and awe as I have described them.

The possibility of arriving at the same or similar results in a variety of ways strengthens the credibility of these results and demonstrates the unity of this region.

We will conclude this chapter with a few reflections on the relationship of the aesthetic region to other regions of experience. This discussion of word-*event* and linguistic *structure* has made use throughout of categories derived from the aesthetic region. This may reflect an ascendancy in our era of aesthetic modes of experience, replacing the ontological categories predominant in Greek thought and the historical ones predominant in the Judeo-Christian tradition. This ascendancy of the aesthetic could be attributed to the double-character of our epoch as one of increasing structuralization (bureaucracy, technocracy) and of crisis (revolution) all too often productive of the peculiar conjunction of anomie and apathy to which we have already referred. Yet such characterizations can be no more than very rough approximations. Certainly all three regions of experience are to be found in any culture or era or world view. Only the relative importance assigned to each is likely to vary and that rather subtly.

The aesthetic region seems to have been more strongly associated with ontological modes of thought than with those more closely identified with the historical region of experience. Traditionally this has been especially evident in the association of the question of Order or Law with that of Being or the Whole. There is, as well, a counter-tradition which links the question of Being more closely to that of energy and power. In the modern period this has been characteristic of romantic (as opposed to rationalist and classical) world views. More recently the philosophical work of Whitehead and of Heidegger and the systematic theology of Paul Tillich exemplify this close interrelation of questions of the whole with those of power. It is by means of such a correlation of the ontological and aesthetic regions of experience that the question of temporality (and thus aspects of the historical region of experience) comes to assume a more important place in philosophy (as, for example in Heidegger).[23]

These remarks are really no more than hypotheses for reflection—indicative of ways in which it is possible to make use of these 'regions' as heuristic tools for further inquiry.

8

The Historical Region

Much philosophical or natural theology is content to describe the ontological region and the experiences that articulate it as the basis for god-language. This is no doubt partly because so much of the philosophical vocabulary derives from this region: whole and part, being and existence, finite and infinite, contingent and absolute. This vocabulary *is* however often enriched by the terminology of the aesthetic region. Thus 'being' may be understood to designate the power or energy of part (existence) or whole (Being). Similarly the figure of order as 'light' or 'law' may play an important role in the philosophical vocabulary.

I. Description

But the philosophical lexicon with its characteristic appeal to the apprehension of the whole, of order, and of the power of being is always in danger of forgetting the arena of discourse and of experience within which we most often find the meaning and point of our lives. This is the sphere of our encounter with one another, and thus with time. It is the region of ethical and historical existence. Some preliminary illustrations may assist us in grasping what is at stake in this region of our experience.

We learn to speak by being spoken to, by being addressed. Often the first word we pronounce is a name—the name of Mother or Father. This name does not 'identify' the other but calls and claims. We learn to speak by learning to call out for the help, the love, the care of an other. Our first speaking is a summoning.

Very early in our education in language we hear words of command: Come. Go. Stop. Don't. We enter into the world of language by being addressed by another. This word of address gives to even our inarticulate behavior the character of an answer or response, of obedience and revolt.

We learn about the character of a promise. We learn to extract promises: "Will you take me to the movies? Do you promise?" Words of promise bind us to one another and give us a future. We say "I do" when asked whether we will commit ourselves to another person "till death do us part." The word of avowal is a word whereby we commit ourselves through time. The words that bind us to one another also bind us to time.

The name for this life together in time is history. Whether we are concerned with the fate of nations or perplexed about how we can promise fidelity for a future we can scarcely imagine, let alone control, we are confronted with history whenever we are confronted with the question of the other or the question of the future. As we shall see, these are not separate and unrelated questions.

What I will be terming the historical region of experience is defined by "relationships in time," just as the ontological region was defined by the categories of whole and part. It is in terms of personal relationships and temporality that we develop such historico-ethical categories as guilt, freedom, destiny, redemption, and condemnation. The two categories—temporality and relationality—belong inseparably together. Apart from these in combination there is no question of ethics and no question of history. For purposes of analysis, however, we will deal with them sequentially, turning first to a summary of "temporality" and then to "relationality."

II. Temporality and the Question of the Future

Our existence is an existence in time. For most of us, most of our experience of time is an experience of continuation, or of change in the midst of continuity. Viewed this way time is but the container and measure of our experience—a pattern or sequence without which we could not experience at all. As such, time constitutes a dependable structure within which our experience and language is ordered.[1]

But we may also be aware of a different experience of time. We may call this 'historical shock' or in this case 'temporal shock'. Time, instead of the homely house of our existence, becomes a question and a threat. Such a 'historical shock' is sometimes occasioned by retirement, or graduation, or by the recognition that 'nothing has changed' (therefore nothing will change, therefore there is no future for us). Whether out of boredom or in panic we may find ourselves asking—is there a future for me?[2]

The character of this trauma in temporality is such that we can have no assured basis for an answer. The extrapolation of the present into the future is precisely what is rendered questionable and thus cannot serve us. Of course we may try to reassure ourselves and one another on the level of the time we know—the past. We may remind ourselves that we have survived many "graduations" before, that other people have faced retirement with equanimity. We may even desperately shut out the question of the future by withdrawing into the past, through nostalgia, or joining movements for the 'restoration of the old order' or by approximating the gestures of infancy. But for many of us there are points in experience when the question of the future cannot be deflected into the past. The past to which we run for an answer to the question of the future may simply echo that question—as the past too discloses itself as a tomb which disgorges its prey "nevermore".[3]

When this occurs, it is no longer possible to take time for granted. The sequence of succession is no longer the self-evident structure of our existence. Our existence seems to depend upon having a future, but there is no temporal 'hold' on the future. I believe that it is at this point that a quest for meaning awakened by temporal trauma may relinquish the historical region altogether and subordinate it to the ontological region. Here the experience of the timeless (eternal) whole, or Being, serves to anchor the meaning of existence, partly by asserting the illusory or unreal character of time and thus the unreal character of the threat that time (as an uncontrollable future) poses. In my judgment this also occurs when temporality is 'transcended' by means of the category of the 'moment' understood as an "Eternal Now." Here, recoiling from time, the subject locates a privileged point in time—a present moment secured from the threat of the future and the imprisonment of the past. This point is "timeless" though it is "in" time. It serves as a kind of 'launching pad' into the equally timeless eternal. This way of reducing the historical to the ontological region characterizes much of the work of Tillich and Bultmann.[4]

But this deflection of historical shock into a quasi-ontological domain is by no means the only way to deal with the questionableness of temporality. Historical (or in this case, temporal) shock entails the radical questionableness of the future. There are, I believe, within the historical region itself, word-like events that correspond to this questionableness of the future and

so serve as the appropriate source within this region for expletive and predicative uses of 'god'. These may be characterized as the positive and the
negative termini of the question of the future. Briefly, the future may be
apprehended as advent and felt as hope, or apprehended as annihilation
and felt as dread.[5]

Hope and Advent

The positive apprehension of the future as advent in hope is to be distinguished from the confidence in time that operates within the given temporal
structure. It is this self-evident confidence in temporal structure that is
shattered by 'historical shock', which thereby raises the question of the future
in a radical way. It is to the question of the future as thus raised that hope
corresponds. Thus hope is to be distinguished from optimism or confidence.
Hope corresponds to the rupture of temporal structure, optimism to the
unbroken integrity of temporal structure. One way of expressing the difference between them is to say that in optimism I 'have' a future; that is, my
possession of a future is not in question. But with hope I do not 'have' or
possess or control my future. Instead the future 'comes' to me. It is an advent
that befalls me in such a way that while I cannot possess what I need (a
future) it is nevertheless granted me. The struggle to articulate this difference
is present in Paul's curious phrase "hope against hope" (Rom. 4:18).

The positive character of hope then is expressed in its correlation to a
future experienced as if it were given, granted or a gift. The future is an
advent, a coming, an arrival rather than an extrapolation or extension. Hope
then governs or 'restructures' our participation in time. The future is "anticipated" in the present either in terms of *contrast*—'misery gives rise to
hope'[6]—in terms of *analogy*—something is taken as a prolepsis of or down-
payment of the radical future.[7]

Corresponding to this sense of hope or 'hope against hope' are a whole
series of metaphors for the future as the advent of a transformed and height-
ened mode of existence. The images of the kingdom of God, the resurrection
of the body, the new Jerusalem and of Paradise have long played an important
role in the Judeo-Christian (and, in somewhat altered form, in the Islamic)
traditions. Secular examples abound as well in the West: Marx's vision of
final communism; the visions of the utopian socialists; even some of the
imaginings of "science fiction" have this character. The cargo-cults of the
Pacific and the ghost dance of the American Plains Indians also illustrate
this apprehension of the future as advent.[8]

The apprehension of the future felt as hope is then word-like in its contrast
to the self-evident structure of time (which is language-like). It corresponds

to a rupture in this structure and may both relativize (bring into question the self-evidence of) that structure, and 'found' or re-found the temporal structure. This last occurs by re-positioning the subject in time in such a way that the future (rather than past or present) becomes the basis for the relation to time.

Dread and Annihilation

The future may also be apprehended negatively as annihilation and felt as dread. Here the question of the future precipitated by the rupture in the structures of a self-evident possession of a future receives a negative response: There is no future for me, that which comes is annihilation.

This negative apprehension of the future as annihilation must be strongly distinguished from all forms of pessimism that function within the temporal structure, just as hope is to be distinguished from all forms of intra-temporal optimism. Both optimism and pessimism 'control' and 'domesticate' the future by extrapolating and extending past and present into the future. But dread, like hope, brings this structure of temporal management into question, thereby making extrapolation impossible. The coming of annihilation, like the advent of a promised future, shatters the temporal frame of reference.

The sense of dread in the face of the annihilation of the future refigures the 'meaning' of time. In the shadow of this dread the past may take on the shape of an inescapable determination toward annihilation. The past then 'pursues' the present, driving it toward the anti-future. The future may then be figured as the consequence of a past that dooms the present and the future. The temporal structure has become a structure of *guilt*[9] or, in the East, of karma. Thus the shattering of the self-evident structure of time moves toward the reconstitution of this structure under the sign of a guilty dread. The sequence of expectation becomes a sequence of doom, wrath, and judgment.

Corresponding to this feeling of dread we encounter again a variety of metaphors or images for the future as inescapable annihilation. The images of divine judgment, of the lake of fire, and all the paraphenalia of damnation play an important role, especially in Christian and Islamic (but also in some Jewish) traditions. Although the secular Western imagination is more often "optimistic" in tone, nevertheless the foreboding of apocalyptic catastrophe is by no means absent. Whether in the Malthusian anticipation of global starvation or the more recent (and even more overt) threat of nuclear conflagration we may readily detect the metaphors of dread. This dread receives expression on the level of pop-culture in the success of 'catastrophe epics', in the cinema and in fiction. Nor is this set of metaphors restricted to the

West, for in Hinduism and in other "traditional religions" we find images of a world conflagration not unlike those of the West.

The experience of dread in the face of annihilation is 'word-like' in its form. It both interrupts and refounds the meaning of time. As such it is an event standing outside the self-evident structure which it presupposes (no temporal trauma—no dread) and within which it 'occurs'. The experience of dread apprehends the future as a sentence of doom addressed to the subject in time, just as the experience of 'hope against hope' apprehends the future as advent and promise.

The Rupture of Temporal Structure

Hope and dread, promise and doom, advent and annihilation point to the end of time within the temporal structure. In them the sequence of temporal succession is radically undermined by the question of the future. The experience-events of hope and dread correspond to this temporal-historical shock to give rise to expletive and predicative uses of 'god'.

Neither the occurrence of hope nor that of dread presupposes a special religious, psychological, or cultural precondition. They transcend the dichotomy of the religious and the profane, the sacred and the secular. In this rather obvious way we may describe them as generically human. But this is true in a more fundamental sense as well. As Kant has shown, temporality is an a priori structure of human experience generally, and Heidegger has shown that this not only determines our experience of phenomena but is also determinative of our awareness of and concern for our own existence as such. Because this is so, temporal shock, the crisis posed by the questionableness of the future, is embedded in our consciousness as a possibility for us. Indeed the temporality of our existence is inscribed in the structure of language itself. This is strikingly evident in the way in which language orders time in simple and composite tenses (present, past, future, past perfect etc.) and in the universally narrative character of actual speech (narrative as the temporal distribution and interrelating of events, meanings).[10] The crisis posed by the question of the future and those experience-events which correspond to this question are possible for us simply because we are human. This of course by no means entails that the word-like events of hope and dread are actualized for all persons. As we have seen, the crisis posed for us by the future may be contained (prevented from becoming radical in scope) or deflected (for example, into what I have termed the ontological region of experience). Perhaps the most effective way of neutralizing the threat of temporality is to adopt a world view which maintains that temporality (and thus a fortiori, that which is a crisis for and in temporality) is an illusion. But such a defense only serves to underline the perennially threatened and threatening character of the temporality of existence. The temporality of our experience (Kant) and of our existence (Heidegger) ensure that temporal shock (the questionableness of the future) and the word-like events which correspond to this crisis are possible for us on the basis of our shared humanity.

The occurrence of such a crisis entails the rupture of the structure of temporality and thus is transcendent of that structure. The structuring of temporality by extrapolation, projection, or reversal is brought fundamentally into question by the apprehension of the future as advent or as annihilation. This breaking in of the future is at the same time the breaking up of this temporal structure. Thus we may speak of a word-event which lends itself to expletive and predicative uses of 'god'. This, of course, does not entail that we are obliged to speak here of 'a god' which stands behind, causes, or explains this rupture. We are here pointing to the quality, the felt 'how' of the event, not to that which, by hypothesis, stands behind this event. It is 'as if' a sentence of doom or a promise of advent is enunciated within and over-against the temporal structures of our experience, existence, linguisticality. Such a word-event cannot be contained within but only more or less successfully warded off by the temporal structures within which our everyday life is organized.

Yet the occurrence of hope or dread (distinguished, we recall, from all forms of optimism and pessimism) is not only the rupture of the structure of temporal extrapolation and control. It does not stand simply outside or alongside this structure but 'bears upon it'. It is a crisis in and for our language and existence. Though it eludes expression it also requires expression, even at the risk of trivialization into mere optimism or pessimism. Thus the occurrence of hope or dread has importance for language. Such occurrences are not 'local' but 'global' in character. We may even say that they 'found' discourse in the sense that they motivate discourse whether in the discourse of denial (time, and thus the threats one encounters there, is unreal) or in the eschatological discourse which typically contorts and distorts ordinary discourse.[11]

The occurrence of hope and dread, the apprehension of the future as advent and as doom thus meet our criteria of the generically human, of transcendence and importance. They are word-events which are appropriately given expression through the expletive and predicative uses of 'god'.

III. Relationality and the Question of the Other

We exist in relationship to other persons. Our language, customs, culture provide, most of the time, reliable structures within which we pattern these relationships. These patterns and institutions may so regularize relationships as to render them self-evident. Relationships then become a strict though ramifying system of exchange. One knows one's place, role and function and correspondingly knows what is to be expected from the other. Indeed it is precisely at the point of an analysis of 'kinship' structures, the most pervasive way of patterning relationships, that Levi-Strauss discovered the pertinence of the tools of structural linguistics for cultural anthropology. Relationships are patterned like a language.

But we may also experience our relationality quite differently. These structures (or conventions) may be experienced as inadequate, unreal, or arbitrary. In such a case we may have an example of historical shock. This means here a rupture in the structure of relationality. The self-evident systems of exchange become questionable.

People who have known one another for years, been married to one another, or lived with one another through many changes in circumstance may suddenly, in some action, word or gesture see the other as a stranger. The self-evidence of structures of relating is brought into question when in such a circumstance we are driven to say: "I thought I knew you" or "I don't know you any more." The possibility of such an experience always lurks in the interstices of our familiar ways of communicating with and relating to one another. The convenient conventions of relationality seek to assure us that we really do know one another, that we do understand one another. Yet this assurance is fragile—and we may find ourselves breaking through this 'crust' into the icy 'recognition' of its arbitrary character. Such a rupture in the structure of relationality may bring this structure as a whole into question: "Do I really know anyone?" "Have I (has the other) only been going through the motions?"

The rupture in relationality may precipitate a flight from the historical region into the ontological or aesthetic region of experience. For example, I may distract myself from the now questionable sphere of relationality by occupying myself with the objects of my world or with the reconstruction of a totality. Thus technology or philosophical (or mystical) contemplation may function to compensate for the ruptured system of relational exchange.

Or I may seek to 'contain' the rupture in relationality. In this case I may accuse the other of simply 'playing false' in the patterns of relationality, committing myself all the more vigorously to their maintenance and rein-forcement. In this way I seek to re-enforce my control over and possession of the other.[12] For it is precisely this control and possession that is brought into question through the historical shock—the rupture in the structures of relationality. The project of reasserting a questionable control over the other is threatened by any unconventional behavior which must therefore be excluded. Part of the horror felt by some Americans in the face of the "counter-cultural" movements of the nineteen-sixties may be understood along these lines. What these movements represented was an alternative convention or set of conventions for relational exchange.[13] But the very presence of such an alternative convention in the midst of our typical mores radically threatened the latter and thus posed the threat of historical shock to those who identified with these mores. Those thus threatened reacted to the "flower children" (often their own children) as though physically assaulted by them.

When the rupture in relational structures can neither be compensated for by preoccupation with some other region of experience nor be contained by a reassertion of the conventions of relational exchange, then the question of relationality is raised radically and unavoidably: Am I alone or am I 'really' in relationship to another? Just as the rupture in the structure of temporality raises the question: "Is there a future for me?"—so the rupture in the structure of relationality raises the question: "Is there one whom I know and who knows me?" Just as the question of the future arises at the point at which I know I cannot possess or control it, so the question of the other arises at that point at which I can no longer control or possess the other.

In this situation I may experience the other either as finally alien or as a 'Thou'. My experience may be one of isolation or of love, of banishment from relationship or as being granted (beyond all expectation) the presence of a true other. Let us briefly explore each of these kinds of experience in turn.

Abandonment and the Loss of the Other

I may experience the other as not there for me, as absent, as alien or as enemy, as one from whom I am finally estranged. My feeling then is one of isolation, banishment, separation or exile. It is an experience of loss, grief and remorse; the other, previously assured to me by the structures of relationality, is now lost to me in the rupture of these structures. My aloneness stands over against and is an expulsion from relationality.

This experience of radical loss of the other stands in contrast to experiences of loss regulated by the systems of exchange and relationality. Radical loss is 'uncompensated' and is thus undermines the system of exchange itself. Within the structures of relationality loss is typically compensated or regularized. The loss of attachment to the parent is compensated for by attachment to spouse or children and so on. Or in situations of great grief, consolation is provided by the community. Indeed much of the literature on 'grief work' which seeks to explain and assist the 'grief process' may be understood as a series of attempts to prevent loss from disrupting the structure of relational exchange. On these terms 'good grief'[14] is grief which is neither denied nor globalized but is 'worked through' in such a way as to reintegrate the person into the structure of relational exchange. In such cases the structures of relationality control (through compensation or consolation) these losses so as to prevent radical loss or expulsion from relationality.[15] But the rupture of these structures means that loss must be uncompensated and inconsolable. There is not an other who is there to compensate or console since the structures of relationship whereby others are present to me have themselves crumbled, leaving me alone.

In the radical loss of the other I too am lost, cast adrift, cut off.[16] Thus the grief is a double one—loss of other and of self. In the loss of the other I am abandoned and this abandonment also defines me. It befalls me as a sentence of exile and banishment which determines or conditions me as lacking what I need in order to be a self.

The sense of radical abandonment has played an important role in the religious imagination. Since the time of the eighth-century prophets, the threat of the abandonment of Yahweh's elect has been an important theme in the religious traditions of the West. This theme is focused with unequaled sharpness in Mark's version of the crucifixion, in which the word of god-forsakenness culminates the life of Jesus as the one sent and empowered by God. Reflecting upon this theology of the cross, Jürgen Moltmann has spoken of "God abandoned by God." The very different mystical tradition uses the metaphor of the "dark night of the soul" to articulate this sense of ultimate abandonment. For all its presumed secularity the modern period nevertheless may be understood as virtually presupposing this sense of abandonment articulated as the death of God (Hegel, Nietzsche). What is expressed by these metaphors, whether religious or secular, is the sense of a radical loss, absence, withdrawal, and abandonment. The sense of a radical (as opposed to partial and consolable) abandonment is possible for us not on the basis of a "belief in God" but on the basis of the relationality of our existence. The attempts to 'explain' the sense of radical abandonment either as the withdrawal of 'the god' or as the mythicization of some more mundane grief experience are in any case secondary to the phenomenon itself. Both posit something (God, the unconscious) that stands behind the experience. We are concerned, of course, with the experience and the uses of 'god' not to 'explain' but to 'express' the quality of the experience.

Love and the Other as 'Thou'

In the rupture of the structures of relationality I may nevertheless experience the other as there with me. The other is present as a Thou in and through the collapse of those structures which have functioned to domesticate and control the other. It is precisely in the loss of these systems of control that the other may appear to me as a true 'Thou'. This sense of relationship beyond the structures of control may be called love—the love of the other, the other as lover.

In this experience the structure of relationality may be restored not as a self-evident system of exchange but as a sphere of play within which persons 'play out' the love that is transcendent of the structures of relationality.

In order to make this clear it is especially important to see how this experience of love is qualitatively different from that structure of reciprocity within which we also may and do use the term 'love'. Within the structures of relationship 'love' signifies our attachment to another and the other's attachment to us. This attachment is secured within a structure of reciprocal roles and obligations. Where the attachment is asymmetrical we speak of longing and desire (I am attached to you but not you to me) or unreasonable demand and expectation (you are attached to me—but not I to you.) It is the function of structures of relationality (systems of courtship and marriage for example) to facilitate the development of reciprocal relations (even when these are hierarchical in character).[17]

Within this structure 'love' always designates a relationship controlled and regulated by reciprocity. These structures assure or reassure me that I know who the other is, that the other is grasped by me within this structure. This use of 'love' stands in contrast to its use to designate the sense of the other's presence and favor which lies beyond any possibility of control and regulation. In this last sense love shares with abandonment the non-possession of the other.[18] Both are experienced in the situation of historical shock which renders the self-evident structures of reciprocity, compensation, and exchange questionable.

Positively the experience of the other as a Thou is one of being found, of being recognized, and of being restored to relationship, through the unmerited (uncoerced, uncontrolled) favor of the other. The other whom I need but whom I cannot possess is nevertheless with and for me. Such an experience of another (a spouse, a friend) may as well be appalling as comforting for it resists domestication into a structure of exchange. The other who is thus with and for me is nevertheless 'beyond' me, outside my control. Love is here neither "cozy glow" nor "wild desire." Instead it is beyond mutuality and satiation. It gives life but eludes one's grasp.

This sense of encounter, of love which exceeds and also undermines the structures of reciprocity, has played a significant role in the religious traditions of the West. The faith of Israel is characterized by a sense of gracious election which exceeds any possible reciprocity (as perhaps most powerfully expressed by the prophet Hosea). Both Jesus and Paul speak of God as 'abba' and develop in parable and theological proposition a view of grace that always stands in fundamental tension with the reciprocal exchange structures of legality and morality. The ensuing theological perplexity concerning the relation between law and Gospel may be viewed as but the reflection of and upon this sense of gracious encounter. A similar sense may be discerned in the tradition of romantic poetry with its articulation of desire for and celebration of the favor of the beloved which can neither be coerced nor controlled. The Greek maxim, "it is a god when friends meet," further exemplifies this sense of gracious encounter felt as the occurrence of 'love' in the radical sense in which we have been using the term. But it is not only in these Western traditions that this sense of gracious encounter finds expression. The similarity of the Christian idea of grace to the Hindu notion of 'bhakti' as exemplified in the Bhagavad-Gita has long been recognized. Moreover, the tendency to use 'personal' images for deity may be related to precisely this sense of gracious encounter or radical love, but by no means functions here as a covert argument for theism as the belief in a person-like god. Ronald Hepburn has, I believe, shown the extreme precariousness of such a mode of argumentation.[19] We are concerned here with the character of the experience not with an 'explanation' which would advert to that which, by hypothesis, stands behind the experience.

Love, as I have been describing it here, is word-like in character. The structure (language) of relationality is broken open by an experience which makes nonsense of reciprocity and exchange, and which is therefore 'outside' or beyond these structures. Yet the occurrence of love presupposes these same structures of relationality, without which the question of the other could not arise. Moreover this experience of love refounds or restructures the system of relationality, transforming it from a self-evident system of exchange into a sphere of love. Love that transcends the conventions of relationship cannot exist without them. Without such structures I am left alone with a fantastic other. To abandon (renounce) the signs of love for the sake of the purity of one's love is to abandon the other and to be abandoned.

The Rupture of Relational Structure

Both abandonment and encounter correspond to the radical question of the other that is the crisis of relational structure. Both are word-like in contrast to the language-like structure of reciprocity and exchange. The crisis in relationality, the question of the 'Thou', are possible for us simply on the basis of the relational character of our existence. That our existence has this character is already clear from the linguisticality of that existence. Whether we think of language as a 'system of communication', or of discourse as dialogue and address, we are confronted with the co-inherence of linguisticality and relationality. The systems of exchange and reciprocity by which this relationality is ordered are themselves the only prior conditions for the occurrence of the crisis posed by the question of the other. In this way the question of the other and the corresponding sense of being befriended (encountered) or abandoned meet our criteria of the generically human. Once again we may remind ourselves that to say that these experiences are possible for us on the basis of the shared character of our humanity by no means entails that all persons have such experiences. As we have seen, the crisis in relationality may be contained and localized (and so prevented from becoming a true crisis) or it may be deflected into some other mode of experience (for example the ontological—in which the crisis of relationality is subordinated to the monological logos of the Absolute). [20]

Not only does this crisis in relationality (and the experiences which correspond to it) presuppose the structuring of relationality as a system of reciprocal exchange—it also ruptures and, in a sense, abolishes it. Both in encounter and abandonment the other eludes the structure of reciprocal exchange and renders it fundamentally and completely questionable. It is in this sense that we may speak of the transcendent quality of these experiences. Indeed it is remarkable in this connection that the radical sense of encounter and that of abandonment have similar consequences for ethics as the science of obligation. Dostoyevsky and Nietzsche draw the conclusion that the moral order is subverted by the death of God. Kierkegaard draws the same conclusion from the would-be encounter with God (in his reflection upon the story of Abraham's sacrifice/murder of Isaac). [21]

These experiences do not stand simply outside or alongside the system of relational exchange. Instead they constitute an ongoing crisis for that structure. They "bear upon" the structure. As the ongoing debate in theology concerning law and Gospel shows, the occurrence of encounter produces a kind of counter-structure which does not actually replace but stands in tension with the structure of reciprocal exchange and law. On the other hand, it is precisely 'encounter' that the system of reciprocal exchange intends or pretends to be about—as the ambiguity in the term 'love' makes apparent.

The occurrences of love and of abandonment then are word-like in character. As such we may say of them that they appropriately give rise to expletive and predicative uses of 'god'.

IV. The Unity of the Historical Region

Under the heading of the 'historical region' we have looked briefly at four kinds of experience-events, which are to the structures of relational exchange and temporal succession as the occurrence of 'word-event' is to the structure of language.

We must now turn to the relationships among these experiences and between them and the historical region of experience generally if we are to make good our claim that this is in fact a unitary region of experience.

It should already be clear that the feelings of abandonment and love arise from the questionableness of relational structures. They are experiences arising in response to the question of and quest for the other. Abandonment is the loss of the other, love is being found by the other. Similarly the feelings of dread and of hope occur in the context of the questionableness of temporal structures. The loss of a controllable future brings with it the question, is there then a future for me? The figuring of the future as Nemesis and as Parousia, as annihilation and as promised advent answer to the question of the future.

But is the question of the other bound to the question of the future? The way in which these questions are bound to each other and the relationship between their different 'responses' may be briefly indicated.

The experience of the future as annihilation and of the other as absent, stranger, or enemy belong intimately together. The sentence of doom which the future pronounces upon me is at the same time a sentence of exile and banishment. To be without the other is to be without a future. On the other hand, to be found or encountered by the other is to receive a future. In both cases (advent and encounter) we receive that which we cannot possess or control. But the connection between love and hope is still more intimate than this similarity of structure. The Anglo-Saxon word 'holpen', which means both hope and help, points to the intimate relation between hope and the presence and favor of another. The presence of this other gives me hope, that is, grants to me a future. The absence of another, however, means that I have no future save that of a sentence of doom. The presence together of an other and of a promised future is thematized religiously as 'salvation'. The absence of a future (the future as annihilation) and the absence of an other (abandonment) are religiously thematized as damnation.[22]

Similarly, the structures of relationality and of temporality coinhere. The system of exchange that characterizes the structure of relationality depends upon reliable expectation and extrapolation characterizing the structures of temporality. The control and possession of the future involves the control and possession of the other within conventions of expectation and exchange. Thus the historico-ethical world is a single though complex interweaving of structures of temporality and relationality. This historico-ethical world is challenged, shattered, and restructured by the occurrence of experiences of salvation and damnation which stand as the end of history (and of ethics).

It may be helpful to indicate how our discussion of the historico-ethical region links up to what is ordinarily discussed under the separate headings of history and ethics. Ethics may be understood either as the consideration of appropriate human behavior as regulated by the structures of relationality or as a consideration of behavior which incorporates into itself the rupturing and restructuring of those structures. In the former case we may attempt to reduce the prevailing structure to its most fundamental principle, which may appear as a basic or categorical obligation (deontological), as a calculus of pleasure and pain, as means to an end (teleological) or in some other way. When ethics attempts to take the rupture of these structures into account then a 'suspension' of the ethical in the first sense may be the theme, as in Kierkegaard, Nietzsche, or Bonhoeffer (to cite only a few examples).

The investigation of history may involve itself principally in the display of sequences and contexts and ramifications of persons and peoples within a self-evident temporal structure. Again we may find attempts to reduce the data to fundamental principles of explanation—whether teleological, economic, ideological or some other. On the other hand, this historical inquiry may eschew such an analysis of principles in favor of the data themselves, in the quest for a 'positive history'. In contrast to these approaches to history, which treat the structuring of temporality as self-evident, we may have historiographies which seek to include the rupture in the temporal structure. In this case history becomes drama either on the grand scale (epic saga) or on the perhaps more intimate scale of an analysis of the existential bearing of some event upon our (or another's) subjectivity, as with Heidegger and Bultmann—to cite the most obvious examples.

The disciplines of ethics and history are thus situated squarely within what I have called here the historical or historico-ethical region of human experience.

V. The Historical Region and the Other Regions

The mutual exclusion of ontological and historical modes of thought is a result of the tendency of ontological thought to regard history as belonging to the order of the part rather than to the order of the whole and so as being "less real". The ontological values of aseity and simplicity (being without relations) and of eternity (being without time) thus mitigate against a positive comprehension of history. This situation has seen remarkable modification in the modern period beginning with Hegel and continuing in the philosophical reflections of Heidegger and Bloch. In the movements of thought they represent, history is taken up into ontology, resulting in the mutual transformation of both. Of course it is possible to maintain with respect to Hegel and also perhaps with respect to Heidegger that the end result remains the abrogation of history in favor of a reconstructed ontology.

Despite the ambiguous character of this rapprochement between ontological and historical thought we may notice some intriguing connections between this movement and certain of its antecedents in the development of the doctrine of God. One of the tasks of medieval theology was the development of a theory of relations which would answer to the problem of establishing the intra-Trinitarian relations among Father, Son, and Holy Spirit. This question was historically focused by the debate concerning the addition of the *filioque* into the Nicene Creed. In Anselm's *De Processione Spiritu Sancti* we have an especially arresting example of the development of such a theory of relations.[23] This failed to become the principal concern of medieval ontology, however, because of the preoccupation (following Aquinas) with the investigation "of the one God" as the *locus classicus* of ontological inquiry. We may wonder to what extent Hegel's achievement may be understood as at least in part determined by the placing of the earlier theory of relations in the forefront of ontological reflection. This would mean that specifically Christological and intra-Trinitarian questions substantially shape Hegel's philosophy—a supposition greatly strengthened by various recent studies.[24]

But a theory of relations does not necessarily entail the introduction of temporality into ontology as its fundamental form. After all, intra-Trinitarian relations are (presumably) atemporal in their pure form, although they are displayed or actualized in time. Temporality achieves a more positive ontological status in Heidegger, for whom time is to be understood "as the transcendental horizon for the question of being."[25] In terms of the traditional theological categories we could say that this represents a shift from the immanent (atemporal theory of relations) Trinity to the economic Trinity, or from the "person" of Christ to the "work" of Christ. The ontology of Heidegger, and still more that of Ernst Bloch, is a soteriological ontology. This may account for the attraction which these ontological perspectives have for much contemporary theology. These are, and can be, no more than suggestions. They only serve to indicate that the relation of ontological and historical modes of thought is an open question, thematized in important movements within the sphere of ontology, and that this development has important antecedents in and consequences for aspects of theology.

But this interpenetration of ontological and historical regions of experience may occur also from the side of history. The articulation of historical experience may appropriate and transform the categories of ontology and aesthetics. This is especially clear in the case of an apocalyptic or eschatological form of historical experience, thought, and language. The question of the whole or totality is appropriated into an eschatological vision of apocalyptic consummation or totality. Similarly, apocalyptic language appropriates the talk of light (doxa) and joy from the aesthetic region to articulate its own vision of a radical future. Similarly, appropriation of the negative apprehension of totality (abyss), order (darkness, iron decree) and energy (conflagration, annihilation) are to be found in apocalyptic figurations of damnation.

Of greatest interest in this connection is the capacity of the historical 'imagination' to coordinate these diverse elements into its own articulation of an absolute future grounded in the advent of a promising or threatening 'other'. Thus apocalyptic, far from representing an especially retrograde feature of collective psychosis or of literal-minded credulity, is a 'work' of constructive intelligence by which an historical consciousness assumes responsibility for ontological and aesthetic apprehension.

It has been precisely by appropriating apocalyptic categories that ontology has been reconstructed as an ontology of the future in the work of Ernst Bloch,[26] as well as in the more theologically oriented reflections of Wolfhart Pannenberg. In a later chapter we will have occasion to reflect again on an apocalyptic discourse as the articulation of an historical word of address.

VI. History and Linguisticality

We have briefly noted that the historical region of experience and, in particular, the articulation of the rupture of historical structures, constitute a more fundamental penetration into the linguisticality of our experience than that occasioned by the rupture of ontological and aesthetic structures. The questionableness of the other and of the future is what engenders or provokes our speaking. The first words we learn to speak are a call for and a claim upon an other. Whether in delight or dismay we learn to call the name of another and, by calling, to claim the regard, the care, the help of another. Throughout our lives our most important utterances are of this type. For by the word of address and claim we commit ourselves to one another, speaking words of promise or threat, of command or revolt, of avowal or refusal. Even in the small talk of friends, acquaintances, and strangers our words convey not 'information' but the desire not to be alone. Words establish community before they 'communicate'.

Yet as we have also seen the question of the other is also the question of time and of the future. When I give my word I commit myself to a future that I can by no means control. When I pledge myself to another, a friend, a lover, a spouse, I venture myself, place myself at risk through time. Even when time is rendered in the past tense of narrative, it is, at least in classical narrative, the recounting of the future of a vow, of promises rashly or resolutely made, of betrayal or of fidelity. Narrative is set in motion by the words of promise and covenant—whether we think here of the vow of Agamemnon, the promise of Abraham, the covenant of Moses, the oath of Alexander or of Caesar, of the oaths which bind us to our nation's cause or our spouse's weal. By our word we commit ourselves to a future that is rendered by narrative in the past tense as the story of the vicissitudes of avowal.

The rupture of the structures of exchange and of extrapolation by which we secure for ourselves a hold upon the other and the future is that 'experience-event' which is most truly a 'word-event'. For thereby the most intimate and fateful character of our linguisticality is disclosed and rendered questionable. Thus the advent of the other and of the future beyond all possibility of control is the word of promise, while the abandonment and annihilation which threatens in the absence of future and other is the word of judgment. The word of promise and of judgment is no 'esoteric' word that can be confined to and rendered 'harmless' by religion. It is the word that echos and necessarily echos in every calling and claiming, promising and threatening, commanding and entreating, blaming and accepting utterance. It echos in every situation of concrete address whereby, however trivially or fundamentally, truthfully or deceitfully we encounter one another.

The occurrence of this event cannot be 'figured' otherwise than as 'voice' for it is the event of speech itself. The experience-event of the rupture of ontological or aesthetic structures *may* be figured as vision, as epiphany and 'revelation'; and precisely in being figured in this way provide the distancing and objectivizing that is the essence of speculation and of theory. Moreover, by this appeal to vision, ontology and aesthetics may secure themselves in that which 'appears' to stand outside of language and only incidently and inadvertently to become manifest as speech. But voice abolishes distance and the security of the 'objective' and the theoretical. Voice calls, claims, and so encroaches upon us and our 'world' in such a way as to summon us to an altered or shattered identity: "I pledge you my love"; "I don't know you any more"; "you are to blame"; "no matter what you are my friend." Here linguisticality is not incidental or external. It is the only possible site of word.

It is sometimes said that ours is the era of an emerging historical consciousness. By this it may be meant that it is an era in which we are discovering that our life with one another is no longer bound by the self-evidence of convention, that our life in time is no longer assured by the strategies of mere 'continuation'. Yet we cannot escape from the vicissitudes of an uncontrollable future by a leap into the 'eternal', timeless and unchanging sphere of the 'inward', 'upward', or 'downward' really real. Relentlessly we are being driven to accept responsibility for ourselves, for one another, for our time. The assured and self-evident identities in which we wrap ourselves are ceaselessly and relentlessly challenged as 'bad faith'. Certainly the philosophy of our own time from Heidegger to Sartre to Derrida turns us away from metaphysical speculation to face the call and claim of an altered and responding 'identity'. More recently Altizer has suggested that the sphere of art and poesis has, in our time, itself taken on the character of voice, which shatters received identities and calls us toward a new or transfigured identity.[27]

The question of whether or in what way our age may be characterized in terms of the emergence of an historical consciousness remains a vexed one. What appears incontrovertible, however, is that we are learning that our past cannot shelter us from our future and that our inherited language seems incapable of securing us a self-evident identity within a stable means of socially conventionalized relationships. With the 'discovery' of history and the re–sounding of the question of the future and of the other has come another 'discovery'; we have come to be suspicious and perplexed about language itself.

9

Experience and 'God'

In the last three chapters we have analyzed three regions of our experience, asking whether there are kinds of experience constitutive of each of these regions that have the character of a word-event. We began this inquiry into the linguisticality of our experience to determine whether there are aspects or 'events' of this experience that provoke or generate god-language generally, so as to determine whether there is here some point of contact for the uses of 'god' in Christian discourse. While it is not possible on the basis of so brief a discussion to maintain the theoretical exhaustiveness of the results of this investigation, it is nevertheless, I believe, relatively complete. The kinds of experience events which meet our criteria are as follows:

(1) *Peace* or ontological confidence, which is the apprehension of the Whole or totality as *Ground* or source of being.
(2) *Despair*, which is the apprehension of the Whole as an *Abyss* or a void.
(3) *Awe*, which is the apprehension of Order or form as fateful and stifling *Law*.
(4) *Wonder*, which is the apprehension of Order as pure *Light*.
(5) *Joy*, which is the apprehension of Energy (dynamics) as exhilarating power or *Spirit*.

(6) *Terror*, which is the apprehension of Energy as disintegrating *force*.

(7) *Dread*, which is the apprehension of the Future as annihilation or *Nemesis* or judgment.

(8) *Hope*, which is the apprehension of the Future as *Advent* of promise, or salvation.

(9) *Abandonment* (Grief, Dismay), which is the apprehension of the Other or Thou as finally absent or alien or of *Loss*.

(10) *Love*, which is the apprehension of presence of the Other as *Grace*.

This list summarizes the results of our inquiry into the experiential locus of 'god-talk'. Throughout, we have kept in view the linguisticality of our experience (and thus our experience of language) as the framework for our investigation. Throughout, we have attempted to identify the traces of the occurrence of a 'word-event' that ruptures the linguistic structure of our experience. In each case the events transcend the structure of experience; this structure is however the only precondition for their occurrence.

Accordingly we have maintained that the uses of 'god' most closely associated with these experiences are expletive and predicative. The expletive use of 'god' signals the rupture of the structure as an explosion into language of that which eludes linguistic domestication. The predicative use of 'god' identifies the 'how' of this experience which we have schematized by our criteria of transcendence, importance, and 'the generically human'. The predicative use of 'god' in conjunction with the expletive use has provided us with a 'line of sight' for identifying those events which are 'word-like' in character.

The model that has been elaborated in the last five chapters enables us to shed light on a number of questions generally brought together under the heading of 'God and human experience'.' In this chapter we will address ourselves to these questions in the hope of demonstrating the interpretive capacity of this model. Among the issues to be addressed are: the role of experience in religion, the experiential basis for a belief in God, and the appropriateness of the use of god-language to designate aspects of experience.

I. Experience and the Question of Religion

The preceding chapters have produced a description of word-like experiences that may found or provoke a predicative or expletive use of god-language. How are these experiences related to what may fairly be called "religion"? Throughout, I have maintained that such experiences are not themselves 'religious', but generic in character—that is, they do not entail or require prior commitment to religion. Yet it is also true that the initial reason for analyzing such experiences was the necessity of grounding or otherwise relating some kinds of religious assertions (Christian use of language about God) to our experience. The discussion of the previous pages makes possible and also necessary a more precise formulation of the relationship between such experiences and religion.

It is important, first, to distinguish these experiences from religion if our claim that they are generic is to be upheld. Part of the dilemma for contemporary apologetics is that our cultural situation is neither specifically 'religious' nor reliably 'secular' (chapter three). If we are to find some point of contact with our situation, then the experiences to which we turn cannot themselves be constituted by this distinction between religious and secular. The events that have been the subject of our discussion are dependent not upon a particular religious or secular orientation but upon ordinary and typical ways in which our experience is structured. Of course not everyone need have such experiences for them to be generic in the sense being used here. For most of us most of the time the ordinary ways of structuring our experience work relatively well—we experience no rupture. Even when such a rupture of the structures of our experience occurs it may be dealt with in a variety of ways. It may be ignored or forgotten—especially if there are no ways of articulating and thus maintaining its importance; that is, if the 'Word' does not alter or found our 'Language'.[2] If such experiences do found or re-found our language in such a way as to enter decisively into our ways of structuring experience, there are still a number of possibilities—not all of them 'religious' in character. For example one or more of these types of experiences may serve as the generative impetus for a philosophical position or be importantly focussed in the literary work of an individual. Examples of this sort are not hard to find. It does not seem fair without further ado to label these individuals or their works specifically religious. Many of us may have such experiences which we then integrate and interpret with language borrowed from our favorite psychology, philosophy, literature, or even 'folk-wisdom'. Does every difference in the way of doing this constitute a difference in religion, and are we obliged to persuade people who do this in ways *they* understand to be secular or even anti-religious that they are secretly really "religious"?

It is more helpful, I think, to reserve the term 'religious' for particular ways of valuing, articulating, and interpreting these events. The term 're-ligion' is notoriously resistant to attempts to clearly and persuasively define it. I have elsewhere proposed that religion be defined as the representation of the conjunction of the 'Sacred' in the world through myth (narrative), ritual, and symbol in such a way as to represent, orient, communicate, and transform existence in the world for a community.[3] For purposes of our discussion it may be most useful to say that the experience-events that we have been describing may be given 'religious' meaning when they are valued and interpreted in accordance with such a communal set of narratives and rites which identify them as the presence of the Sacred in the world.

This way of distinguishing these experiences from some possible religious interpretation of them is important not only to safeguard the integrity of the experiences themselves but also to safeguard the integrity of religion. No Protestant theologian has taken the experiential character of religion more seriously than Jonathan Edwards. His analysis of the 'Religious affections' remains the basic work in exploring and analyzing the forms of experience that are integral to Christianity, despite increased attention to this topic by contemporary theology. One of Edwards's most important, and most frequently ignored, contributions is the distinction between even the most basic 'affections' (experiences) and a 'religious' appropriation and organization of them.[4] For Edwards this distinction was crucial since the religious revival which he led had considerable success in evoking certain experiences which turned out not be 'saving' in the expected sense. The experiences associated with faith could be separated from faith. If the integrity of faith was to be maintained without sacrificing its necessary connection to vivid experience, then it would be necessary to distinguish between these experiences and their proper appropriation and formation. Edwards's work on this problem remains a salutary warning to any over-eager and self-defeating apologetic that effaces this distinction.

It is no less important to acknowledge Edwards's other major contention, namely that religion is dependent for its force and vitality upon this experiential base. We have seen that the value of our language about God has become deflated by the loss of a connection between our language and our actual or possible experience. This also has the effect that experiences which we no longer have a persuasive way of naming are simply lost to view or consciousness. Thus the religious life may depend both upon the power of experience and upon the ways of naming that experience. The loss of either of these contributes to the loss of the other. In the last five chapters I have sought to provide an account of those experiences which, while not themselves specifically 'religious' in character, are nevertheless often valued and interpreted in religious language. In the tradition of Edwards, Schleiermacher, Otto, and Tillich, I have sought to provide a kind of phenomenology of such experiences (or rather the outline of such a phenomenology).

But unlike Schleiermacher and Tillich and a number of contemporary theologians I have not identified these experiences as religious or crypto-religious. In this the present essay is more indebted to Edwards.

In summary, then, we may say that the list of experiences which have the character of a word-event is a list not of the religious affections but of what we may term the '*radical affections*'. These radical affections taken together as a set constitute a kind of '*anti-structure*' which is the ever-threatening 'other' to the linguisticality of our experience. This *alterity* (otherness) is inscribed in linguisticality itself as that which both founds and confounds it, as its end and its beginning. It is, as it were, the shadow of the mind.

It is this which has led others to speak of a "religious a priori" (Otto) or of religion as the 'depth dimension' of experience (Tillich), but these for-mulations are inadequate. They are inadequate first because by these for-mulations we are often led to suppose that religion is a necessary and universal phenomenon. This is simply not the case. It is not even the case that this alterity is universally 'experienced'—only that it is a universal *possibility* for experience. It is universal in principle but fundamentally atypical in experience.

While it may certainly be granted that religion may be understood as concerned with the sacred and that the sacred may be understood as a thematization of this alterity, it is by no means the only way in which this alterity is thematized nor is this alterity the only concern of religion. Religion is best viewed as a social phenomenon. In terms of this discussion we may view it as, in part, the representation through tradition, institutions, and corporate practice of these radical affections. But there are other ways in which these radical affections are represented—we may think for example of various forms of madness, of poetry, and even of many of the achievements of speculative philosophy. These are by no means to be confused with one another nor with religion. Yet on the basis of this model we are able to give an account of how these discrete phenomena are related to one another. They share at least the common concern with that which is 'other than' the everyday structures of experience. Each has its origin in the astonishment occasioned by the rupture of these structures and each attempts to reintegrate discourse with this astonishment. But they do this in characteristically dif-ferent ways.

Despite the distance that must be maintained between religion (and the Sacred) and the fundamental alterity of our linguisticality, the understanding of the latter does shed light upon the phenomenology of religion. The list of radical affections may, for example, serve as an instrument for characterizing particular religious traditions in terms of the prominence of one or another subset of such affections. Such a procedure would enable us to account for some of the differences between religions and for some of their similarities. Moreover we could distinguish between articulations of a religious tradition that seriously engage these affections and those which appear to ignore them (i.e., are more purely 'language-like'). Such a distinction would not provide us with a way of distinguishing "higher" from "lower" forms of religion (a bad habit inherited from the nineteenth century) since the distinction will cut through rather than between most religious traditions (Bergson).[5] A religious tradition that altogether ignored these radical affections or the events which are signalled by them would be unable to survive them.

Finally we should note that religion is not properly understood as merely a secondary elaboration of these radical affections or of the alterity which, together, they signal. As we shall have occasion to notice in part three of this essay, much religion is at least as concerned with structure as with anti-structure, with the everyday as with the astonishing. The experience of structure is at least as important to religion in general as is the experience of the rupture of that structure.

II. Experience and the Question of Theism

The discussion of the relationship between religion and the radical affections prepares us to deal with the question of to what extent these affections provide us with an argument for a belief in God. Much of the literature on the relation of god-talk to experience has attempted to build just this sort of bridge between experience and 'theism'. So the work of John Cobb, Langdon Gilkey, Schubert Ogden, and others use experiences of a particular kind as 'evidences' for the presence of that which is their source—a source construed on the basis of a revised theism.

I believe that such a move is mistaken or at least precipitous not only because of the unpersuasiveness of theism itself (see chapters two and three), but also because it tends to deflect attention away from the very experience-events upon which it rests and to ignore the variety of ways in which the language related to such word-events may work. The danger here is that we fall into a "fallacy of mis-placed concreteness." Put simply this means that we will deflect attention away from the actual and concrete (the experience-events and their qualities) to an abstraction which is postulated as lying behind (or above, or under) these. This abstraction is then objectified or reified as the real or actual; the experiences become merely episodes or manifestations of that which is real. What has then occurred is that the concrete, real, and actual is transferred from the experience to that which, by hypothesis, explains or causes the experience. Concreteness (and hence, reality) has been "mis-placed."

These radical affections may of course be assimilated by religious language as something like the epiphany of the Sacred. Similarly, Christian discourse may assimilate these word-events as 'Word of God'. But these moves depend upon the antecedent plausibility of the religious discourse itself since there are non-religious (and certainly non-Christian) ways of interpreting these events. The connection between radical affections and belief in God (or the Sacred or what have you) is necessarily indirect and complex. An analysis of these radical affections does answer the question: to what in our experience may our talk of god refer? It does make clear that religious language and god-talk do relate to experience. But it does not legitimate the claim that such experience *requires* religious language, still less 'god-talk' of a particular (Christian or quasi-Christian) type.

We may of course be persuaded that these experiences (or some of them) are best interpreted by means of a particular discourse. We may even be persuaded that this discourse is the language of Christian faith. But it is unlikely that the mere occurrence of such experiences will be cause for adopting this language—especially in situations in which a variety of other ways of interpreting these experiences is available, such as the situation of early Christianity in the Hellenistic world and of contemporary Christianity in the context of cultural pluralism.

Nor can we argue from the capacity for these experiences (the capacity is universal though the occurrence of the experiences is not) to a belief in God. In terms of the Christian theological tradition it would be far more appropriate to speak of this capacity as related to the *imago dei* rather than to the existence of God.[6] The capacity belongs to anthropology, it is a part of our constitution as language-using beings.[7] Thus neither in the occurrence of the radical affections nor in the occurrence of alterity that is their possibility can we find grounds for a direct conclusion to the existence of God.

III. Experience and the Question of 'god-language'

But if we cannot make the direct move from the radical affections to 'belief in God' what is the point of using god-language in connection with these experiences? I have suggested that such experiences *may* give rise to god-talk, most immediately to what I have described as the expletive and predicative uses of 'god' language. But what are the advantages or disadvantages of such a naming? How does such a naming function?

This may seem to be but a restatement of the question of the relation of these experiences to religion but such an assumption would be mistaken on two grounds. First, not all of the phenomena that we would ordinarily describe as religious have an equivalent for our term or concept of God. The spectrum of such religious phenomena ranges from relatively primitive forms of animism to the most sophisticated forms of Zen Buddhism. Secondly, not all ways of employing god-talk to name these experiences or to identify their source can rightly be termed religion. So, for example, Plato may use an equivalent to 'god' to name the source of the experience of the Beautiful but it would not be fair to say that Plato is proposing a new religion. At the other end of the scale we would not be justified in supposing that the frequent use of 'god' as an expletive could be taken as a sign of special commitment to a religious perspective or tradition.

Our present question is therefore different from the question of the relation of the experience to religion. Our question is how the term 'god' functions in relation to this sort of experience. I will first point to some functions of this sort of naming that are common to religious and non-religious uses and then consider possible religious functions. It will also be necessary to point to some liabilities of such naming.

At the most elementary level the use of the name 'god' in connection with experiences serves to designate their extra-ordinary character. In this way they are marked off from the ordinary levels or structures of experience which they rupture (and possibly found). This is true whether or not these experiences are positively valued. Even the simple use of the expletive 'god' (or more colorful combined forms) in swearing attributes importance to an event or experience even if the expletive is used to ward off or refuse the experience (as in the literal even if not typical meaning of 'goddamn').

Beyond this the use of the term 'god' in connection with these experiences may serve to indicate a positive valuation of them as constitutive or founding of the world of experience and discourse. Thus to say "it is a god when friends meet" is to ascribe a basic rather than ephemeral importance to that event. The use of god-talk here may serve to focus attention upon the constitutive experiences of life—experiences which might otherwise be missed, ignored, or left without effect upon the structure of life itself. The use of god-talk here then is a way of focussing upon values that are otherwise not obvious, a way of keeping steadily in view the ultimacy of what, all too often, we may lose track of or lose hope for. The way our tradition ascribes such importance to these experiences is to say that they are 'of God'.

A third function of the use of god-language to name these experience-events is to draw attention to their special character of standing outside the ordinary ways of structuring our experience that is, to assert their transcendence. Thus the use of god-talk here draws attention to the fact that these experiences elude the ordinary ways of patterning our experiences and occur in such a way as to "befall" us—that is come to us from 'outside' ourselves and remain 'outside' our world of ordinary discourse. This double character of transcendence is focussed by the use of the word 'god' or one of its cognates.

A related, though apparently contrary function of the use of god-talk in connection with these experiences is to point toward the integration of all our experience on the basis of these events. That is, the ordinary structures of experience are related to these word-like events so as to find their meaning and orientation in relation to such events. The use of god-language then serves to 'center' existence upon these events and to position existence within a horizon of meaning derived from them. Such a use of god-language is not necessarily religious. It is the common heritage of the religious (Judaism, Zoroastrianism, Christianity, Islam) and philosophical traditions of our culture (and others). It is important to notice however that this use of god-talk to structure our experience on the basis of word-events apparently contradicts the way in which the same language serves to designate the transcendence of such events. More attention will be given to this issue in chapter eleven.

Despite the usefulness of god-talk to focus upon the character of the experience-events we have been describing, it is also important to notice that such a way of naming these experiences may also confuse us with respect to their character. Having attended to some of the functions of god-language, it is also important to attend to some of its dysfunctions.

The principal danger of the use of god-language for naming these word-events is that it may tend to deflect attention away from our experience or to 'alienate' us from our own experience. This occurs in a variety of ways. First the god-talk used to name our experience may carry with it such idealized connotations that we may be unable to recognize our own experience in that which is so described. Thus if I use 'god' to name the sense of the presence of an other I may be led to suppose that the experiences thus named must be extraordinary in a way in which my own experience is not. I may then reserve 'god' to name 'mystical' experiences requiring a special religious orientation which I do not possess. Thus the very language that is invoked to draw attention to the importance of (my) experience ends up drawing attention away from my experience to an 'ideal' experience.

Beyond this there is the tendency of this language to focus attention upon the 'source' of the experience and thus, again, away from the occurrence itself. Our cultural associations with the term 'god' conspire to objectify or 'reify' our experience. More than a century ago Ludwig Feuerbach noticed and denounced this tendency of god-talk to dislocate our experience and to project the qualities of that experience onto the alleged source of that experience—i.e., 'God'. Thus in using god-language to name our experience we lose the experience.[8] Feuerbach's philosophical intention (not limited to his critique of religion) was to recover the priority of experience itself.[9]

This complex of difficulties can only be resolved by clarifying the variety of ways in which god-language functions—especially the relationship between what I have called the predicative use of such language and other uses, both philosophical and religious. Only on the basis of such a clarification will the analysis of our experience be able to under-gird our use of god-language without being obscured by the use of that language. This clarification will occupy us in the next several chapters.

At this point it is important to hold steadily in view the expletive and predicative character of god-language in relation to experience—resisting the temptation involved in that language or, indeed in any language, to abstract from the 'event' to that which stands behind it. We will be aided in this by the analysis of different language 'games' in part three.

That the expletive and predicative uses of 'god' serve to focus attention upon certain kinds of experience has the further implication that different ways of construing the concept of "God" will result in the highlighting of different experience-events. Just as these experiences become 'religious' by being interpreted through the symbolic system of some particular religion, so also these symbolic traditions may impose a certain selection upon these experiences in accordance with the way God (or the "Sacred") is represented in their mythos.

One example of this selective screening of the radical affections is the way in which religious traditions variously relate positive and negative affections. Some may posit an ultimate dualism in which the positive affections are correlated to a benevolent deity while the 'negative' ones are correlated to Satan (or a Satanic deity). Or the negative affections may be understood as not ontologically 'equal' to the positive but as merely 'privative' (as in Augustine's understanding of evil).

But the disjunction between negative and positive affections is not as self-evident as it appears. So for example, some forms of Buddhism value the experience of the totality as 'nothing' or 'Nirvana', thus appearing to reverse the Western valuation of totality as 'plenum' or 'ground'.

Other differences among religious traditions may be correlated with differences in the stress placed upon particular regions of experience. Thus the Judeo-Christian tradition stresses the historico-ethical region while the religious traditions of ancient Greece stress the aesthetic region as the primary locus of the divine and the quasi-religious metaphysical traditions of the West (Platonism) and of the East (Buddhism) lay greatest stress upon the ontological region.

Thus we may be able to distinguish different religious and/or metaphysical traditions by noticing the differing valuations and correlations of these radical affections.

IV. Experience and The Question of Monotheism

One function of the use of god-language to name the quality of some of our experiences is to unify the experiences thus named, to draw attention to the features that they have in common. This function may variously be construed as an advantage, in that it draws attention to these common features, or as a disadvantage, in that it may reduce their real diversity and even introduce a preference for one or another of these kinds of events to the neglect of others. If we are persuaded that god-language may be the most appropriate way of designating the quality of these word-events on the grounds discussed above, but we are troubled by the monistic reduction of the variety elaborated in the last three chapters, we may opt for a phenomenological equivalent of polytheism. If on the other hand we either unreflectively identify the use of god-language with a monotheistic tradition, or upon reflection are most impressed with the unity of these experience-events as a class, or with the primacy of one of the kinds of events described, we may be inclined toward the phenomenological equivalent of monotheism. A brief discussion of these alternatives is therefore in order if we are to know what sort of god-talk is warranted by our analysis of experience.

What is at issue here is the way in which the god-language we may employ to designate our experience also patterns that experience. This is the power of language which we noticed in chapter four. The question then is whether the god-talk we use is sufficiently flexible to account for both the unity and the variety of the experience that may occasion its use. Thus the question of choosing a monotheistic or polytheistic pattern is a question of which paradigm best represents our experience. This is not a question of the attributes of 'divinity' but of the attributes of our experience.

At first the 'mono-theistic' implications of god-talk may seem simply self-evident. For most of us in the Western tradition no other alternative seems available. To contemplate a radical diversity in divinity seems a retrogression to the long since superseded superstitions of antiquity or of contemporary 'primitives'.[10] Yet as even these reflections show, god-talk does not always and everwhere mean unity and identity. If it did we would be in the odd position of having to deny that polytheism employs god-talk.

A more phenomenological basis for stressing the 'oneness' of god-language (and thus its appropriate tie to monotheism) may be advanced however. The preceding analysis of experience has used a single set of criteria to isolate those kinds of experience that share the structural characteristics of a word-event. It is precisely that which they have in common which suggests the appropriateness of god-language in our linguistic tradition for naming these kinds of experience.

Despite the advantages of the monotheistic implications of god-talk, there are good reasons to suppose that precisely these implications have functioned to separate god-talk from our experience and to limit the kinds of experience associated with that language. Some years ago David Miller proposed that on account of these difficulties (and others associated with the theistic tradition as discussed in chapter two) it would be appropriate to opt for a kind of phenomenological polytheism.[11] This proposal, which has been discussed for several years, is not reducible to a simple cultivation of ancient religions or an atavistic reconstitution of 'paganism'; from a phenomenological point of view it offers considerable advantages.

Our analysis of three regions of human experience has produced a variety of experiences which do not seem reducible to one another. It is this irreducible variety that gives credence to a 'polytheistic' logic for god-talk derived from experience. A monotheistic paradigm for our experience tends to influence us to look only for one sort of experience (of 'depth', of 'presence', etc.) which will correspond to such a paradigm. Undeniably, the monotheistic bias of some who have attempted a phenomenology of 'religious' experience has led them to focus upon some one experience—for example the experience of the 'whole', as with Schleiermacher or Tillich—as correlative to god-language. Others have sought this experience in a separate region of experience—as, for example, Rudolf Otto's phenomenology of the holy. The result is to render the experiential connection to god-talk arcane. Only a frankly polytheistic paradigm seems equipped to expose the genuine variety of our experience and to relate this variety to our use of god-talk.

This tension between unity and multiplicity in our experience, including our 'ultimate' experiences, seems to be an irreducible one. If too much weight is given to unity, then the actual texture of our experience is lost; if too much attention is given to the multiplicity, then the common features may be lost as well.

It is at this point that something like a 'Trinitarian paradigm' may be of use to us. I do not mean that the doctrine of the Trinity is derived from experience or that there are 'vestiges' of the Trinity in our experience. For our purposes, the doctrine of the Trinity may serve as a paradigm for relating a unity of structure with a variety in experience without collapsing the one into the other. The doctrine itself was formulated in order to insist, against the monism of philosophy and the monotheism of Judaism, upon the irreducible variety of ways in which God is manifested in the experience of history and nature (three persons), while still insisting upon an unfragmented unity in the divine being. Translated into a paradigm for our experiencing of 'word-events' this would mean insisting upon the diversity of the kinds of experiences to which god-talk is related while insisting upon the unity of the experiencing subject and upon the unity of the 'class' of experiences which are appropriately connected with god-talk. What is crucial here is not so much the numbers of three and one (though that has guided me to a certain extent in discriminating regions), as the coincidence of unity and diversity. The use of such a paradigm would be primarily regulative; that is, it would function as a kind of rule to prevent the excesses of unitarian or pluralistic interpretations of our experience, without 'solving' the question of how unity and multiplicity can coincide. In this it functions negatively and critically in much the same way as the doctrine of the Trinity.[12]

V. Experience and The Question of Language

Raising the possible use of the doctrine of the Trinity as a paradigm for our experience reminds us of the aim of the present inquiry, namely to discover in our experience and in our language that which may serve as an analogue to or point of contact for the way in which god-language is employed in the Christian tradition.

The model that has been proposed in the last few chapters has been offered as an alternative to theism in an apologetic situation within which theism no longer functions as a reliable bridge between Christian discourse and a culture no longer specifically Christian in its language or presuppositions. For this reason no conclusions concerning the 'being' or 'existence' of God have been drawn from the experiences we have described. To go in that direction would have been to attempt to justify some form of theism as a bridge between human experience generally and Christian discourse.

Instead I have proposed a model for the use of god-language that is embedded in generic experience and does not entail a particular religious or metaphysical commitment to the 'existence' of God. This model has been what I have called the predicative or expletive use of god-language—

a use of god-language that signals the rupture of the structures of our experience and is therefore rather like swearing. I have argued that there are some features of our more reflective associations with the use of the name 'god' which make this term especially appropriate for designating these sorts of experience.

Thus far we have focussed our attention upon the experience of the subject. We have termed the rupture in the structure of language an 'experience-event' and a 'word-event'. We are now in a position to clarify this terminology. The "radical affections" signal the rupture in the structure of language. They are not themselves that rupture. Thus the lexicon of affections, like the corresponding lexicon of basic or 'root' metaphors, serves as a kind of index of this rupture. The affections are debris of this event and so are the trace of this event. Insofar as this event occurs within and against our linguisticality it is a word-event. Insofar as linguisticality is the character of a specifically human experience it is an 'experience-event'.

That the character of our experience is to be understood in terms of linguisticality does not mean that the only thing important about human beings is our use of language in the narrow sense. Rather it means that our use of language reveals an even more pervasive structure of our life. Thus Freud has been able to show that the unconscious is structured like a language, so that it is possible to decipher dreams, fantasies, hysterical paralysis and so on by understanding their 'linguistic' or 'language-like' character. Similarly Levi-Strauss has shown how elements of myth, ritual and social organization may be better understood as instances of a pervasive linguisticality susceptible to 'semiotic' analysis. Less technically we may speak of the language of dance or of music or say to someone "your actions speak louder than words." What is intended is the linguisticality of our entire experience.

Even when we find it difficult to 'put into words' our intentions, meanings, experience, they still have a linguistic character. This linguisticality will characterize all the alternative modes of expression we may choose as well as the body-language or even the dream-language that eludes our "choosing" or subverts it.

If we use 'Language' to designate the structured or patterned character of this pervasive linguisticality then 'Word' or 'word-event' will indicate the rupture of this structure. When this rupture is articulated within the structure of language as narrowly understood we have an expletive. When this is articulated as an event that modifies our existence, we have a predicative. If the term 'god' is deployed here it is deployed as an expletive or, subsequently, as a predicative.

Such an event generates a lexicon, a terminology, that serves to pinpoint its location or site within language. In fact we have a double lexicon: that of radical affections and that of basic metaphors. These are correlative. The list of radical affections is also a list of basic metaphors (peace-ground, hope-advent, etc.). The lexicon of radical affections designates the event as a modification of the subject. The lexicon of basic metaphors (light, law, etc.) designates the event as coming to or befalling or transcending the subject. Radical affections are an index of 'importance'; basic metaphors are an index of 'transcendence'. Both designate an event within our linguisticality which is possible on account of that linguisticality and so is 'generically human'.

Thus the question of experience is not a question of that which is somehow prior to or more basic than linguisticality. The question of experience provokes a more fundamental question of linguisticality. The question of the relation of 'god' to our experience is the question of 'god' in our language, our discourse, and so our linguisticality. So far we have seen that this question points to the rupture in the structures of linguisticality, and thus to expletive and predicative uses of 'god'. But there are clearly other ways in which this term functions in our discourse—both in the discourse of faith and in other discourses. We will turn to the question of the character of these 'other' discourses in part three.

Part Three
Theology as Grammar

10
The Problem

In part two of this essay we have focussed upon our experience of language as providing the clue to understanding the relation between 'god-talk' and the linguisticality of experience. This focus has required us to restrict our analysis of god-talk to two uses of 'god'—the expletive and predicative—as indicators of a crisis in the structure of our experience and so of language. This restriction has meant that we have continually had to distinguish these uses of 'god' from uses which are perhaps more familiar and which we have simply grouped together as 'nominative'. The distinction between predicative and nominative uses of 'god' entails that there are at least two ways (three, counting the expletive) in which 'god' is used in language. It thus entails the existence of importantly different "language games" (Wittgenstein).

It is to this issue that we must now turn in the clarification of the use of the term 'god'. This is by no means a purely contemporary issue, as we have seen (chapter one). The long history of discussion regarding analogy in the theological tradition of the West is but the most obvious indication of the persistence of this question. In our own era this question has been given a new basis with the emergence of various philosophies of language and in particular by Wittgenstein's famous musings on language in his *Philosophical Investigations*. It is from this treatise that the title of this final set of chapters is taken.[1]

The notion of diverse language games arises in response to the attempt of positivist language analysis to reduce all (meaningful) language to two varieties: tautological ($2 + 2 =$ four) and empirical (the ball is blue; the cat is on the mat.) The fact that discourse in which 'god' featured prominently could not satisfy either of these sets of rules for language use meant that it should be relegated to the poetico-ethical dust bin. Wittgenstein's approach is more empirical than this in that he proposes that we discover how language 'means' by attending to the ways it is actually used in ordinary (as opposed to "ideal" or positivistically reconstructed) language. When such a functional analysis is employed we discover that there are a variety of ways in which language is used and that these usages appear not to be 'mistakes' (incorrect tautologies or defective designations of matters of fact) but have a discernible structure and logic. In such cases we may speak of a particular 'language game'. Accordingly, some theologians have maintained that theological or theistic or religious language may be understood as just such an alternative language-game.

But what does this entail? Clearly we are not speaking of completely different languages. This is evident from the fact that the same lexicon is used—that is, the same vocabulary. In the case of religion, where some terms appear to be peculiar to its concerns (sin, apocalypse, etc.), we soon discover that these terms have been appropriated from far less specialized discourse and given (by particular forms of usage) peculiar meanings. Moreover, the superficial connective operations for the construction of sentences (grammar) also remain in force. Thus the rules of good English (or some other language) usually apply with undiminished force to a variety of such language games including, presumably, those which invite the attention of investigators of religion. It also appears that the canons of logical argumentation generally apply to a variety of such language games.[2] In these ways religious language appears to be much like a number of other ways of using language.

We may begin to get a clearer sense of what is entailed in the identifying a different language game if we look at a few examples. The phrase "My wife is five feet eleven inches tall" functions differently than the phrase "My love is like a red, red rose." The prediction "it will rain tomorrow" functions differently than the promise "I will still love you tomorrow." The notice in the newspaper that highway 80 is now open to traffic functions differently than the Governor's declaration "I declare this highway open." A correspondent's description of hostilities on the border has a different 'way of meaning' from that of a declaration of war on the part of the government.[3] Where we find systematic traces of a consistent difference in the use of language (promising, declaring, describing, etc.) we are justified in supposing that we have a difference in 'language game'.

But in order to make this claim good we must also discover the rules in accordance with which such a 'game' functions. It is on this basis that we will be able to know whether the game is being played correctly. Thus if 'promising' really is such a language game then it will be possible to discover whether in any particular case it is being correctly used (can I promise that it will rain tomorrow?). Even where it turns out to be formally correct it may turn out to be 'false' or falsifiable. The assertion "This glass is empty" may be correct formally (meaningful—as the positivist would say) but false. Similarly the phrase "I will love and cherish you . . . til death us do part" may be correct form for a promise but may go wrong in other ways (I may be faithless, we may grow apart, etc.). Thus to speak of a language game is not to absolve some discourse from regulation but to draw attention to the rules by which it is governed.

The rules of language use are called grammar. But such rules may lie at different levels. At the most general (and superficial level) grammar simply indicates the way in which sentences are properly formed by the combination of words in their various forms. These rules apply to all language games within a particular language (like English) with only minor variation (or "poetic license"). Similarly the rules that govern a particular language game may be termed a grammar. Thus to speak of religion as employing a particular language game is to raise the question of the grammar, the rules, of this language.

This question (or rather, set of questions) is the focus of the next chapters. We will be asking about the way in which 'god' is used in a variety of language games, about the relation among these language games, and thus about the rules that govern these uses and relations.

There has been considerable attention given by religionists to Wittgenstein's suggestion concerning language games. But all too often this has gone no further than to suggest that religion (or 'theism', or 'theology') uses language in ways importantly different from say, scientific, or philosophical, or 'secular' language and then to draw attention to some of the oddities of this language game. The distinction between religious and non-religious uses of language has too often contented itself with discussing certain symptoms rather than uncovering basic structures (or grammars). The most often cited symptom has been the use of 'god' or some equivalent term. Such discussions then go on to focus upon the oddity of this particular lexical item.

This approach to the problem is wholly unsatisfactory. It gets the inquiry off to a false start (1) because it focusses upon symptoms rather than structures, thus leaving the discussion of "god-language" without foundation in the fundamental character of language; (2) because the symptom chosen, the term 'god', is assumed without argument to be primary, thus covertly importing an entire range of theistic assumptions; (3) because it assumes without troubling to inquire, that religious language (or god-language, or theological language, etc.) is *a* language game, that the use of a single lexical item constitutes a language game.

No progress is possible on this front unless and until we have at our disposal a far more sophisticated procedure for identifying, discriminating and relating 'language games'. Moreover, any such procedure will need to take far more seriously the question of the relation of such discrete language games to the more fundamental features of language in general. Talk of the 'oddity' of religious language or of 'god-language' has often served to obscure rather than to clarify these issues.

To make even a beginning here we must attend to some important discriminations between god-language, religious language, and the language of (Christian) faith. It should by now be quite clear that there are a variety of uses of god-talk which are in no way 'religious'. The prominent use of 'god' by no means indicates a 'religious' use of that term. So, for example, the expletive use of 'god' or the use of 'god' to designate a metaphysical principle may only by virtue of confusion be termed 'religious'. It should also be clear that there is religious language which has no cognate for 'god'. We need only to think of the 'primitive' forms of animism or of ancestor veneration on the one hand and of the highly sophisticated forms of Buddhism on the other. The obvious but regularly ignored distinction between god-language and religious-language should immediately put us on guard against supposing that there is some one language game which employs 'god' over against 'normal' language which does not. The failure to notice this distinction stems, I believe, from the way in which the question of god-language has been subordinated to the extraneous issues of the atheism-theism debate in the Anglo-Saxon context. The simple conflation of 'religious language' and 'god-language' imports the whole paraphernalia of theism into the discussion, with its notion that religion amounts to a belief in God and vice versa.

A further discrimination is necessary as well when we come to the use of language to articulate Christian faith. Clearly this religious language does employ god-language. But it should be equally clear that it is not the language of faith only because and insofar as it uses 'god'. In chapter two I have shown how this distinction came to be lost with the emergence of theism as a particular form of the doctrine of God. We need not repeat that discussion here but we do need to remind ourselves of some of its consequences. There are uses of 'god' in Christianity which are not "theistic" (Trinitarian ones for example). There are theistic uses of 'god' which are not specifically Christian (think, for example, of the theism of Voltaire). Clarification of the oddities of theism may therefore not bring us very much nearer to an understanding of the oddities of Christian discourse. We may have here quite different 'language games'.

This brings us to the problem of focussing upon 'god-language' as the clue to the oddity of religious language generally or Christian language particularly. It is often maintained that it is the peculiarity of the use of 'god' which determines or governs the peculiar character of Christian "theological" discourse. This claim is plausible on two grounds. First, the etymology of "theology" suggests "language about God," therefore clarification of god-language is the first (and perhaps even the only) task of theology. Second, it appears possible to account for the odd use of other terms (sin, faith, salvation, etc.) on the basis of the oddity of 'god-talk' since they are regularly employed in some connection or other to god-talk.

This thesis is plausible but misleading. It is certainly true that in any coherent discourse the meaning of any of its terms is related to the meaning of the others. This is what is meant when in structural linguistics one says that the meaning of x (let us say a term like 'god') *is* its location in a system of differentiations. But precisely this entails that no one term is by itself "primary." This means that the term 'god' cannot be isolated from other important terms in the discourse (or language game). An understanding of 'god' that makes it irrelevant how this term is related to, for example, 'sin' is of no use whatever for understanding the language game in which these two terms (and a number of others) co-determine one another. The isolation of one term in a discourse cannot give us much insight into the discourse. It is indeed a complete violation of the most basic principles governing the use and meaning of language. It is as if we transferred the attributes of the 'being of God' to the term itself. Thus we are asked to believe of the term 'god' that it is without relations (simple, absolute), all-determining within the discourse where it occurs (omnipotent), all-pervasive, (omnipresent) in that discourse, and in any case not derivative from any other term or group of terms (aseity). Surely an odd sort of 'word-magic'! The use of the concept of a language game may be of great assistance in clarifying the use of 'god' in a particular discourse. But only if we discard the unjustifiable word-magic of supposing that the term 'god' constitutes 'the' language game which employs it. The rule we must follow is that it is not the use of the term 'god' which makes the discourse odd but it is the peculiarity of the discourse which gives the term 'god' meaning.

If we focus in the following chapters upon the various ways in which 'god' is used it will have to be in the context of giving an account of the language of faith as a whole. In the course of giving an account of the uses of 'god' we will, of course, come into contact with religious language generally (for there are religious uses of 'god') and with the language of Christian faith particularly (not only because Christianity employs god-language, but because our task is, in part, to show how it does). But even if we were to succeed in giving a relatively complete outline of the uses of 'god' we would not have given an account of the oddity of religious discourses or of the peculiar character of Christian theology. In order to accomplish this latter task it will be necessary to identify the structures or rules that govern the deployment of an entire complex of interrelated terms in each of the discourses within which 'god' occurs.

The task that lies before us is to indicate the principal ways in which the term 'god' (or its cognates) functions in language. This will involve us in identifying a number of different 'language games' whose 'grammar' will have to be indicated. We will restrict ourselves to usages and language games that have obvious relevance for Christian theology since our overall task (see chapter three) is to show how the Christian use of 'god' is related to more general features of experience (part two) and language (part three).

This talk of 'grammar', 'language game', and so on may seem rather forbidding until we remind ourselves that we are concerned with the most ordinary and even obvious (although often overlooked) features of language. At bottom our questions are rather simple: how does 'god' function in prayer, in proclamation, in philosophy? What are the differences between these usages? How does an understanding of these differences help us to 'know what we are saying', to avoid confusion and misunderstanding?

Unfortunately confusion and misunderstanding are not rare. Thus it is necessary to attend carefully to the use of language and to important differences between various uses. This is especially true for theology, even when it is specifically dogmatic or confessional theology. After all, heresy is defined as the violation of the rule of faith, and what is this but the rules governing the use of language to articulate faith? Even some of the most common 'pastoral' problems stem from confusion about the meaning (function) of language used to articulate faith.

In order to be of much use a theoretical framework for an inquiry into the meaning of 'god' in language must satisfy a number of conditions. We must avoid confusing symptoms with structures. The mere presence or prominence of 'god' in a discourse tells us very little. It is not the case that the presence of this term marks a different or new language game. Indeed we will discover a number of importantly different uses of language which employ this term. It is the language game that governs the meaning of the term and not the reverse. Thus we will have not some one 'god-language game' but a variety of these. In addition to the expletive and predicative uses of 'god', we will also attend to the use of 'god' to designate not the 'rupture' but the 'structure' (descriptive discourse) of language and thus experience. We will also have to take into account the use of 'god' to name the speaker (prescriptive discourse) and the hearer (ascriptive discourse) of an "address."[4]

The discrimination of multiple language games and thus of multiple uses of 'god' must also involve us in showing how these usages are related to one another. This will mean that we will have to be able to give an account of how misunderstandings arise through a confusion of one language game with another and to show how it is possible to avoid such confusion. It is not enough for language to be odd for it to constitute a discrete 'language game'. It must also be possible to show the rules that govern this 'oddity', which make it possible to discriminate between correct and incorrect "plays in the game." To be either 'language' or 'game' it must exhibit such regulation. What makes perfectly good sense in basketball (dribbling the ball) is nonsense in football. What makes good sense in metaphysics may be absurd in physics.

But we do not live in airtight compartments—particularly with respect to language. As different as they are we cannot suppose that metaphysics has nothing whatsoever to do with physics or that what we say *to* God has nothing to do with what we say *about* God. Thus an adequate theoretical framework will have to show how moves are made from one language game to another, from one use of 'god' to another.

Finally it is important not to lose sight of the relationship between god-language(s) and language generally. This is not only because we otherwise turn god-talk into a form of esoterica—but also because no theory of god-language that ignores 'language' can hope to be illuminating. In these ways the concern of the next chapters may be properly understood as an elaboration of "theology as grammar."

In the next three chapters it will be possible only to provide an outline of such a theoretical framework and occasional suggestions of the way in which its application may resolve certain problems. Yet even as a preliminary survey of the terrain it may serve both to provoke further discussion of the problems and to provide a perspective on the relations of the problems to one another.

11

God in Explicative and Meta-Explicative Discourse

The description of the basis of expletive and predicative uses of god-language (in part two) has stressed the episodic and eventful character of this use of language. I have maintained that such language is most clearly rooted in the event of the rupturing (and restructuring) of the structures of linguisticality. This direction of thought has been suggested by an attempt to take seriously the problematic of word and language on the one hand and by a consideration of the contemporary problematic of the 'experience of transcendence' on the other. The result of this direction of thought, however, is one whose oddity may be made most clear by comparing it with other ways of locating god-language within the range of activity of *homo symbolicum*. Put most abruptly: is not the most obvious function of god-language the naming and legitimating of the structures of experience rather than the breaking open of these? Doesn't the very phrase "god-language" properly suggest that the term 'god' belongs more to the structuring of language than to the rupturing of word-event?

The seriousness of this question may be seen if we review briefly some of the ways in which god-talk functions to name and legitimate conventional or traditional or 'normal' structures of experience and action. The study of the phenomenology of religion, especially as carried forward by Eliade and his school, identifies religion with the articulation of original structures and the legitimation of present structures through connection to a 'time of origin'.[1] The language about the Sacred, in this case, seems to name the power, order, or reality that resists the rupturing of the human world and restrains the forces of chaos. Of course Eliade also gives an important place to the hierophany, which is an interruption of the profane and ordinary by the sacred and extraordinary, but the weight of emphasis seems to fall upon the function of religion (and therewith, of the Sacred, and by extension of god-language) to name, legitimate and preserve structures.

Similarly Durkheim earlier identified religion with the social structure and power of the community as a whole.[2] This insight has been modified and greatly elaborated in subsequent analyses of the sociology of religion—especially under the impact of the sociology of knowledge, on the one hand, and the analysis of civil religion on the other. Once again religion and thus god-language has been principally identified with social, conventional, and traditional structures rather than with their rupture. This identification holds in many of the human sciences regardless of the attitude taken toward religion (apologetic, polemical, or 'descriptive').

In Christian theology as well the triumph over Marcion of a doctrine of creation and providence and the subsequent linking of these doctrines (via Stoicism and then Aristotelianism) to doctrines of natural law has resulted in the growing association of god-language with the legitimation and preservation of structures—especially ontological and social structures. This tendency has taken hold as a fundamental presupposition in the course of the emergence of theism sketched earlier.

I. The Explicative Use of god-language

These few illustrations are sufficient to show that god-language is not reducible to expletive and predicative uses of 'god'. If we are to give a satisfactory account of a god-language in general we must be able to account for the uses of 'god' that are analogous to 'language' as well as those which are analogous to 'word-event'.

It is essential therefore to relate the expletive and predicative uses of the word 'god' to its more generally structuring uses. In this second more general use of 'god' we find a close approximation to the function of language, in terms of our basic contrast of Language and Word. God-language is here employed to domesticate events into an over-arching structure or pattern of meaning. Thus, for example, in popular religion, the phrase "it's God's will" is most commonly used to explicate the meaning of an event (usually an unsettling or disruptive one) into a wider frame of reference, thereby lessening its power to interrupt the structure of experience. The event is made an exemplary case of the structure which it threatens to rupture. It seems appropriate to term this *the explicative use of god-language*. It is the use of god-language to explain or 'domesticate' an event by explicating its connectedness within a pattern of meaning sanctioned or legitimated by reference to 'god'. The term 'god', then, functions to evoke the explicative power of a given pattern or structure of experience.

The explicative (legitimating, structuring) use of 'god' may be discovered in three related kinds of discourse corresponding to the old stoic distinction between the theology of the philosophers (theology of nature), the theology of the state (political theology), and the theology of the poets (myth).[3] Together these discourses constitute the domain of a "natural theology" which, in the modern era, has been taken to be both an alternative to (deism) and, in some cases, a prolegomenon for (theism), specifically Christian theology (doctrinal, dogmatic, or confessional theology). A brief consideration of the way in which 'god' functions in these discourses will give us a better understanding of the explicative use of 'god'.

Natural Law and 'Nature's God'
The orderliness and regularity of nature, whether observed in the constellations of the stars or the succession of the seasons, frequently occasions an explicative use of 'god'. In the period of the rise of theism, this frequently expressed itself in the elaboration of cosmological and teleological arguments for the existence of God. In contrast to the expletive use of 'god' to mark the rupture of these regularities, the explicative use of 'god' functions to bolster confidence in these regularities. The 'laws of nature' are ascribed to a divine origin and guarantor whose supremacy insures their reliability and wards off chaos.

This is the usage of god-language that is perhaps most familiar to us and has already been considered at length in the discussion of the rise and fall of theism, in chapter two. Accordingly we may give it somewhat briefer attention here. The use of 'god' to account for and to render dependable the regularities of nature has contributed to making science, as the study of this regularity, possible. For without confidence in this regularity no such inquiry could be fruitful. As science succeeds in rendering this order 'self-evident', however, the need for god-language to draw attention to and secure this order diminishes. It thus becomes an 'unnecessary hypothesis'. Some (Ogden, for example) continue to argue that any confidence in regularity must have an ultimate ground and that god-language continues to serve the purpose of identifying or supplying that ground. This argument is not particularly persuasive. Indeed it can only become persuasive if the categories of order, law, rule, regularity are or become less self-evident than talk of god. This is by no means our present situation.

It is of particular interest to notice how talk of "divine providence" appears to reflect the tension between an expletive and explicative use of 'god'. Such language about providence appears most often to guarantee the regularity and regulation of nature and history. But it also functions to 'explain' the interruption of this regularity. Thus such an interruption is termed an "act of God" (most often in connection with a catastrophic event). This use of the language of divine providence to 'account for' catastrophe predominates in popular religious discourse, while the use of providential language to draw attention to regularity and order is more typical of 'academic theology'. Yet these apparently contrary uses of 'god' are related. Both use 'god' to account for or explain phenomena in the world. In fact when 'god' is used to account for a breach in the order of nature it suggests that the event only *appears* to be a breach but is in fact an exemplification of a (perhaps hidden) order, law, or pattern. In both cases 'god-talk' functions to insure against a radical break in the regularity and order of nature.

Civil Religion and Political Theology
Since the time of Durkheim it has been generally agreed that an important function of religious language in general and of 'god-talk' in particular has been to draw attention to and to sanction the social order without which a particular community or culture could not exist. This is exemplified not only in the so-called 'primitive' societies which Durkheim studied, but also characterizes the polity of republican and imperial Rome, the assumption of the divine right of kings, and the nineteenth-century alliance between Throne and Altar[4]; it is at the heart of recent investigations of the 'civil religion' of American and other 'industrial democracies'.[5]

Characteristic of this use of 'god-language' in civil religion is the use of 'god' to legitimate the given patterns of relationality and temporality. This contrasts sharply with the expletive use of 'god' to mark the radical rupture of these structures. Through the explicative use of 'god' these structures are sanctioned, and their power to withstand rupture is assured. Civil religion thus provides a kind of "social glue," which binds together competing interests and claims. In the American context, civil religion also serves to "bind time" (hold together past, present, and future) through such notions as "manifest destiny" or "the American dream," which are more or less secular equivalents of a more traditional doctrine of election. The explicative use of 'god' in civil contexts then focusses and legitimates patterns of relatedness (the sanctity of marriage and family and of group or national loyalties) thereby securing these patterns against the threat of their rupture.

This 'political theology' need not be simply conservative. It is quite possible to employ the language of civil religion to call for a reform of a given order which is perceived as 'disorderly' or as bearing within itself an "inner contradiction" that is the seed of its destruction. Thus movements of modest or even profound socio-political revision may resort (as did the American Revolution or the Abolitionist movement) to the same explicative use of 'god' to sanction calls for an importantly different social order. In this connection it is important to recall that the term 'revolution' itself has typically been employed (especially in eighteenth- and nineteenth-century political thought) to signify a return to a more 'natural' or 'original' civil order,[6] one more directly in accordance with the laws of nature and nature's God.

This last observation reminds us that civil religion and natural theology tend to supplement and reinforce one another. In the early part of the modern period (seventeenth and eighteenth centuries) civil religion seems to have been governed by the metaphor of "natural order" or "law." As we saw in chapter two this gave way in the nineteenth century to a more direct relationship between theism and the social and moral order, as the connection between theism and the laws of nature was weakened. Conversely the very notion of 'natural *law*' appears to reflect the application of a social or political perception to nature or cosmos. Thus the term 'natural theology' may be, and often is, employed to cover both of these kinds of discourse.

Poesis and god-language

The natural theology of the philosophers and the political theology of the state were classed by the stoics with the theology of the poets, whose stories of the gods were a principal vehicle for artistic expression and creation. The meaning and import of this poetical theology has been the subject of vigorous and long debate which it would be inappropriate in this essay either to rehearse or to attempt to resolve. We only propose the following observations.

(i) When the focus is upon the religious language of 'primitive' societies this language is typically assigned the function of referring existing structures and dilemmas to a "time of origin." The retelling or reenactment of the 'myth of origin' then serves to overcome the distance separating the community and its world from the "strong time" of the beginning. This characterization, familiar to all students of the phenomenology of religion, makes no distinction between the myths of nature and of society. All are part of a seamless fabric of myth.

(ii) If we attempt to employ the stoic distinction among natural, political, and poetical theology, the definition of myth as a narrative of beginnings will not assist us to make this distinction, since it characterizes all three types. The specificity of poetical theology lies not in its mythic form, which it may share with natural and political theology, but with its peculiar subject matter. One characteristic of these myths (especially the ones to which this stoic classification applies) is their depiction of the jealousy, the anger, the loves of the gods. These 'stories of the gods' offer paradigms of typical conflicts of emotion and desire: the contest with death, the quest for power and revenge, the loss or attainment of the object of desire. Thus the anthropomorphism of the gods is not an accidental or incidental feature of particularly retrograde myths and legends but is essential to their function; they serve to dramatize and 'regularize' the conflict of emotions in which our life is played out.[7] The transition from myth and legend to drama and thence to the literary poesis that is so important a part of modern culture represents a similar change in the ways in which this intra- and inter-psychic drama is represented. Certainly we must reckon with the fact that in this sphere god-language has been almost wholly replaced by an anthropocentric perspective anticipated by the anthropomorphic language about the gods.[8] That the fundamental themes and plots (myths) of poesis have survived this transition intact is shown by the way in which Northrop Frye can use the ancient mythic themes as a principle of classification for modern literature.[9]

To say that god-language functions explicatively in poesis is to suggest that it 'serves to normalize' the conflicts of desire by providing paradigms at the level of 'the gods' for these otherwise threatening emotions. Thus this use of 'god' in the 'stories of the gods' functions to defuse the threat to the psyche of a repressed and uncontrolled conflict of emotions. In this it may be contrasted with an expletive use of 'god' to mark the rupture of intra- and inter-psychic structures.

In the modern period the work of psychoanalysis has in part substituted for and in part rehabilitated the mythic language of poesis. Freud's development of Oedipal structures or of myths of the 'primal scene' and 'primal horde' to account for the conflicts of desire illustrates this rebirth of a mythologizing poesis in the context of the human sciences. With the subsequent designation of Eros and Thanatos as the presiding powers governing the intrapsychic process, a rather advanced stage of poesis is attained. If a re-mythologizing of psychic structures as a strategy for explaining (analyzing) and for re-ordering (therapy) has its root in Freud, then we may say that it comes into luxuriant flower in the work of Jung for whom all the old gods reappear, not from the heavens, but from the chthonic depths of the psyche. While many have hailed this reappearance of the gods as a 'point of contact' for Christian theology, it would first have to be established that Christian uses of 'god' have some necessary or positive relationship to the gods of mythopoesis and a fortiriori with the explicative discourse which both accounts for these myths and deploys that account for therapeutic purposes. I believe this approach is a dead end. I am inclined to suppose that Christian (as well as Jewish and Islamic) uses of 'god' entail a 'demythologizing' of the world, the state, and the psyche. The rebirth of what the older theologians called paganism is by no means a positive development from the standpoint of these religious traditions. This is especially important to recognize since there appears to be so much uncritical adoption especially of Jungian language motivated by the naive supposition that religiousness is *eo ipso* closer to Christianity than secularity. The result can only be the 'reverse apologetic' discussed in chapter three.

The use of the three-fold schema of natural, civil, and poetic 'theology' borrowed from stoicism serves to elaborate the ways in which god-language has often functioned to legitimate the structures of our life and to buttress them against the threat of rupture. This three-fold schema is *not* intended as a replica of the one which we employed to discriminate regions of experience in chapters five through nine.[10] Its function is not to carry forward that analysis but to show how in a variety of ways 'god' functions in discourse to structure experience just as 'god' also functions (expletively and predicatively) to mark the rupture of the linguistic structures of experience.

The Structure of Explicative god-language

Having explored some of the ways in which 'god' may be employed with this explicative or structuring function we turn now to a consideration of some of the characteristics of this use of 'god' and of its relationship to expletive and predicative uses of 'god'.

The explicative use of god-language is important not only because it is so apparently widespread, but also because it so clearly answers to a basic human need: the need for pattern, order, regularity. From the proverbs of ancient wisdom to the work of systems analysts, from the labors of astrologers to the speculations of sociobiology, human beings relentlessly search for and celebrate the regularity, rhythm, and order without which life veers over the edge of chaos. We have already seen how this may be understood from the point of view of the rupture of structure in the discussion of the aesthetic region of experience. But with the explicative use of god-language we are no longer dealing with the epiphany of doxa, which the ancient Greeks might have termed the appearance of Apollo, but instead with the sanctioning of a received order and pattern against its interruption and thus against the epiphany of doxa/logos itself. From the standpoint of our analysis of the predicative and expletive uses of god-language, it is difficult to escape the impression that the explicative use of god-language is a secularization (in the sense of a 'normalization') of god-language.[11]

This impression grows stronger when we attend to the way in which secularization increasingly renders this explicative use of god-language unnecessary or, at least, less compelling. Though even for Newton the laws of mechanical physics were evidence of God as Creator and Preserver, the effect of the discovery of these "laws of nature" had the long-term result of rendering talk of "nature's God" superfluous. This could only happen because the explicative use of god-language operates in the same way and in the same sphere as laws of nature. Thus they are capable of coming into conflict with one another as explications of the secular. That this is so can be seen in the steady retreat of this explicative use of god-language before the advancing explanatory power of science. It is this that has rendered the explicative form of god-language problematic as an apologetic strategem. The development of alternative modes of explanation renders 'god' redundant, a no longer necessary hypothesis.

It is not my contention here that the explicative use of god-language is no longer possible or somehow illegitimate. It may be that the explanatory force of science is exaggerated or that as these explanations become more arcane and their results more ambiguous additional and more compelling explicative structures including those which employ god-language may again come into play. Whatever may come to pass in this area, however, it is clear that the explicative use of god-language does not now have the requisite character or compelling power to make it useful as a first stage in rendering a Christian use of god-language intelligible; it cannot serve as an anchor for a Christian apologetic without necessitating the kind of moves I have described as a "reverse apologetic."

Despite the limitations of the explicative use of god-language it is both possible and important to specify more precisely its relation to the expletive and predicative uses of 'god'. At first this relationship appears to be one of simple opposition, but upon closer examination it becomes clear that the relationship is somewhat more dialectical.

In the first place we may notice that the explicative use of god-language presupposes and derives from the expletive use of god-language. It is the interruption of structure that brings the structure itself into view. The presence of a regularity or rule is highlighted, brought into focus, by the exception to or breach of that rule or pattern. (I take this to be the meaning of that singularly opaque phrase: "the exception proves the rule.") In this way the explicative use of god-talk depends upon and derives from the expletive or predicative use of such talk,[12] just as language as a structure depends upon the actuality of word.

At the same time the use of god-talk to identify and reinforce the received structures of experience has the function of warding off the possible or potential rupture of such structures. Thus the use of explicative god-talk serves as a buffer against the ontological, historical, or aesthetic 'shocks' that provoke expletive and predicative uses of 'god'. The explicative use of god-talk is in this sense antithetical to the expletive use of god-talk. This antithesis is not a simple opposition, however. The negation of expletive god-talk is dialectical in that it contains within itself the potency of that which it opposes. Thus the use of god-talk in civil religion sanctions the given structure of values in a society by reference to something outside that social order. The use of god-talk in this connection signals the fragility of the structure (it shows that it needs sanctioning) and thus preserves a sense of the threatened character of that structure even while defending it. The attempt to eliminate god-talk from civil religion (as in some forms of "scientific socialism") is, in part, an attempt to eradicate this latent threat to the structures that is preserved in the language of their legitimation. If this is so then we are some way along the road to understanding how such societies (that is, Marxist ones) render themselves relatively impervious to change from within.

If we stick to our example of civil religion we see that the use of god-language to legitimate social structures also keeps open the possibility of their rupture. This rupture is made possible by the ultimacy of the language used to legitimate the given social order. The very ultimacy of god-talk makes it possible to sense a disparity between the empirical structures and the god-talk used to legitimate them. Thus what is taken to be the point or basis of these social structures (the ultimacy represented by god-talk) is also the possibility of their collapse or rupture. In this odd way the rupture of social structures is also the point or basis of the structures themselves.

The relationship of explicative and expletive uses of god-talk reflects the relationship of Language to Word outlined in chapter four. While language and word are opposing terms, their opposition is a dialectical one in which language both opposes and presupposes, both prevents and anticipates the rupture of language by the word.

II. The Meta-Explicative Use of god-language

The discussion of the relationship of expletive or predicative to explicative or nominative uses of god-language does not yet clarify the role and function of god-language in philosophical and especially metaphysical systems of thought. This is a use of god-language that has greatly affected Western intellectual history and it continually offers suggestive insights for the development of natural theologies whether of an apologetic character or not. It is obviously impossible in this essay to survey all the ways in which this language is employed in metaphysical systems. Instead I will offer some general observations concerning the relationship of the metaphysical use of 'god' to the way in which god-language is employed in expletive and explicative languages.

The metaphysical use of 'god' may be best understood, I believe, as meta-explicative language. While explicative language uses god-talk to 'explain' an event in terms of a structure or to 'explain' a structure, the meta-explicative use of this language seeks to illuminate the principle, or 'prove' the possibility of, explanation itself. In an explicative context 'god' functions to 'explain' an event or structure; in a meta-explicative context 'god' functions to 'explain' explanation. This hypothesis concerning a meta-physical use of god-language as meta-explicative becomes plausible when we attend to particular features of metaphysical language.

At least since the time of Aristotle the basic form of explanation in the West has been explanation by way of causation. Knowledge is identified, in this tradition, with knowledge of causes. The various departments of knowledge identify the causes of particular kinds of entities. Metaphysics, however, seeks to identify not particular causes but universal causes, not the fact of causation but the basis of causation, not a multiplicity of causes but the unitary character of causation itself. It is in pursuit of this goal that, Aristotle maintains, we come to 'theology', which investigates the cause of being *qua* being.[13] God-language is here identified with the "unmoved Mover," that is, with the uncaused cause. It is only by identification of such an uncaused cause that the principle of causation may be rendered fully intelligible in Aristotle's view.

Now to a great extent this inheritance from Aristotle determines the character of god-language, insofar as it occupies the crucial and central role in the explanation of cause. Thus proofs for the existence of God, especially those of Aquinas, may best be understood as proofs of the necessity and reality of the principle of causation itself.[14] We have then the following progression: the sciences explain by identifying causes, philosophy establishes the character of causation, "first philosophy" or metaphysics establishes the necessity and reality of causation as such. God-language functions as a meta-explication of the dominant mode of explication, in this case, causation.

This progression helps to clarify some of the peculiarities of this metaphysical or, more generally, meta-explicative use of god-talk. The so-called proofs for the existence of God serve to identify and establish the antecedent conditions of knowledge. They do not add some additional datum of knowledge but establish knowledge itself. This accounts for the 'emptiness' of such proofs. Even if we find the logic of such proofs compelling we may wonder about the object of such proofs. The 'God' whose existence has been 'established' seems to be devoid of 'religious interest'.[15] This is, of course, the case. The God of the philosophers is related to the God of the religions only in that both indicate a kind of ultimacy. But the movement between these two ways of speaking (even when both are 'descriptive', e.g., civil religion and metaphysics) entails fundamental grammatical transformations. The charge that the god identified as necessary, simple, impassible, etc., is devoid of religious significance is of course true. But this charge is beside the point, even when made by metaphysicians like Charles Hartshorne or theologians like Karl Barth.[16] It overlooks the different depth structures of these ways of employing god-language. A metaphysical use of god-language is formed in accordance with the function of offering a meta-explication (that is an explication of explication). The 'attributes' of God in this language are controlled by this abstractive and formal intent and function and are thus removed from the situation of religious discourse and reflection upon that discourse.

When Feuerbach notices that "the essential attributes or predicates of the divine being are the essential attributes or predicates of speculative philosophy,"[17] he has come very near to defining the meta-explicative function of this discourse. In contrast to Feuerbach however we are not maintaining that "speculative philosophy" is thereby eliminated, but rather that its specific function is clarified.

The work of David Hume struck a blow at this philosophical tradition, a blow aimed both at metaphysical god-language *and* at the notion of causation. In the *Dialogues* Hume undermines the metaphysical function of god-language by demonstrating the difficulties in the notion of God as first or final cause. In A *Treatise of Human Nature* Hume further proceeds to deny that we have any knowledge of causation derived from observation or perception. It is this double blow to the metaphysical tradition (perhaps especially the second) which Kant credits with awakening him from his dogmatic slumbers. Kant's response was to propose a model of explanation quite different from that which had dominated the philosophical tradition. For Kant the "second Copernican revolution" consists in making the activity of the knowing subject the paradigm of explanation. By changing the paradigm in this way, Kant attempts to save for the emerging modern sciences the character of knowledge.

Kant's shift from knowledge of causes to the knowledge of the (subjective) foundations of knowing changes the paradigm of metaphysics. Metaphysics shifts from an analysis of causation to an analysis of the subject. In this shift god-language also changes. "God" designates not 'first cause' but 'first subject' in the idealist and existentialist philosophies that follow from Kant's Copernican revolution. In both idealism and existentialism god-talk continues to function as a meta-explanation, but this is no longer an explanation of cause but of 'subject'. In the philosophy since Kant this subject is variously understood as the knowing subject (idealism) or the existing subject (existentialism).[18] In the tradition from Hegel and Fichte to Barth, God is understood not as 'first cause' but as 'Absolute Subject'.

In these philosophical contexts god-language is used as a meta-explication of the basic or universal paradigm of explanation.

A not inconsiderable irony in this development in philosophy is the fact that, although it was conceived as an attempt to save for the emerging natural sciences (especially as represented by the work of Newton) the character of knowledge, these sciences have steadfastly refused to be rescued. The modern period has been characterized by the divergence of philosophy and science. While some philosophers have sought to claim these sciences as children (and thus as owing a debt of gratitude to the 'parent') these sciences have, for the most part, had no use for the parent, which they consign to a kind of old folks home for antiquated, useless, and addled pursuits.

But this separation from philosophy leaves science without a clear way of knowing or saying what it is doing. Science as we know it functions more or less blindly. It explains without knowing what an explanation is, that is, without a meta-explanation. Science in effect turns against itself. Instead of a way of knowing (scientia) it has become simply a way of doing (techne). Thus science has been all but swallowed by technology—a technology which, as its critics note, has lost direction, aim or purpose. It is blind.

Thus the rapprochement between science and philosophy has become an urgent task in our time—the task of restoring sight to the sciences before the blind onrush of technology destroys us. This is not only an intellectual but also a profoundly political urgency.

It may be that in this task of facilitating a rapprochement between philosophy and science, even theology may have a role to play.[19] This is plausible in view of the long experience of theology in the use of meta-explicative language, though it is made difficult by the legacy of animosity between science and theology from Galileo to Darwin. In any case, such a dialogue cannot proceed as a tactic within an apologetic strategy. As an apologetic strategy it can only fall prey to the reverse apologetic described earlier. The resort to a meta-explicative use of god-language for apologetic purposes is problematic on two counts; first, because there may be no necessary connection between Christian faith and this sort of language, and second, because of the (perhaps unfairly) discredited character of meta-explicative language in our era. To attempt to gain credibility for theology by linking theology to a widely discredited use of language seems self-defeating. The most appropriate reason for Christian theology to resort to meta-explicative language (and thus to god-language which functions in this context) is the urgent dilemma for modern society of a blinded science held captive by technology.

Whatever may be the potential contribution of a dialogue between theology, natural science, and metaphysics, it remains important to have a clear conception of the character of the meta-explicative use of 'god' in much of philosophy and some theology. This meta-explicative use is correlative to and derived from the explicative use of 'god'. Where the paradigm of explication is causation god-language is used to identify the "first cause." Where the paradigm of explication is the knowing subject, god-language is used to identify the absolute subject. In either of these cases god-language is used to identify and describe the basic paradigm of explication as part of a process of reflection upon the antecedent conditions for explication.

Such a use of god-language within a discourse whose aim is to establish the antecedent conditions of explanation (and thus to offer a meta-explanation) may also be termed "logo-logical." Our basic paradigm of word and language which corresponds roughly to the distinction-in-relation of expletive (predicative) and explicative (nominative) uses of god-language would then have to be expanded to a consideration of linguisticality as constitutive of human existence and experience. This third level would correspond to the meta-explicative use of 'god.' Such a use of 'god' would be "logo-logical" in that it would reflect upon the antecedent condition of the use of word and language *and thus* upon linguisticality as the antecedent condition of explanation.

Reflection upon the intelligibility and thus the explicability of experience produces a type of god-talk which is found both in the wisdom literature of Israel and in the natural philosophies of Greece. Much of the use of god-talk in these contexts aims not to establish the existence of a supreme being (as the proponents of theism seem to believe) but to explore the efficacy of linguisticality as the antecedent condition of explanation. God-talk in such cases is employed to display the prerequisites of human involvement in word and language and is thus logo-logical. So, for example, the phrase "God created the heavens and the earth" may function in a variety of language games, but when it functions logo-logically or meta-explicatively it asserts the antecedent conditions of human interaction with word and language—namely that both human being and the world are created by 'the word' and thus are susceptible of (linguistic) explication. The phrase then serves as a kind of description of human existence in the world. The sort of description it gives is meta-explicative—that is it identifies the prerequisite of understanding existence in the world.

The notion of god-talk serving such a logo-logical function is developed by Kenneth Burke in his *The Rhetoric of Religion*. In this essay Burke analyzes the use of god-talk within a logo-logical discourse isolated in Augustine's *Confessions* and in the first three chapters of Genesis following up the hypothesis that "statements that great theologians have made about the nature of God might be adapted *mutatis mutandis* for use as purely secular observations on the nature of *words*."[20] Whatever we may think of the details of Burke's rather ingenious argument, he has established that the term 'god' does function logo-logically at least some of the time, that is, may be understood as displaying the fundamental conditions of the use of language and word. The use of god-language to display the antecedent conditions of causality as a mode of explication (in the tradition of Aristotle and Thomas) can be seen as a specific form of such a logo-logical or meta-explicative use of god-language.

I have already maintained that explicative god-language is the use of god-language to identify a structure which explains an event or to explain or 'legitimate' structure. This explicative use of god-language depends upon the rupture of a given structure—a rupture that brings the structure into view and requires an explanation, defense, or legitimation of the structure in the face of its actual or possible rupture. Thus the explicative use of god-language (as in civil religion or natural law) derives from and is secondary to a predicative and expletive use of god-language. If this is so, then a metaphysical (and perhaps also a meta-poetical or meta-political) use of god-language to reflect upon and establish the antecedent conditions of explication, legitimation, explanation, etc., is a "third order" use of god-language.[21] While the practical urgency of reflection upon the antecedent conditions of explanation is made clear by the consequences of a "science" that has been swallowed up by technology, it must remain for the moment an open question whether the term 'god' is the best way (still more—the only way) of focussing this reflection. I have only sought to claim that the term 'god' has functioned in this way. That it has also functioned as an explanation (rather than a meta-explanation) and as a way of giving expression to the rupture of the structures of experience (and thus to the collapse of their explanatory power) should be no less clear.

We may ask whether it is not a source of much confusion for god-talk to function in such disparate ways. The answer is that much confusion does arise when we fail to keep clear the way this term is being used. The difficulty most frequently comes from transposing meta-explicative or predicative god-talk to the explicative use of that language. This happens, for example, when the cosmological 'proof' of God's existence is taken to apply directly to the use of 'God' in natural law. In this case god-language comes perilously close to serving as a substitute for explanatory structures of significantly greater power, as for example 'scientific' ones. This results in a "God of the gaps" where god-talk is employed only on the fringes of an explicative discourse and is increasingly pushed out of the center of human interest and involvement. Similarly a predicative or an expletive use of god-talk, when it is reduced to explicative or explanatory god-language, produces additional confusion. Here the predicative use of god-language is unreflectively transferred into a context within which 'god' functions nominatively— frequently as the name of an agent whose "causal efficacy" is to be discerned in the miraculous. In this context a 'miracle' is not the epiphany of 'Word' but is simply the evasion or contravention of the laws of nature—especially as these are defined by natural science. The deformation of predicative into explicative god-language produces an anti-science (miracle) just as the deformation of meta-explicative into explicative language produces a pseudo-science.

III. Conclusion

I have sought to clarify the relationship of the expletive use of 'god' to two other uses of god-language which normally have played a major role in a "natural theology" either as a distinct field of inquiry or as apologetic prolegomena to Christian theology. Together these ways of employing god-talk may be labeled 'descriptive' since, in a variety of ways, they describe or purport to describe aspects of our experience.

At the level of a predicative use of god-talk we find a way of describing the quality of an event or complex of events in our experience. The use of god-talk in this connection points to the experience of the rupturing, destructuring and (possibly) restructuring of the patterns of experience. At its most basic and unreflective level this use of god-talk is an 'explosion' into language (which is the structure of our experience) of an event that ruptures and thus transcends language. This verbal rupture is what we have termed the expletive use of 'god'. In the case of explicative language, on the other hand, god-talk is used to account for the structures of experience, describing these structures in such a way as to explain, legitimate, or otherwise establish them. This description functions to display these structures just as the predicative use of 'god' describes experience in such a way as to display the rupturing of these structures. The use of god-language in 'civil' or political religion serves to display the socio-political structures in such a way as to enhance their explanatory power with respect to a particular event or custom.

The metaphysical use of God-language serves as yet another order of description—in this case displaying the antecedent conditions of one sort or another of explanation. So for example the Thomistic (and Aristotelian) uses of god-language serve to display the prior conditions of explanation through causation. In most general terms we have designated this meta-explicative mode of god-talk as logo-logical, following the suggestion of Kenneth Burke.

12

God in Kerygmatic Discourse

In the preceding chapter I have sought to distinguish the ways in which god-language has been employed in the sphere of "natural" theology. I have termed these uses of god-talk "descriptive." In this chapter and the next it will be necessary to inquire whether there are not important differences in the ways god-talk is employed. In so doing we will move from the sphere of "natural" theology into a consideration of the ways in which god-talk is employed within a religious community. Our focus will be upon the Christian community, though observations made here may be applicable to other religious traditions and communities. This concentration upon the Christian community is required by the character of the problematic we have been discussing. The questionableness of god-language emerges in relation to the apologetic function of Christian theology, that is, in relation to the attempt to give a generally intelligible account of the language of Christian faith and community. The decomposition of theism as the form of the doctrine of God has been accompanied by the general loss of credibility for explicative and meta-explicative uses of god-talk. This loss of credibility has given rise to the crisis of religious language generally and of god-language particularly. In preceding chapters I have argued that an attempt to render the god-language of a religious community intelligible through an appeal to explicative or even meta-explicative functions of this language cannot succeed.

It cannot succeed first because of the collapse of theism together with its context of plausibility and second because the explicative and meta-explicative uses of 'god' are themselves too far removed both from the religious language itself and from the "linguisticality of experience." If we are to engage the latter more clearly it is first necessary to have recourse to the sort of analysis I have attempted in part two. The result of that analysis was the description of expletive and predicative uses of 'god' to designate the rupture of the structure of language (and so experience) in confrontation with a radical alterity.

But this exploration of expletive and predicative uses of 'god' and (in the last chapter) of their relation to explicative and meta-explicative uses does not yet clarify the Christian use of god-language to which we have sought to discover a 'bridge'. To do this it is necessary to inquire into the specific structure of this Christian discourse and to see how it is both related to the 'radical affections' discussed in part two and distinguished from the explicative and meta-explicative discourse described in the previous chapter.

In the pages which follow I will identify two primary modes of discourse used in the Christian community. They are the kerygmatic, or "prescriptive," and the doxological, or "ascriptive," modes of discourse. Within each of these kinds of discourse god-language functions distinctively to identify the source (prescriptive) or object (ascriptive) of address. While descriptive discourse has an essentially monological character and structure, both ascriptive and prescriptive discourse have a dialogical character. In addition to describing the use of god-language in these modes of discourse I will attempt to indicate their relationship to descriptive uses of god-language and to the radical affections discussed in part two of this essay.

The attempt to identify the basic structure or grammar of a discourse is fraught with hazards. First of all, it is important not to confuse superficial symptoms with fundamental structures. Yet we have no access to these structures apart from careful attention to symptoms. Even if we succeed in gaining some sense of 'the way the language works,' however, not all difficulties are over. Inevitably there will be tension between the formulation of the structure and the actual ways of speaking which we suppose to be governed by this structure. Some of this tension is explainable simply by the difference between rule and performance, grammar and actual sentences, structure and 'appearance'. Once one understands the basic rules of the game there is still considerable room for variation and free play. But we may also encounter forms of speech which seem to violate the rules of the game or to obey quite different rules. Part of our task is to be able to distinguish among basic language games so that we will be able to determine

when language is functioning explicatively and when it is functioning kerygmatically or doxologically. Thus it may be that when language 'goes wrong'
it does so as a consequence of an inadvertent shift from one sort of discourse
to another.

This means that our analysis of Christian discourse can by no means be
purely 'inductive'. It will also entail normative judgements about when this
discourse is proper (articulated in accordance with basic rules) and when it
has gone wrong. We will then not only be describing how language is used
but prescribing—saying how it ought to be used if it is to be an articulation
or elaboration of the basic or fundamental character of that language. In
this sense our approach is not only "apologetic" but also "dogmatic."

In this chapter I will offer a description of the kind of discourse that may
be found within the Christian community in proclamation and exhortation.
My aim is to describe this language rather than to establish its "legitimacy"
by reference to something outside itself. I will identify some of the basic
features of this discourse and its use of 'god', which stand in contrast to the
god-talk of descriptive discourse as outlined in the previous chapter.

I. Word of God: The Structure of Kerygmatic Discourse

Kerygmatic language is often identified within the community of faith as
the "Word of God." This phrase "Word of God" includes not only specific
"revelatory events" as these are focussed above all in the Christ-event, but
also that body of early Christian discourse (scripture and tradition) which is
produced in response and in conformity to such events. The phrase is also
employed to include that speaking within the community which bases itself
upon Scripture (and tradition) or the events to which Scripture is a response:
preaching, testifying, admonishing, and exhorting. The phrase "Word of
God" then, may designate an astonishing variety of objects: the second person
of the Trinity, the person, message, and fate of Jesus, the canon of Scripture,
formal preaching, informal talk among Christians and the experience of
being addressed (by God) even apart from Christian identification. These
apparently heterogeneous contents constitute elements within a Christian
discourse whose structure it is now our task to uncover. The simplest identification of the structure that links this heterogeneity together is the phrase
"Word of God." We will take this phrase to identify not the surface content
but the basic structure that is the foundation for such ways of speaking. Our
task then is to "unpack" the *structural or grammatical implications of the
phrase "Word of God"* insofar as this phrase designates the character of
Christian discourse.

The most obvious, and for that reason most readily overlooked, implication of this designation is that it indicates that this discourse has the structure of actual and concrete address. It removes this discourse from the sphere of the monological and the speculative and places it in the sphere of dialogue. We are here in the sphere of command and promise, of words that do not so much describe as pre-scribe and pro-scribe. We do not have here a description of the way things are but a *calling*, a provocation, a summoning, which intends the transformation of the way things are.

As such this discourse has an *ad hominem* character. Unlike the explicative language of description this discourse implicates speaker and hearer directly. Let us take the case of preaching. In particular cases of preaching we may, of course, discover strongly didactic forms of discourse which may or may not be "edifying." In these cases we may be justified in supposing that this language functions explicatively, that is to describe or to explain our life in the world. But in other cases the mode of direct address comes more clearly to the fore. When Nathan tells David of a man with only one sheep whose single and beloved beast is stolen by a rich man with many sheep, he may be remarking upon the general power of injustice (the rich get richer and the poor get poorer) or he may be reporting on the breakdown of law and order in a particular case. In either case he would be simply reporting, only describing. But when he turns to his outraged king and says, "you are the man" we have direct address, and we have the form of proclamation. Proclamation is *ad hominem* in character.

The word "god" is used in this manner of speaking to name the agent or subject of the address, to name the one who speaks. Thus Christian discourse that takes the form of proclamation speaks *about* God only indirectly and then only to identify the one who is responsible for the speaking, the one whose "message" or "tidings" is being conveyed. We will see shortly in what way such a word *from* God may imply words *about* God and thus god-language in more familiar ways. But first it is necessary to notice that kerygmatic discourse uses the term "God" to identify one who speaks and whose speaking is directed in *ad hominem* fashion to us.

Already the possibility of misunderstanding presses itself upon us here— leading us to think piously or disdainfully of some 'heavenly speech' which has nothing to do or has to do only incidentally with our ordinary words and language. It is therefore important to insist that we are describing purely human speech here and rather ordinary and commonplace human speech at that. The most obvious instance of such speech is that which takes place on Sunday mornings in some sermons. Some of this discourse has a kerygmatic structure—one feature of which is that it identifies the original or actual speaker of this address with the term 'god' but in such a way as *not* thereby to warrant the conclusion that 'god' is the name of the man or woman occupying the pulpit. Thus this kerygmatic discourse is understood to be *structured as if it were the repetition of a message whose original speaker (and therefore the one responsible for the message) is identified as 'god'*. It is in this derivative and secondary sense that this preaching is also identified as the "Word of God." By this designation we are reminded of the basic character of this discourse, namely that it is structured as if it were a message whose speaker is God and whose hearers we are.

II. The Elaboration of Kerygmatic Discourse

The above observations concerning the grammatical implications of the phrase "Word of God" may be made more clear and precise if we attend to the specific forms which this discourse has taken. I will therefore propose a series of such forms beginning with the most basic and least 'reflected' forms. These forms may be understood as sub-grammars of the basic grammatical structure of kerygmatic discourse.

Audition as Vocation
We must begin by showing how this kerygmatic discourse is related to the event of the rupture in the structure of discourse, which we discussed in part two of this essay. There we noted that the only prior condition required for such a rupture is the linguisticality of our experience. We also noted that there are a variety of ways it may be felt, figured, and articulated. In order to say what these events have in common I have spoken of the irruption of or encounter with 'alterity' or 'otherness' that both shatters and founds our language.

That which characterizes the encounter with or irruption of this alterity in our language insofar as this language has the character of kerygmatic discourse may be provisionally designated as—audition as vocation! This must be briefly explained.

In the first place it must be clear that we do not have in mind a different set of 'word-events' than those we have described in chapters four through nine. Thus the criteria for determining such word-events remain the same here as those which we have discussed for expletive and predicative uses of 'god': that is, on account of the generic features of our linguisticality such an event can bring into question or rupture our ordinary or everyday ways of ordering or naming our experience; it is taken to be of fundamental (or catastrophic) significance for our way of being in the world; in short, it both shatters and founds our (linguistic) way of being in the world.

What is different however is the way in which this rupture is figured, the 'root metaphor' that is deployed. The sequence expletive-predicative-explicative-meta-explicative, figures this encounter or rupture as "appearing, seeing, vision." But kerygmatic discourse substitutes the metaphor of voice for that of vision. The rupture is a word, the event is a word-event. The predominance of voice over vision suggests the predominance of the historical region over aesthetic and ontological regions of experience. It does not entail the elimination of aesthetic and ontological regions but it does mean that these are appropriated into the historical sphere.[1] Conversely, the metaphor of vision may entail the subordination of historical experience, and so of linguisticality, to ontological and aesthetic experience.

This shift is not to be accounted for only by a shift in the relative degree of importance attached to the various regions of experience, however. It may also be understood as a deeper penetration into the problematic of linguisticality as such. Language is not only the structure of our experience (Langue) but also the medium of our communication (Parole). Concretely, communication is address implicating not only a subject matter and the structuring through language of that subject-matter but also implicating a speaker and a hearer. The metaphor of vision abstracts from this speaker-hearer. The metaphor of voice is situated squarely within this relationship and makes it central.[2] Through this more intimate engagement of linguisticality the 'radical affections' become also radical 'inflections' modifying not only the structures of experience but the subject of experience.

The alteration of the subject through the occurrence of alterity takes the form of the transformation of the hearer into a speaker. Audition is vocation. It is in this way that the rupture of the structures of discourse enters into and founds discourse. That which occurs (the rupture as word-event) *as if* it were address, actually and concretely *becomes* address in the transformation of the hearer into a speaker. The subject 'repeats' the word-event. To be addressed is to be summoned into speech by speech. Just as the infant (literally the "non-speaker") is initiated into speaking by being addressed, spoken to, and called, so also with the more radical situation of 'audition as vocation' which characterizes the occurrence of the radical affections as word-events.

If we take the historical region of experience as the seedbed of kerygmatically generated discourse then the character of "audition as vocation" becomes all the more clear. The rupture of the structuring of our linguisticality is "heard" as "address." That this occurs within the structure of language as well as 'against' that structure generates a discourse within language which repeats this address. Language is itself volatilized in the service of this address; thus the address that ruptures language (promise, judgement, command, etc.) itself ramifies through language as the address of the 'prophet' to the 'people', of the 'people' to the nations, and as the elaboration of and reflection upon this address. It is the advent of the other as address that produces the repetition and ramification of address as kerygmatically generated discourse.

If this is correct, and it must still be substantiated by discussion of actual forms of discourse, then we may be approaching a way of distinguishing kerygmatic address from explicative language. For kerygmatic address reiterates the rupture which explicative language 'covers'. That is, the address that repeats the rupture, articulates it, elaborates it, is likely to be profoundly different from the sort of language that seeks to prevent, seal off or "explain" this rupture. There may then be corresponding differences in the way in which 'god' functions in these very different kinds of discourse.

The apprehension of alterity as voice rather than as vision characterizes the traditions of Israel, Christianity, and Islam, although we cannot either restrict it in principle to these religious traditions nor maintain that it is even specifically religious (chapter nine). That it is a generically human possibility is shown by the fact that the metaphor of voice focusses the universal character of linguisticality as address. It does not require the importation of some special presupposition from outside this linguisticality.

Despite this it is clear that the religious traditions which descend from ancient Israel are characterized by an especially noticeable stress upon address rather than vision. The prohibition of graven images is a particularly strong indication of the insistence of the primacy of voice over vision. Any attempt to clarify the use of god-language in Christianity (one of the descendants of ancient Israel) must therefore attend to the primacy of this structure of address which I have characterized as 'audition as vocation'.

Prophetic Discourse

This reflection upon the fundamental character of word-event as speechevent enables us to account for a number of features of biblical discourse. Indeed we may understand much of this discourse as the articulation and elaboration of 'audition as vocation'. The most fundamental articulation of this speech-event may be found in prophetic discourse. This articulation takes the form of a repetition of that which is heard, a repetition provoked by the hearing itself. This characteristic of prophetic discourse is regularly indicated by such formulas as "thus saith the Lord" or "the Word of the Lord which came to . . . ".

The message or address that is to be 'repeated' has the character of an identification of the speaker and the hearer of the address (there may also be an identification of the one who is both hearer and speaker, i.e. the prophet, as in the case of Jeremiah, who exhibits the wrenching compulsion to speak laid upon him by hearing). Perhaps the simplest enunciation of kerygmatic structure is the phrase "I will be your God and you will be my people." All kerygmatic discourse in Judaism and Christianity (and perhaps Islam) may be regarded as a variation upon and elaboration of this structure.[3]

The first feature which must strike us about this structure is that the message or content of the address is entirely subsumed into the identification of speaker and hearer. The content of the address is not a "what" but a "who," not a "subject-*matter*" but a "subject." This corresponds to Barth's recognition that the content of revelation is not some information (for example, *about* God), but rather is "God-himself".[4]

A second feature of this formula is the parallelism of the identification of the speaker (your God) and the hearer (my people). The naming of the one entails the re-naming of the other. This reciprocal naming corresponds to Ebner's and Buber's view of the reciprocal constitution of I and Thou in which this relationship is not one between substantially unalterable monads but constitutes the identity of each.[5] Thus Barth's formula would have to be expanded to include the identity of the hearer (Israel, the Church, etc.) as well as the speaker. This double naming may be abbreviated to the name of the speaker (e.g., Emmanuel) or to the name of the hearer (Israel, ecclesia); the full structure is implicit in the naming of either pole of the dialogic situation. Thus the name Emmanuel (god with *us*) as well as the names Israel (the chosen of God) and ecclesia (those who are called together) name both speaker and hearer in naming one.

Related to these features is the fact that *de*scription is entirely subordinated to *pre*scription. The word imposes itself upon "the way things are" in such a way as to create a state of affairs, rather than to mirror a state of affairs. The language is thus performative in character. (As in a wedding service the language of avowal not only describes my feelings and intentions but also brings into being a new state of affairs—with legal, social, and economic consequences.) The word thus generates a state of affairs in such a way, in the case of our biblical example, as to create its own hearing. In this way it is preemptory.

The word of address as word of God is thus creative (it creates for itself a hearing—indeed it creates the hearers).[6] It is also elective in that it chooses, and binds itself to, the hearer. Here it is also imperative or vocational in character, in that it summons the hearer into a new mode of being—as hearer and as "repeater" of the word.[7] All of this is congruent with what we should expect of a "word" within the historical region of experience based upon the analysis of chapter eight. On that basis we should also expect there to be an intimate connection between relationality and temporality, and indeed that is what we find here. Here too we have the opening up or granting of a future, which is inscribed in the future tense (I *will* be, you *will* be) of the address. It is in this sense that the form of the word of address as word of God is basically that of promise as Moltmann has made clear.[8]

This also helps us to understand how it may happen that prophetic discourse comes to be misunderstood as a *description* of a future state of affairs, that is as a prediction or forecast. We have seen in the description of the historical region of experience that what is as stake in the structuring of this region is the possession of an other and of a future. The rupture of this structure abolishes the secure possession of other/future which are then either absent (abandonment/annihilation) or 'given' (love/promise) outside and over against any possibility of possession. In prophetic discourse we have the annunciation that ruptures the structure of historical possession through the advent of an other. The advent of this alterity may be articulated as annihilation/abandonment (as in Amos) or as a gracious 'return' (Hosea, deutero-Isaiah.) In either case the question of a future and the character of the future is co-implicated in the question of the identity of the one who comes and of those who are the object of this advent.

The future tense of prophetic discourse then does not take the form of a predictive description, which would be merely the re-instatement of a structure of possession, but instead the form of promise. This 'promise' is essentially the address: "I will be with you," "You will be my people," and so on. It is the 'naming' of the speaker and hearer. It may conversely be expressed as the "un-naming" of the hearer: "not my people" (Hosea) "are you not like the nations to me" (Amos), etc. In either case what is at stake is the identity of the hearer (Israel) in relation to the identity of the speaker (God).

It is the disclosure of this situation and identity of the people in relation to that alterity which confers, creates, or abolishes that identity which is at the heart of prophetic address. Thus when we hear of the encouragement of prophecy in the early Christian community (1 Cor. 14) what is there valued is not the capacity to predict the future (explicitly rejected as 'false prophecy' in Mark 13) but rather that speaking which discloses the actual situation of the community in relation to its call. Prophecy is then the specification of this call or commission within a concrete circumstance or in relation to a particular situation.

Prophecy then does not itself disclose, still less predict, a future; rather prophetic discourse summons the hearers to be those to whom such a future is promised. In this discourse "God" (and a variety of other names) functions to identify the one whose advent as address is this call, claim, and commission. At this level of kerygmatic discourse, then, the name "God" serves to identify the authority of that which is heard so as to make clear the sovereignty of that address vis a vis the hearer(s) and to assert the utter reliability of the speech-event which is initially heard as "self-authenticating." Moreover the "name" of God may serve to summarize the entire event of speaker/hearer/message as in the name Emmanuel or perhaps even Yahweh.[9]

Command and Law

We have drawn attention to the *ad hominem* and therefore imperative character of kerygmatic discourse generally and of prophetic discourse in particular. This imperative has the force of a command: be those to whom God, the future, comes. Kerygmatic discourse does not simply disclose who we are. It indicates who we are to be but in such a way that this indicative is an imperative: be who you are summoned to be. This imperative 'moment' is command and command is elaborated as 'law'.

The function of law in this context is not simply to 'organize society'. It is instead to differentiate the new or transformed identity from the old. Thus law may in fact have a "Utopian" character as in the Levitical instructions for the Jubilee year.[10] It functions in this case to indicate not who Israel *is*, but who Israel would be or will be if/when Israel corresponds to that call or commission which constitutes it. Much the same is true of the 'eschatological ethics' of Jesus in Matthew 5–7. Thus the saying concerning plucking out an eye if one is tempted by lust serves not to organize a social structure or contract (comprising, one may imagine, a high percentage of persons with self-inflicted blindness) but to indicate the distance between a prior identity and a new or eschatological one.

This function of law to distinguish a transformed identity from a prior identity (before and after having been addressed) also carries over into laws of purification. Of course much of this Levitical material may be elaborated from other motives but it is always articulated against the backdrop of the call to a new identity (hence the identification with Moses). Rules for ritual cleanliness then are appropriated into the context of a differentiation of a new from a prior identity. The 'logic' of this differentiation then propels law toward increasingly rigorous formation and elaboration.

Even when this has not yet occurred or is prevented in principle from occurring (for example in certain Pauline formulations) we notice the prefacing of moral or ethical admonition with phrases like: "don't do as the heathen do but . . . " or "don't do as you did before you heard the gospel . . . ".

Yet both in Judaism and in Christianity the inner logic of law used to differentiate the community and those who have been addressed leads to rigorism and legalism. In both cases this tendency is countered by the very address that has been construed as command, law, and legalism. In the cases of Jeremiah, Paul, and Luther (to cite only the best-known examples) the movement from command to rigorism is interdicted. This occurs by no means through a revocation of the element of imperative or command, but through an attempted clarification or re-iteration of that command. This apparently paradoxical relationship to the law may take many forms. In Matthew the Jesus who abolishes Sabbath law and who abolishes rigorism by hyperbolizing it (the saying about the eye for example), also says "I am come not to abolish but to complete (fulfill) the law." Paul, who inveighs against the law as concentrated in circumcision, also condemns the un-freedom of bondage to desire. Both are, in Paul's terminology, "flesh." This critique of legalism from the standpoint of the advent of the Kingdom of God or grace of God is by no means limited to Christianity. It is also to be found in Judaism and especially in the texts associated with Jeremiah and Ezekial. In these texts an external and fixed legal structure is contrasted with the interior and living (heart) law. The new law, or that form of command which supplants the law as code, is, in both Judaism and Christianity, associated with an eschatological reality—with the inbreaking of the future, the advent of God.

In the elaboration and suspension of legal structures found in biblical literature and in the subsequent history of the communities that trace their identity and vocation from this literature we are confronted with a by now familiar dilemma. It is the dilemma of linguisticality itself. That which ruptures language also founds it. And the language that "aims" at address also prevents it. This is the dilemma we have traced in part two of this essay. To the extent to which the kerygmatic discourse we are considering may be understood as an internalization of this rupture into language—to that extent it is confronted again and again with the tendency of discourse to become "language." We may object that discourse is of course language. Where else may discourse occur? Precisely. This is why we find in kerygmatic discourse the consistent interdiction of its own apparent or surface "logic," but this does not occur by way of an arbitrary or "irrational" intrusion. It occurs in accordance with a precise and determinate grammar.[11] This is the grammar of the vocative. We may therefore expect to discover it not only here in the discussion of command and law but in all other elaborations of this kerygmatic structure.

Narrative and Apocalyptic Elaboration

A further elaboration of kerygmatic discourse is the narrative identification of speaker and hearer. In the case of biblical narratives (though not only these) the narration of "God's mighty acts" serves to identify the one who speaks in a given situation and to link together various situations within which such speaking has occurred. These narratives may be simple or complex, depending upon the number of links to prior hearing-speaking events that appear.[12] Since the identity of speaker and hearer are correlative the narrative may have as its principal subject the history of the hearer—Israel or the Church.[13]

It is important to notice that the elaboration of the identity of hearer/speaker takes a basically narrative form. This is because it is an elaboration upon a speech-event which discloses, modifies, or founds personal identity. It is precisely this which makes dramatic narrative necessary, for it is precisely in this way that "character" is disclosed, "developed," and transformed in relation to the other. Story (plot) and person (character) are correlative. A survey of Old Testament literature reveals what an astonishing variety of narrative forms are pressed into this task: heroic saga, (Samson, David, Moses), Near-Eastern myth (creation, Babel), legend (Elijah), folk tale (Balaam's ass), annal or chronicle, genealogy, etc. Moreover the material shows unmistakable evidence of the extension of narrative to include previously heterogeneous traditions (Sinai, Davidic, etc.) as well as differently "named" deities (Elohim, Yahweh, etc.).

This narrative elaboration is also to be discovered in the New Testament not only in the genre of "Gospel" but also in the way in which Paul's self-designations take on the form of a summary narration of "sufferings" patterned upon or reflective of the passion of Christ.[14] The inclusion of the Acts of the Apostles further extends this narrative identification of hearer (the church) and of hearers who have become speakers (the apostles).

However constructed, such narratives reflect the basic structure of address in its relationality and temporality. It is for this reason that the genres of history, story, and parable are crucial components of Judeo-Christian traditions.[15]

It is especially important to notice that this narrative material has in any case a "confessional" character. It is to be understood as the unfolding of the identity of God in relation to his people and of the people in relation to their God. This recognition is at the heart of the revolution in biblical exegesis associated with the name of Rudolph Bultmann for the New Testament, and of Gerhard von Rad for Old Testament. It entails that the kerygmatic structure determines the composition of these materials both in general and in detail.

The kerygmatic basis of narrative character depiction is likewise seen in the way in which this narrative may also take the quite different form of apocalyptic. A purely narrative depiction tends to locate identity in the past and so to give it a reliable, stable, and hence 'possessed' character. To the extent to which this occurs, the narrative approximates to a descriptive or explicative discourse. The narrative is then sealed off from the rupture of the structures that provokes it. The rupture of the narratively assured structure takes the form of apocalyptic. Apocalyptic is the annunciation of a new identity that dispossesses or exorcizes an identity which is merely past. In both Old and New Testament apocalyptic the old or past identity is confronted with a new identity: "for behold I am doing a new thing" (Isa. 43:18–19). This 'new thing' entails a new identity: new creation, new heaven and new earth (Isa. 65:17; 2 Pet. 3:13).

This apocalyptic does not simply abolish narrative however. Indeed it too must take the form of a narrative (Daniel, Revelation of John) or be inserted into a narrative (Mark 13 and parallels). It retains this 'narrativity' precisely because it too is concerned with the character of speaker/hearer in and through time. But at the same time it is juxtaposed against the tendency of narrative to become a strategy for the possession of this identity by rendering it in the past tense.

Perhaps the most intriguing feature of apocalyptic discourse is its abolition of the question of identity.[16] We have noticed that prophetic discourse may be summarized as the naming of speaker and hearer, and indeed as the naming of one through the naming of the other. Thus we have, at least implicitly, not two separate identities but one complex, dialectical identity. Now narrative may become simply the separation of this identity of speaker/hearer—on the one hand Israel or Church, on the other, God. The separation of these identities is abolished in the apocalyptic anticipation that "God will be all, in all." (1 Cor. 15:28). This entails that the identity of 'world' as that which is separate from God is abolished. It entails that the Church as that which is 'other' than God or world is likewise abolished (Rev. 21). It finally entails that the identity of God as the Other over-against the world and/or community is also abolished. The name for the eschatological reality of God is 'doxa' (glory or splendour). The name of the resurrected body is likewise "doxa" (1 Cor. 15:35ff). Outside or apart from this

volatilized identity is—nothing. This may be expressed either in universal-
istic terms or in terms of the utter annihilation of all 'other' identity. In
either case that which is anticipated in apocalyptic annunciation is that God
will be all in all. Thus 'God' names not one identity among others or over
against others but the volatilization of identity as such.

Thus both with respect to the confrontation of a narrative past with an
apocalyptic future and with respect to the abolition of the separation between
speaker and hearer apocalyptic 'fulfills' the narrative elaboration of kerygmatic discourse.

Paradigms and Compendia

A further development of kerygmatic discourse leads to the identification of
paradigms, which function retrospectively to summarize the content of kerygmatic discourse and the identities of speaker and hearer and which also
function prospectively to determine the authenticity of subsequent kerygmatic speech. Such summaries or surveys tend to presuppose the narratives
discussed above, to which they may only briefly refer or which they may
include in *toto*. One type of such discourse is a brief creed or confession
that identifies the basic paradigm or norm intensively and more or less
abstractly as in the case of the Apostle's Creed or in the *Shema*. These serve
as 'plot summaries' or 'outlines' of the narrative complex as a whole.[17] But
the development of normative paradigms may also occur extensively through
the establishment of a canon of Scripture. The development of the canon
does not itself take the form of a separate discourse but rather the identification of those examples of discourse, prophetic, legal, narrative, or apocalyptic, which will serve normatively as the basis of the speaking of the
community.

These compendia then, whether intensive (creed) or extensive (canon)
serve as complex protocol statements securing the basis for further speaking
and as the norm against which such further speaking is to be tested. The
authority of such complex protocol statements derives from the way in which
they reflect and represent the structure of an address whose author is identified as God. To be sure, these protocols have in themselves only the
questionable character of communally determined norms; they are not themselves the address that ruptures all structures. Only insofar as they reflect
that address do they function authoritatively in a fundamental sense. Luther
expressed this in his formula for the internal criticism of the canon: "that
which bears Christ" alone is "canonical."

While we will return to the character of creedal formulations later in this
chapter ("dogma") and in the next, it is important to notice a further feature

of canon as norm. The very diversity of genres of discourse as well as the diversity of exemplars of these genres (four narrative gospels for example) serves to prevent the consolidation of this norm into a single "party-line" or perspective. Thus the canon that 'legitimates' subsequent discourse also prevents the over-stabilization of that discourse into a simple homogeneous language. That it in fact does this despite all attempts to consolidate the language of the community into a single structure is shown by the way in which explosive or volatilizing forces within the community have been able to 'legitimate' their overthrow of legal, institutional and authoritarian structures by appeal to this shared norm. Significantly, this happens most often by appeal to prophetic and apocalyptic texts within the canon. But it may also occur by means of appeal to 'legal' texts as well, as the examples of the Franciscans and of the Puritans illustrate.

It must also be said that the canon only serves its appropriate function as "Word of God" if it provokes discourse—that is if it transforms hearers/readers into speakers/writers. Only insofar as it does this does it become not inert letter but volatilizing address. That it has served this function in the past is evident especially if, with Ebeling, we regard the history of theology as the history of the interpretation of Scripture.[18] Whether and in what manner this will continue to be true is the challenge that confronts every speaker/writer in the community of faith and, most evidently, each one who undertakes to 'proclaim' or to engage in theological reflection upon that discourse.

Proclamation

In post-canonical preaching we encounter the exposition and application of a previously articulated word-event to the end of gaining for that event a new hearing in a new situation. Thus, insofar as a sermon is proclamatory or kerygmatic in character it undertakes the task of provoking the hearing of the hearer to draw that hearer into the vocation of proclamation itself. We may designate several aspects of this discourse which illuminate its peculiar structure and function.

In the first place we must note the peculiar role of a text in proclamation. The text here is the quotation of a passage of Scripture which then is elaborated and applied by the 'address' or sermon. The presence and function of a text distinguishes proclamation from prophecy on the one hand and from more general edifying discourse on the other. The latter may be an articulation of religious or ethical sensibility in which the speaker seeks to express his or her own view, opinion, or judgment. Prophesy also dispenses with a text but in order to present by way of repetition the direct address of

God. In preaching, the text (or perhaps Scripture viewed topically) intervenes to become the source of the address. Preaching is thus "Word of God" at two (at least) removes. It is the reiteration of the word of God in Scripture, which itself is the repetition of the word of God in prophetic or apostolic address. The task of preaching is then to bring to speech in our language that which came to expression in *their* language (that is, in the language of Israel and the primitive community).

That which came to expression or is to come to expression is not an "eternal" or "timeless truth" but a concrete word of address. Proclamation is to be distinguished thus from various forms of exegesis that either ignore the historical chasm between then and now (producing timeless truths) or concentrate entirely upon past meaning (as in some forms of "scientific" exegesis). Proclamation has the task of reiterating kerygmatic discourse. This means that its structure must make possible the identification of the final author of the address as God (in this is the derivative authorization for the authority of the preacher) as well as to embody in itself the *ad hominem* character of kerygma (the address must be "applied" in such a way as to summon the hearer to an altered identity).

Of course proclamation as the discourse provoked or set in motion by a "text" may become simply the stale repetition of a text, which is then heard not as address but as an alien "tongue." To the extent to which this death of address is attributed to the text, the text will be understood not as that which provokes but as that which silences speech. In such a case proclamation can only be revitalized as prophecy—that is, as a discourse that dispenses with a text in order to iterate the situation of the hearers vis a vis the advent of God as address. Despite the biblicism of much Protestant theory of preaching as "exposition and application of a text," it must be understood that proclamation is first of all prophetic discourse and that the text is to be understood as a propaedeutic to such a discourse, not as a prophylactic against it.

Doctrine
Derivative from the kerygmatically structured discourse of "prophets and Apostles" and aiming toward the kerygmatically structured discourse of proclamation is the language of doctrine.[19] Despite its origin and end in kerygmatic discourse, doctrine displays a significantly different character. It is almost entirely discursive, didactic and "explicative." If we were to employ the analogy of explicative discourse, we might say that doctrine is to explicative god-language as prophetic discourse is to predicative god-language. Yet this is only an analogy, since doctrine remains oriented to kerygma and

is in this way to be distinguished from the various kinds of explicative discourse discussed in the previous chapter.

Doctrine has the task of transposing kerygmatic address and its narrative elaboration into conceptual form, so as to display the coherence of that discourse and its correspondence to the widest possible range of human experience. This task is that which is normally understood to be the work of Christian theology as such. It is, of course, impossible in the context of this essay to discuss in detail the task and method of this "theological" discourse. It is only possible to indicate briefly how it is related to the kerygmatic and prescriptive structure that has been our theme in this chapter.

Doctrinal discourse is necessitated on the one hand by the astonishing diversity of canonical materials and on the other by the necessity of applying these materials qua canon to fundamentally altered cultural and linguistic contexts, so that in whatever linguistic structure the word of address may be both heard and understood.[20] These twin exigencies of biblical interpretation produce doctrine. In this sense we are in agreement with Gerhard Ebeling's thesis that the history of theology *is* the history of biblical interpretation.

As Augustine argues in *On Christian Doctrine*, the task of the theologian is to demonstrate in relation to Scripture: "a way of discovering those things which are to be understood and a way of teaching what we have learned."[21] But the theologian is immediately confronted with the difficulty of diverse and even apparently contradictory expressions in canonical material. Thus Augustine must first suggest a rule that will determine whether assertions in canonical literature are to be understood "literally" or "allegorically." He discovers this rule in the centrality of love. Subsequent theologians employed a four-level hermeneutic, distinguishing among grammatical-historical, typological (Christological), tropological (moral) and anagogical (eschatological) levels of meaning. In our time the question of hermeneutics has once again become acute for theology. The reason for the centrality of this issue is the understanding that theology as doctrine is derivative from and governed by the kerygmatic structure normatively exemplified in canonical texts.[22]

If we attend to the relationship between doctrine and kerygma we can understand more clearly some of the peculiar features of doctrine as a form of discourse and thus understand the role that god-language plays here. Kerygmatic structure, we have seen, is the structure of address involving speaker and hearer and the transformation of the hearer into speaker (audition as vocation). As such, kerygmatic discourse effects the disclosure, transformation, and founding of identity. Doctrine is the transposition of this structure into conceptual formulation. On this basis we may discriminate two kinds of doctrine: theological anthropology, which is concerned with the identity of the hearer who is summoned into speech, and theology proper, which concerns itself with the identity of the primordial speaker who is "heard." Theological anthropology gives a conceptual account of "who we are," who are addressed, and to this end deploys such conceptions as image of God, creatureliness, fall, original sin, justification, sanctification, etc. The task of theological anthropology then is to carefully construct these fundamental concepts from the kerygmatic and narrative materials at its disposal, to place them in proper relation to one another, and to elaborate and apply them in ways that permit them to function as descriptions of actual human existence in the world. The task of theology proper is to clarify the basis of this description of human existence. That basis is God as the subject of address. In theological anthropology, then, god-talk is not the theme or subject-matter but rather indicates the point of view or perspective from which the subject-matter (human existence in the world) is to be viewed. In theology proper, god-talk becomes the focus of attention as doctrine seeks to clarify the basis for its description of human existence in the world. Thus the loci or topics of Christology, Pneumatology, Patrology, and "Of the Unity of God" are brought into view as doctrine uncovers the foundations for its conceptualization of human existence in the world. What is particularly in view here is the "economic Trinity," that is, God as the one who encounters, addresses, and summons human being.

The god-talk of doctrine then is motivated by the attempt to provide a conceptually adequate account of what it means to be addressed in such a way that one's existence in the world is fundamentally altered.[23] If we were to carry this principle through we would be able to show how it is possible to avoid fundamental misconceptions occasioned by the confusion of this doctrinal language with the explicative and meta-explicative language discussed in the previous chapter. We must content ourselves with a suggestive illustration. Talk of God as Creator may function in the following ways: (1) explicatively, to validate, sanction, and explain the structures of experience in nature and society—this is the use of god-talk characteristic of theism; (2) meta-explicatively, to establish the basis of such explanation and legitimation—this is the use characteristic of metaphysics and illustrated by Thomas Aquinas' proofs for the existence of God; (3) narratively, to provide a narrative account of the one who speaks (God), of the radicality of the speaking (it is creative—*ex nihilo*) and of the identity of the one addressed (called into being or created by this word of address—this is the use to be found in Genesis 1:1–2:4) doctrinally, to transpose this narrative account into a conceptual one. In this last use the talk of God as creator does not provide us directly with a theory about the world but with a way of interpreting our existence in the world or, more precisely, with the articulation of the basis for such a normative interpretation.

But our existence in the world is by no means a straightforward affair in this "language game," for that existence is subject to radical transformation, from not hearing to hearing, and from hearing to speaking. Thus the account of 'who we are' in doctrine has a necessarily paradoxical and dialectical character created by the juxtaposition of contrary categories such as *imago dei* and original sin, *simul justus et peccator*, etc. These paradoxes result from the attempt to clarify existence from the point of view of its alteration by being addressed. The peculiarity of doctrinal discourse over-against the more usual forms of explicative and meta-explicative discourse is that it takes into itself (or attempts to) a radical alterity. It does this insofar as it is a reflection upon and conceptual elaboration of a word-event that fundamentally alters the existence of the hearer. Thus even when its theme is something like the nature of God it deals with it in distinctive ways. For doctrine, God is neither one object among others, nor the principle of their existence, but is the one who speaks in such a way as to alter (not just establish) the way things are. In any case doctrinal language *about* God is governed by kerygmatic discourse which is structured as the word *of* God.

Dogma

Dogma is the logology of kerygmatic discourse, serving the function that metaphysics serves in relation to explicative discourse. The task of dogma is to identify the fundamental grammar or structure of the discourse of the Christian community. The basic dogmas for this purpose are Trinitarian and Christological. They belong together and constitute a single though complex grammatical structure. Just as metaphysics has the task of identifying the antecedent conditions of some mode of explication (or of explication as such) so dogma has the task of identifying the antecedent conditions of theological "explanation" (doctrine) or of that discourse as such. Like metaphysics, dogma does not ask *whether* explanation or discourse is possible but, since it is actual, *how* is it possible.

If we attend to Trinitarian dogma we discover that it functions in two ways: as a normative outline of Christian doctrine (a protocol statement whose elaboration and explication *is* Christian doctrine) and as the logological identification of the antecedent conditions of Christian discourse. In the first case we have the "economic Trinity." In the second case we have the "immanent Trinity" that is, the Trinity as pure grammar in the form of a definition of the internal relations of God. In Trinitarian dogma, god-language becomes language about language.

If we concentrate on dogma as the logology of Christian discourse and especially as the logology of kerygmatic discourse, a number of important clarifications follow. In the first place we may be struck by the way in which dogma focusses upon 'person'. The two dogmas that are recognized by the Christian community as a whole are the Christological and Trinitarian dogmas. The first defines the relation of two natures and one person; the second defines the relation of three 'persons' and one 'nature' or being. The determination of 'person' is especially significant here. The prominence of the category of 'person' in dogmatic formulation should not mislead us into supposing that what is at stake here is a kind of subjectivity or personalism analogous to modern uses of this category. It has often and rightly been noted that the term 'person' in the Hellenistic context designates the character in a drama and more particularly the mask that manifests the identity of the character *as speaker*. The category of 'person' operates in dogmatic discourse to make manifest the identity of the primordial speaker whose address is the provocation of our discourse. The structure of kerygmatic discourse always entails, we have said, the disclosure, modification, and founding of person as the subject of speaking/hearing. Christological dogma defines the identity of the hearer (very man of very man) and speaker (very God of very God) as the coincidence of opposites that founds or generates all Christian discourse. Trinitarian dogma extends this identity in two directions: (1) the identification of the primordial author of the speech-event (Father) with the agent of the speech-event (Son), and (2) their identification with (and distinction from) the ongoing empowerment of hearing-speaking in the community or world of history (Spirit). Viewed in this way, Christological and Trinitarian dogmas function to clarify and focus the antecedent conditions of the structure of address.

If this is correct (and it can be at this point no more than a hypothesis) then we are well on our way to distinguishing dogma from doctrine. Dogma is not simply doctrine raised to a higher power of "certitude" or extended to 'universal assent' as a good many theories would have it. It is rather of a fundamentally different order of discourse—not logos but logology. In this connection it is worth remembering that the term 'theology' was restricted in Orthodox Christianity to a reflection upon or contemplation of the Trinity as such and "in itself'—that is, restricted to precisely this 'logo-logical' "mystery" which is properly contemplated (in this tradition) not discursively but—in silence. In any case it is this logo-logical function of dogma that distinguishes it from the elaboration and structuring of the kerygmatic logos which is doctrine.

Lest this be misunderstood it must be said that there are also Christological and Trinitarian 'doctrines' in the sense of the elaboration and systematization of talk about Jesus as Son of God, and about God as Father, Son, and Holy Spirit. These are doctrinal insofar as they are attempts to structure discourse founded by kerygma. This discourse becomes 'dogmatic' when it leaves off its function as a "taxonomy" of discourse to become a reflection upon the possibility of such a discourse and its ordering. This distinction then corresponds tolerably well to the classical distinction between the economic Trinity (doctrine) and the immanent Trinity (dogma).

Having introduced this distinction we must nevertheless prevent it from becoming a disjunction. Theology as the elaboration and systematic ordering of doctrine may be termed 'dogmatics' (not dogma) insofar as it is oriented to the fundamental situation of address that dogma has in view. Thus Barth calls his theology *'Church Dogmatics'* because it is governed on the one hand by Trinitarian dogma and on the other by the necessity of proclamation. Similarly Ebeling writes his *Dogmatics of Christian Faith* from the standpoint of a radical attention to the situation of address as the context of a "word-event." 'Dogmatic' theology is not distinguished from other theologies by a presumed "narrowness" of outlook, but by its orientation to the fundamental structure of speech-event defined by dogma and enunciated in proclamation.

These observations also suggest a way of distinguishing between the logological character of dogma and the logo-logical structure of metaphysics. Both establish the antecedent condition of particular discourses. But dogma does this in terms of the identification of the antecedent conditions of address, while metaphysics does this in terms of the antecedent conditions of the explication of being (causation) or knowing (post-Kantian). In metaphysics vision predominates over voice. Thus the substitution of metaphysics (the consideration of the one God) in Aristotelian terms for dogma (Trinity) in Thomas Aquinas renders the dogma merely arcane, deprives it of its logological function, and results in the deformation of Christian god-language into theism. That this move is necessarily accompanied both in its earlier (Augustinian) and later (Thomistic) versions with a displacement of the metaphor of audition by that of the "vision of God" should, by now, be self-evident.

It must remain something of an open question whether or not dogma may be understood as not only the grammar or 'depth' structure of Christian discourse but also as internalizing the crisis of discourse occasioned by the rupture of linguistic structures. Certainly dogma is often regarded as if it had merely a stabilizing, consolidating and structuring function. Yet I believe this view to be seriously deficient. It fails to account for the relation between dogma and that which gives rise to the discourse of which it is the grammar or structure.

Accordingly, any attempt to formulate Trinitarian and Christological dogma must concern itself with the way in which such a formulation may account for and represent the rupture of the structures of discourse—including Christian discourse. In this regard we must ask ourselves whether the juxtaposition of three and one does not serve to prevent the development of a merely explicative discourse concerning God? Is it not the case that this paradoxical formula interdicts any attempt to reduce or 'normalize' any talk of God? The normalization of god-talk could take the form of monism or monotheism but this is prevented by the assertion of 'three'. This 'three' may itself be 'normalized' either through subordination and hierarchialization (Monarchian) or through serialization (age of the father, age of the son, age of the holy spirit as in Sabellius, Praxeus or the medievial Joachimists or in the modern Hegelians). But these movements in the direction of a purely explicative discourse are interdicted by the Trinitarian formula itself. Thus it is at least plausible to suppose that the function of dogma is to prevent the stabilization or consolidation of Christian discourse. It serves then as a permanent provocation of discourse.

III. Conclusion

In this chapter we have been exploring the thesis that much talk about God in Christian (but also Jewish and Islamic) discourse may be understood as the elaboration and reflective transposition of a kerygmatic structure. This structure is summarized by such phrases as word-event, speech-event, word of God and "audition as vocation." It is distinguished from explicative (and thus also predictive and meta-explicative) discourse by the predominance of the metaphor of voice over that of vision to bring to expression the encounter with alterity that ruptures the structures of experience and so of language. This alterity breaks into experience as an address that alters the "experiencing subject," constituting this subject first as 'hearer' and then also as speaker. Kerygmatic speech is the repetition of this address by the 'hearer' who has, by that fact, become speaker. It is for this reason that the discourse of the community is also termed "Word of God."

I have maintained that this structure governs and accounts for the tensions between command as law, which by itself leads to rigorism, and the interdiction of this rigorism by the annunciation of grace (which by itself leads to antinominanism). This structure similarly accounts for the development of narrative as the elaboration of the identity of speaker and hearer, as well as for the development of an apocalyptic complement to narrative discourse, which abrogates all fixed and isolate identity. Similarly, doctrinal discourse is to be understood as the transposition of this kerygmatically, narratively, and apocalyptically articulated identity into the register of conceptual, intelligible, and public discourse. Since this doctrinal discourse is derived from and drives toward this kerygmatic structure it may also be understood to disclose the character of the speaker/hearer in this kerygmatic structure. This also helps to account for the dialectical and sometimes paradoxical character of doctrine, because it reflects not a stable identity but an identity-in-transformation (from non-hearer to hearer, from non-speaker to speaker, etc.). Its dialectical character is derived from the situation of address from which it arises and toward which it aims (proclamation). Finally dogma as the definition of that by virtue of which address occurs (two natures—one person; three persons—one nature) is to be understood as the logology of this kerygmatic structure.

Kerygmatically governed discourse may be most helpfully distinguished from explicative discourse by the distinction between *de*-scription and *pre*-scription. Explicative discourse is concerned with "the way things are" or appear to be and so is descriptive in function. In description 'god' functions to explain, whereas in prescription 'god' functions to alter or transform. These differences are radical and thorough-going, and they result in quite different meanings for the 'same' lexical item or term.

Ironically kerygmatically derived discourse stands in a much closer relation to expletive and predicative uses of 'god' than to explicative and meta-explicative uses. For it is characteristic of kerygmatic discourse that it articulates rather than suppresses the rupture of linguistic and experiential structures. To the extent to which theism is properly identified with valuing structure and preventing its rupture, kerygmatic discourse is 'anti-theistic'. This is not because it avoids or finds meaningless any talk of God—on the contrary—but because its way of speaking of God is necessarily opposed or in unalterable contradiction to theistic structures. It may therefore not have been a mistake to suppose that Jesus was, from the standpoint of elements of Judaism that had temporarily forgotten their own prophetic and iconoclastic tradition, a blasphemer. Nor was it wholly mistaken when early Christians were denounced by their contemporaries as atheistic and impious. This may also indicate why the attempt to develop theism as an apologetic bridge to the understanding of Christianity was doomed from the very beginning.

The urgent task of theology is thus to develop a non-theistic doctrine of God. This task is one that theology has set itself, beginning with the work of Barth and Bultmann (and, to a certain extent also Tillich). The prosecution of this task has resulted in a number of disparate theological proposals—a diversity suggested by the juxtaposition of such names as Gerhard Ebeling, Jürgen Moltmann, and Thomas J.J. Altizer. What these proposals have in common despite their diversity, is the renunciation of explicative and meta-explicative discourse in favor of an attempt to reformulate doctrine as a reflection upon the situation of address. In that respect these theologies, like those of Barth and Bultmann, are post-theistic.

13

God in Doxological Discourse

Perhaps the most widely used variety of god-language among Christians is to be found in the liturgical language of prayer and praise. Its importance in this respect may be indicated by the reflection that while only a few Christians preach and a still smaller number engage in explicit or formal theology, most participate in the worship services of their congregation and thus employ here and elsewhere the language of these hymns and prayers.

Despite the widespread and crucially important use of this language, very little attention is given to it either in linguistic analysis or in theology. The underdeveloped state of research and reflection in this area makes a summary assessment of it rather difficult. Still the beginnings of such a sketch must be made if we are to have a sense for the way in which god-language is used by those who use it (as opposed to those who study it) most. In what follows I will attempt a preliminary sketch of some of the peculiar features of the religious language of prayer and praise.

We must of course remember that this language with respect to its words and its surface structure is exactly the same language we use in other circumstances. It is necessary to remark upon this since some liturgical language is archaic, and these archaisms may cause us to suppose that this language is superficially different from other uses of language. In fact archaisms are entirely incidental to liturgical language. If they have any function at all (apart from sentimentality) it is to remind us of a peculiarity or 'oddity' that exists elsewhere than on the surface of the language. Unfortunately the opposite result is often achieved by their use; too often we do not look beyond these superficial symptoms.

In any case our task must be to inquire into the fundamental structure of this discourse so as to be able to identify the way the term 'god' functions in relation to this structure. For purposes of convenience I shall refer to this discourse as oralogical or doxological language designating, respectively, the structure of prayer and the structure of praise. Except where the difference is explicitly under discussion I mean to use them interchangeably.

Like kerygmatic language but unlike explicative language, doxological language has the character of address rather than that of explanation. This follows from the simple observation that prayer and praise have the form of concrete address and that the one who is thus addressed is identified by the term 'god', or by other terms, titles, elaborations, and circumlocutions which, together, constitute the god-talk of doxological discourse. Doxological discourse then is not language *about* God, nor is it language *from* God (Word of God); it is language directed *to* God. Such language is then not descriptive (explicative) or prescriptive (kerygmatic) but "ascriptive" of the honor, power, mercy which is the basis of praise and petition. Thus god-talk has a vocative character in the language of prayer and praise—it functions to name, call, or summon the one to whom speech as address is directed. While both kerygmatic and doxological language share this vocative structure of address the grammatical position of god-talk in doxological discourse is the reverse of that in kerygmatic discourse. In kerygmatic discourse 'God' designates the one who speaks, in oralogical discourse 'God' designates the one to whom speech is addressed. In the discussion of doxological discourse regular attention will have to be paid to the ways in which this discourse supplements and corrects the kerygmatic discourse whose structure and elaboration we have already indicated. Only in the interplay of these ways of speaking do we find the full range of Christian discourse displayed.

I. Preliminary Description

Before attempting to locate this doxological structure more precisely in relation to the explicative and kerygmatic structures discussed in previous chapters it may be useful to attend to the characteristic 'genres' of prayer and praise, as present in biblical and liturgical discourse. How are these genres presented and understood within the community of faith and what is their basis understood to be in that context?

With respect to prayer we may take the clue of Romans 8:28 which links prayer to the "groaning of the spirit." This groaning or sighing is the yearning of the heart for that which founds existence and generates life. This longing of the heart is also the opening and orienting of existence to that which both transcends and grounds existence. This opening and orienting of existence, this longing and yearning, is based upon the absence of that for which it asks, seeks and opens itself. The absence of God is the beginning and basis of every prayer.[1]

But this absence is not simply absolute. The longing, yearning, opening, and orienting of existence qualifies this absence as a 'no longer present' or a 'not-yet present'. Thus presence is the penumbra, the shadow of the absence which gives rise to prayer. This presence also comes to expression in language—in the poetry of praise—in doxological language. As such, doxological language is the language which anticipates the presence for which prayer asks and to which prayer directs itself. The groaning of the spirit is thus related to the 'leaping' or onrush of the spirit—the joy of anticipation corresponds to the sighing of longing. These two movements of the spirit belong together and, indeed, imply one another.[2]

In the analysis of the regions of experience undertaken in part two it is clear that at the level of experience designated by the rupture of the structures of everydayness, the negative and positive aspects of such a rupture belong together. Thus in the ontological region both 'ground' and 'abyss' figure the experience of rupture. Prayer corresponds to the yearning for the ground that overcomes an actual or virtual abyss. Thus yearning for the ground presupposes the actuality or possibility of the abyss. Praise, on the other hand, is the anticipation and expression of the ground which overcomes the abyss. Praise anticipates and articulates that for which prayer yearns. Prayer is the articulation of the absence of that for which it yearns. Praise is the articulation of the presence of that for which prayer asks.

This same relation of presence and absence may be worked out in relation to the other contrasting pairs of radical affections even more clearly. Thus prayer may be understood as the cry for a future in the absence of that future (thy Kingdom come) or as the cry for the other who is absent (why have you abandoned me?) just as praise is the exultation which expresses the bestowal of gracious presence or of the future.

Similar relationships obtain for the radical affections of the aesthetic region—most obviously with respect to the call for or celebration of energy,

vitality, or life. Similarly the contrast of light and darkness figures prominently in liturgical language which praises the doxa of God or calls out for
the light that banishes darkness and chaos. In each of these cases we may
say that prayer is the call for that wholeness, grace, vitality, and light which
is absent, while praise is the breaking into speech of the presence of that
plentitude for which prayer asks.

Another way of relating and contrasting this double discourse of prayer
and praise is to locate the chief distinction between oralogical and doxological
discourse in the status of the speaker. In oralogical discourse the speaker
stands empty and in need (or, in intercession, in the place of one who is
empty and in need). In doxological discourse the speaker stands in plenitude
and "ecstasis." Fundamental priority must be given here to doxological
discourse since it is the basis (though possibly the hidden basis) of oralogical
discourse. The possibility of praise is the basis of prayer.

The use of god-talk to bring this yearning (prayer) and anticipation (praise)
to expression is rooted in the recognition that that for which the subject
yearns and that which the subject anticipates is transcendent to or fundamentally other than the subject. This radical alterity is recognized and
affirmed by ascribing that for which one yearns and that which one anticipates to 'God' as the one to whom the subject turns in openness whether
in longing (prayer) or anticipation (praise). God-talk is then vocative and
ascriptive in the language of prayer and praise. Both prayer and praise are
articulated in a simple or complex way upon the dialectic of presence and
absence.

Common to prayer and praise is the movement of turning toward that
which is felt as transcendent to, yet constitutive of, the 'subject'—whether
this is felt as absent (prayer) or present (praise). The 'subject' addresses itself
to that which founds or will found the 'subject'. The name of God here
serves as a kind of compass point to indicate the direction of this turning,
addressing, adverting. The rupturing of the structures of existence is not
merely 'named' but 'summoned', not merely 'experienced' but 'intended'.

We may illustrate this thesis by attending to a prototypical prayer. The
maranatha (Aramaic for "Lord come") is probably the earliest prayer of the
community and in any case is the most compressed expression of the liturgical life of the early church. Because of its special place in this regard
it may reward special attention.

The prayer, as I have said, is highly compressed. It may be translated as
an announcement "The Lord comes," "The Lord is come," and as an
invocation "Come Lord." In the first case the maranatha serves to announce
presence and plenitude. In the second case this presence or plenitude is

addressed from the standpoint of its absence (since you are not yet here, and since this is intolerable, "come quickly"). As a petition or invocation the maranatha addresses the emptiness, longing, and yearning of the congregation to the one who is absent. But this absent one is not simply or purely absent. This absence is a no longer and a not yet present. More than this, however, the Lord is virtually present in such a way as to make address possible and necessary. Thus the 'presence' of the Lord is the aim and the hidden basis of the prayer which articulates the absence of the Lord. Thus the announcement (The Lord is Come) is implicit in the petition (Come Lord). The announcement is similarly complex. As an announcement of presence it is the announcement of a presence which has displaced absence. But if the presence of the Lord has overcome the absence of the Lord then this absence is taken up into the presence in such a way as to be a cause for rejoicing and thus of cultic celebration. Thus the phrase "my wife is home" functions one way if she always is and quite another if she has been absent for too long. When this statement of presence is addressed to the one who is present (and not to do so is not to take into account the one who is present) it is then doxological in structure ("you're home!"). What makes the assertion liturgical in character is the vector quality of the assertion—its "directionality." If it is directed to the congregation it may be descriptive (that's the way it is) or prescriptive (be as those to whom the Lord has come). But when it is turned to the one who has come or is to come it is liturgical in character. As liturgical it may 'articulate' absence (oralogically) or presence (doxologically). But as we have noted absence and presence are dialectically related to one another.

II. The Elaboration of Oralogical Discourse

With this preliminary sketch in view we turn now to an attempt to discriminate particular kinds of discourse that elaborate and reflect upon the doxological language of the Christian community. For purposes of clarity we will follow the outline which guided us in the similar exploration of kerygmatic language.

Speaking as Response

As we have seen, both kerygmatic and doxological language have the structure of address. In both cases we are confronted not with discussion about or description of but with address to. In both cases we have the correlation of two subjects: a speaker and a hearer. Thus any elaboration of this discourse is an elaboration of the *who* of these subjects rather than the *what* of an intervening object. Once again there is here no question of the transmission of information (at least this is not the *point* of the language) but a calling, summoning, and in that sense a 'naming'.

If we return to the table of radical affections developed in part two of this essay we see that once again we are confronted with what we have termed the metaphor of voice rather than that of vision. But in doxological language this metaphor has a different application. It is now we who speak. The location of 'god' is thus reversed. Instead of being the way of designating the 'one who speaks' this term designates the 'one to whom we speak'. The basic situation of address therefore receives new dimensions. We may now elaborate this structure in the following way: in kerygmatic structure the address of God results in the repetition of this address by the hearer, who thereby becomes a speaker. In the language of praise we have however not a reptition but an answering or responding. Instead of the hearer addressing her or his neighbor, the address is turned back to the 'prime speaker' to that which has transformed existence/experience and thus language. Prayer is also addressed in this way but is a calling for (invocation) rather than a responding to (evocation) this word.

This dialectic of absence and presence constitutive of the liturgical rhythm of prayer and praise may be understood as the articulation of the rupture of the structures of linguisticality. In the case of prayer as the articulation of and protest against need, lack, and absence, the discourse functions to draw attention to the inadequacy of given ordering structures. Thus the call: "your Kingdom come" articulates the critique of any existing 'state of affairs'; in the face of this call, such structures can no longer appear stable, self-evident, or viable. Prayer may be understood as the call for the abolition of every such structure which is, in the face of such a call, exposed as a pseudo-structure. The radicality and totality of the transformation for which prayer calls (The Kingdom of God) is that which marks prayer as a "sighing too deep for words." We will have to see to what extent the articulation of this sighing in liturgy may be understood as internalizing this critique of every structure and thus of language as such.

The presence which is articulated in praise is, as well, to be understood as the rupture of every given structure. This point may be less obvious than the first since we may think of 'presence' as that which validates or legitimizes (and in this sense "sanctifies") order and structure. Yet this impression is, I believe, a superficial one and one which is contrary to the more fundamental 'logic' of praise. What comes to speech in praise is a plenitude that exceeds (and so transgresses) every stabilizing structure—including that of language.

The way in which language is exceeded by the articulation of praise is most strikingly exemplified by the phenomenon of glossalalia. The phenomenon of speaking in tongues is by no means restricted to Christianity. A good many quite diverse religious traditions have their own way of manifesting and of understanding this phenomenon. What is important for our purposes is the way in which glossalalia is understood in at least some sectors of Christianity as the articulation of praise. In both the Pauline and Lukan texts glossalalia is linked to 'praise'. It is understood by Paul to be an "address to God" (1 Cor. 14:2) and is associated with praising and singing (1 Cor. 14:15–17). In Luke's narrative in Acts the attempt to correlate this phenomenon with proclamation in 'other' languages is discernible (Acts 2:5–11) as well as its association with the joyful response to the proclamation (Acts 10:46). The phenomenon of speaking in tongues is by no means unproblematic even at the earliest and thus most charismatic stages of Christianity as Pauline and Lukan texts also show. Nevertheless it is intelligible as the eruption into discourse of that which surpasses discourse.[3]

If I am correct in supposing that glossalalia is to be understood as the generation of 'praise' then it remains to be asked to what this articulation may be supposed to correspond. Here we find the language of excess, plenitude, and abundance as the key indicators of the situation of praise. Glossalalia then and the praise and song which derive from and articulate it may be understood as the explosion into speech of a plenitude which exceeds speech.

I do not of course mean to suggest that glossalalia or praise as its articulation 'prove' such a plenitude. We are certainly well aware of the possibilities of an artificially or psychologically induced ecstasis. Our argument is not about the reality of experience but about the character of a discourse— a discourse which has a precise and intelligible relation to ordinary language. That relationship is identifiable as the articulation of abundance, excess, plenitude which overwhelms language even as it remains within it and is in an "unknown tongue."

It is noteworthy that both prayer and glossalalia as praise are marked in the New Testament with a certain reserve. Jesus is reported to have prohibited praying in the sight of other persons, and Paul suggests that where there is no 'interpreter' for glossalalia it too should be spoken only in private (1 Cor. 14:28). No such reservation attaches to kerygmatic discourse however. The difference is the difference between speech addressed to one's neighbor, sister, or brother, and speech addressed to God. The former is necessarily public. The latter, which is deformed when it is addressed to one's neighbor into an establishment of one's own privilege, is restricted to the sphere of the private. We shall consider how it reenters the public sphere as 'liturgy' shortly. But first we must examine more closely the relation of doxological and oralogical discourse to kerygmatic discourse.

In the discussion of kerygmatically generated discourse we noted that the advent of alterity as address resounds in discourse as the repetition and ramification of address. This is the meaning of "audition as vocation." From the standpoint of prayer and praise we may amplify this characterization in the following way. To the extent to which this address is spoken and heard as the advent of grace and thus of the other as love and the future as promise it is the address of "plenitude" or abundance, which confers or conveys this plenitude to the hearer who becomes a speaker. Speaking that responds directly to this address, answers it or co-responds to it is praise. Praise is the mark or trace of this plenitude—the eruption into discourse of that which exceeds language.

It is the absence, the not yet or no longer present occurrence, of this plenitude that is articulated in prayer as the call for and desire of this abundance. Thus prayer protests the absence of that which the kerygmatic address promises while at the same time turning itself in longing toward that which is promised or announced in kerygma. The 'god-language' of prayer and praise is the ascription of plenitude from the standpoint of its absence or presence.

At this point a misunderstanding may arise. It may be supposed that we are here attempting to lay the foundation for a new theism—a new way of establishing the existence of God as a supreme object. This is not the case. Such a move attempts to account for language by way of an appeal to that to which by hypothesis, the language refers. We are then well on our way to understanding (or rather misunderstanding) this language as a covert proposition whose meaning (or meaningfulness) is to be determined by asking: is there or can there be evidence for the existence of the state of affairs described by this language? We are then returned to the sterile debate of theism and atheism. Instead of determining the meaning of this language by asking about the extra-linguistic reference of the language it is our task to determine the way this language is structured and the way in which it functions.

Those who suppose that the existence of a supreme being must be proved to account for this language should consider the following: Is it not the case that the explicative and meta-explicative language which purports to describe the nature of God actually renders prayer unintelligible? Are we not confronted there with the reflection: since God is 'all knowing' and wills only good is it not impossible that God should either not know what we want or not give it to us without our asking? Similarly in the case of praise do we not meet with the objection that since God can lack nothing God therefore cannot need or desire our praise? And if the response is made that we do these things for our sake rather than for God's (and this is said by several theologians) then have we not rendered the form of *address* unintelligible? Thus what purports to be an 'account' of address turns instead into an elimination of address.[4] Is then the result of theism any different than the result of atheism with respect to this language? This result is certainly astonishing. It is to be accounted for by the observation that we are dealing here with radically different language-games rather than with more or less deficient or adequate modes of the same language-game.

Our concern then is with this fundamental structure (or grammar) of doxological language and with the way in which this structure generates discourse through elaboration and transformation. We are concerned not with the derivation of this structure from some extra-linguistic state of affairs but with the way in which this structure exhibits fundamental features of our linguisticality—a linguisticality which is not only a 'means of communication' but is also and more fundamentally the mode of address.

Address as Ascription
The basic 'content' of doxological discourse is the identification of speaker and hearer in relation to one another. This corresponds to the initial articulation of kerygmatic discourse. With respect to the identification of the speaker the most obvious form is that of confession. In a prayer of confession the one who prays is fundamentally naming her or himself. In general, however, this self-naming is tacit or implicit in the naming of the one to whom prayer and praise are directed. The naming of the one addressed is done *ascriptively*. That is, the god-language of this discourse is elaborated by ascribing to the one addressed that which corresponds (either in contrast or correlation) to the condition of the subject. The name "Merciful Father" for example ascribes to the one being addressed that mode of being which corresponds to my condition. This correspondence may be contrasting and negative (I am lost, alone, guilty) or positive and correlative (I am found, forgiven). In the first place we have prayer, in the second, praise. Thus the identity of speaker and hearer correspond to one another in such a way as to name the one in the naming of the other. The most rudimentary or primitive content of doxological/oralogical discourse then is this naming by ascription.

Whereas the language of prayer emphasizes the contrast or opposition of the identity of speaker and hearer (sin–grace, need–fullness) the language of praise anticipates and articulates the collapse of this separation and alienation and alterity. The abundance of the one is conveyed to the other in such a way that the distinction is overcome, at least provisionally. Thus the identity of the community in praise corresponds to the identity of God— both may be designated as "doxa" for example. In the tradition of Eastern Orthodoxy this finds expression in talk of the deification of the community, and this deification is proleptically articulated in the praise of the community. This development is anticipated in the liturgical language of the early Christian community, which speaks of God "uniting all things in Himself" (Eph. 1:10). Thus doxological (like apocalyptic) language anticipates and articulates the volatilization of identity into the divine totality.

This abolition of distinction may however become 'demonic' when it serves to ascribe fullness or plenitude to existing structures. In this case it is merely the mystification of privilege, which seeks to prevent any true or radical transformation of existing structures. This is why we find the language of ecstasy and praise subjected to criticism already in I Corinthians and throughout the Christian tradition. For when praise is merely the sanctification of the status quo or the privileging of one's own status, then it no longer articulates the rupture of given structures but rather their maintenance. Thus the articulation of absence, lack, and yearning as prayer is the necessary counterbalance to the articulation of plenitude as praise. It prevents praise from becoming its own opposite by preventing the god-talk of praise from becoming the descriptive legitimation of structure.

Law and Grace

In the discussion of kerygmatically generated discourse we noted that address may take the form of command, which is then elaborated as law. We also noted that this elaboration when unchecked produces rigorism, which is then regularly opposed or interdicted in the Judeo-Christian traditions. The ground of this interdiction may be found in the logic of prayer and praise— especially the latter.

If praise is the articulation of a received or anticipated plenitude and if this plenitude is not 'possessed' or 'grasped' but is the gracious advent of the other and promise of a future, then praise is the articulation of love, a love which answers to or corresponds to that apprehension of alterity as love. Now it is precisely this which interdicts all legalism and rigorism. For it is the character of legalism and rigorism that they attempt to establish or defend, acquire or maintain a separated identity. Their essential point of departure is a threat to the loss of identity and so an attempt to acquire or to defend identity. Thus rigorism 'fends off' the threat to this identity through the legal structuring of existence.[5] The advent of the other as grace, promise or love makes nonsense of this attempt. Thus the annunciation of a gracious plenitude abolishes the possibility of the elaboration of command into legalism.

But it does not abolish command. This would be possible only on the basis of an actual and total correspondence of our existence to that address which calls, claims, and transforms our existence. Thus the abolition of command is an apocalyptic but not yet an existential reality. The tension between command and grace is then formulated as the "law of love." Such a formulation, and it is to be found in Judaism as well as in Jesus, Paul, John, Augustine, and Luther (to cite only the best-known examples), is certainly paradoxical in that it prevents the stabilization of ethical discourse either in legalism or in antinomianism. Instead it volatilizes the subject toward identification with the "neighbor" and toward identification with that gracious alterity which transforms existence in the world. The *command* of love marks the difference and deferral of that eschatological identity which the command of *love* anticipates and represents.

Liturgical Expansion and Elaboration

The liturgy of the community is developed through the elaboration and juxtaposition of oralogical and doxological discourse. Hymns of praise alternating with the invocative formulations of prayer constitute the rhythm of this liturgy. The cry from absence, the cry of yearning, the articulation of need and lack punctuates the song of exuberance, of abundance, of presence. Neither alone but both together constitute the worship, the liturgy of the community. Like the narrative that elaborates kerygmatic discourse, the liturgy which elaborates doxological discourse has a dramatic structure constituted by this rhythm of absence and presence, of yearning and celebration.

In this discussion we must concentrate upon the specifically linguistic aspects of liturgy because of the nature of our problematic (i.e., god-language). However, this should not be taken as implying or entailing that these linguistic aspects of liturgy are the most crucial aspects of liturgy in general.[6] Indeed ritual (to use a generic rather than specifically Christian term) as unity of linguistic and para- or extra-linguistic phenomena (dance, gesture, symbolic action, and matter) brings to expression precisely through this unity, the unity of the 'speaker'/'actor', community/world which is characteristic of the doxological structure. It is the speaking *subject* as a whole who is addressed to God and not only the speaker *qua* speaker. Ritual action brings to expression this prior unity of the intellective, affective, imaginative, and bodily in addressing the subject's existence to that alterity which it names as "God."

This unity of the subject in ritual is at the same time the unity of the subject in participation with community and cosmos. Thus in ritual there is no separation between individual and community, even in the case of the elevation of the priest or liturgist whose function is representative (of community and/or of God) rather than individual. The unity with the cosmos or nature is expressed most clearly in the use of sacred elements (water, wine, bread, oil). It is thus no isolated individual or subject whose existence *coram deo* is enacted in the ritual, but the subject in psycho-cosmic totality.

The universalizing or totalizing character of the language of prayer and praise brings into play the onto-aesthetic regions of experience while subordinating these to the historical. Thus the language of plenitude, light and joy and wonder play a strong role in doxological address, while prayer articulates their absence as a protest against despair and emptiness and iron necessity. All of these are correlated to the advent of 'alterity as address' as that to which praise responds and for which prayer asks. It is this correlation to address which prevents the ontological and aesthetic from overwhelming the historical region and so transforming ascriptive into descriptive discourse.

In the relationship between ritual and liturgy we may also find the basis for the public character of the language of prayer and praise in the Christian community. I have already noted that this language is marked by a certain reserve at its very inception within the Christian community. In subsequent Christianity, however, its public display is astonishingly seldom thought of as problematic. I take this to be one of the most fundamental problems for liturgical theology. It is, I believe, possible to overcome this difficulty only if liturgy is understood to exhibit basic paradigms for existence in the world. Only such a paradigmatic quality and function can justify the display of the language of prayer and praise. But this will in turn mean that liturgy must not be understood as a "religious" action separated from the profane and worldly reality "outside the temple," but as the concentrated enactment of gestures and words whose aim is the transformation of existence in the world. This entails a "non-religious" interpretation of liturgical action and speech.

The liturgy identifies this unitary or total subject in relation to God—a relation characterized by absence and presence in fundamental tension. This tension is that which requires the form of dramatic tension characteristic of liturgy and of its elements.

The god-talk embedded in liturgy may be understood as functioning to direct the subject (the community) to that in the presence and absence of which it has its being. God-talk names the 'audience' (that is, the hearing) to whom the word and gesture is directed, and thus the audience to which the subject/community is directed. God-talk then construes the existence of the community as existence *coram deo* (before or in the face of God).

That liturgical language is an elaboration of the rupture of language through the advent of a radical alterity it names "God" (or Spirit or Word) means that it bears within itself the principle of its own deconstruction. Thus the appropriation of cultic and ritual forms from its parental Judaism and circumambiant Hellenistic world always is accompanied by a critique of these forms and a delegitimizing of their language and action. This may be seen at virtually every stage of the development of the early church. The critique of the cultus is well known in Paul with his abhorrence of the celebration of times and seasons (the liturgical calendar) (Gal. 4:10) and his demystification of the problem of food offered to idols (1 Cor. 8). This same process is at work in the Gospel of Mark with the 'rending' of the veil of the temple and thus the abolition of the separation of sacred and profane that is at the heart of a cultus. The abolition of priesthood and sacrifice in Hebrews and the elimination of the temple in the Gospel and in the Apocalypse of John illustrate the same tendency. Yet precisely this 'demolition' of the cultus engenders a liturgy, and the very texts within which this critique is offered are themselves liturgical texts both in composition (as in Mark and Revelation) and in canonicity (whether they are used, and appropriately and even necessarily used, in the worship of the community is in fact the question of 'canon') and thus in the regular use to which they are put by the community. It would be a serious misunderstanding to suppose that the critique of the cult is only directed against "the others." For it is and must be an internal critique. But this critique by no means abolishes cult and ritual. Instead it appropriates them and volatilizes them. The deconstruction is a dissemination (Derrida).

A theory of liturgical action, language, and order will then be obliged to show how this critical and volatilizing principle is at work here—how this action and word not only stabilizes but also destabilizes and so is continually regenerated.

Liturgy and Canon

This liturgy is elaborated into an entire liturgical cycle extended throughout the year. This cycle is itself articulated upon the rhythm of fasting and feasting reflective of the tension of prayer (absence) and praise (presence).

The liturgical cycle serves also as a canon or rule of communal prayer and praise and thus functions normatively in the same way Scripture functions for kerygmatically derived or structured discourse. We may even postulate that those rituals designated as sacraments (perhaps especially the Eucharist or Lord's supper) function to regulate in a concentrated way the whole of the liturgical cycle in the same way creedal formulations intensively structure kerygmatic discourse.

In the discussion of the elaboration of kerygmatic address in narrative we noted that narrative requires an apocalyptic 'completion' which prevents that narrativity from assuming the character of a past and thus already acquired identity. It may be that sacramental action is to be understood as having a secular function vis a vis the liturgical cycle or rhythm. By itself the liturgical cycle tends to 'normalize' or 'regularize' existence in the world. It may be or become the 'sanctification' of a given and self-evident structure.[7] A counter-tendency may be exhibited in sacrament (especially Eucharist) *provided that* sacrament is understood as the disclosure of apocalyptic consummation. This is the meaning of the "mystery" that is translated as "sacrament." Mystery/sacrament is the manifestation of apocalypse—its "happening in advance." Thus the enactment of sacrament anticipates the eschatological upheaval, reversal, and consummation of all things in the divine plenitude. A consummation, let us recall, which is figured as the abolition of temple, priestcraft, and cult (Rev. 21).[8]

Now, of course we know that exactly the opposite may be signified by sacrament and liturgy—that these may be deformed into the stabilization of a status quo, the separation of identities, the perpetuation of privilege. But it may and must be asked whether this development does not find itself in contradiction to the internal and fundamental logic of Christian liturgy and sacrament.

However understood, an appropriately articulated 'canon' of doxological discourse serves to pattern the informal or extemporaneous or individual uses of doxological discourse. Thus, for example, the formal, liturgical prayers of confession, petition, or intercession structure the informal "prayer life" of the community and its members. They do this by modeling or displaying the linguistic structures appropriate to the expression of need, lack, or absence on the one hand, and of plenitude, abundance, or joy on the other.

The liturgical cycle has a regulative (as well as elaborative) status vis a vis doxological language. It is also the case, however, that scriptural canon and creed have an important relation to this liturgical canon of which we must not lose sight if we are to avoid an artificial abstraction of doxological from kerygmatic language.

In our discussion of kerygmatic discourse we noted that this language is regulated by an intensive (creed) and an extensive (canon) norm in which the former is to be understood as a compression (plot summary) of the latter. This 'rule of faith' may also be related to doxological discourse. The canon includes not only narrative materials (and imposes a narrative order even upon non-narrative materials which are 'located' between Genesis and Revelation, origin and end) but also a considerable body of oralogical and doxological material. For example, the Psalms are sometimes referred to as the 'prayer book' of Israel or the Church. Form criticism has identified a considerable amount of liturgical material not only in the Old Testament but in the New Testament as well. The Lukan and, especially, the Matthean versions of the Lord's Prayer are taken by the theological tradition to be the paradigm of all subsequent Christian prayer. We may also draw attention to the often noticed 'liturgical structure' of the Apocalypse of John as a further (and final) illustration of the way in which the canon includes and (by including) regulates the liturgical language of prayer and praise.

There is an even more intimate connection between canon and liturgy however. It lies in the fact that materials are included in the canon *because* they were, or were to be, included in the liturgy of the community. It appears that debates concerning the inclusion of Hebrews or the Apocalypse were resolved by the consideration that these texts played an important part in the worship of several Christian communities. Thus the canon is as much a product of liturgical (doxological) considerations as of kerygmatic.

Just as we must locate canon in a liturgical as well as a kerygmatic context so also with creed. A creed is both a 'plot summary' of narrative and an element in liturgy. It has its place in liturgy as an 'act of praise' that summarizes the 'ascription' of honor to God as the aim or goal of human existence, experience, and language.

A still more fundamental relation obtains between canon (Scripture) and liturgy. A canonically fixed identity recedes ever into the past and so threatens to become a heteronomous norm. The 'supplement' of liturgy destabilizes this identity by enacting it in new and transfigured ways. At the same time the canonical and creedal norm prevents this liturgical enactment from becoming a mere celebration of the status quo. Thus together and in contrast to one another these poles of liturgy and canon generate ever new articulations of the vocative structure they together exemplify.

Doctrine

Although liturgy is not typically the 'source' of theological reflection in the Western tradition (which focuses upon Scripture and creed) it has long occupied this position in Eastern Christian theology. Basil's reflections in *On the Holy Spirit* for example, arise from a liturgical controversy: whether the hymnn of praise may be directed not only to Father and Son, but to Spirit as well.[9] Basic treatises on Christian life and doctrine are typically developed as commentaries upon liturgical practice in the tradition which begins with the Cappadocians and continues through medieval theology (e.g., Cabasilas)[10] and on through to the present (e.g., in the work of Alexander Schmemann).[11]

This doctrinal reflection has two foci: the formation of Christian life (ethics) and the reflection upon God as the goal of life and liturgy (the triune God).

Ethics The discussion of kerygmatically generated discourse indicated that theological anthropology is developed as the doctrinal reflection upon the narrative—apocalyptic depiction of human existence in the transition from non-hearer to hearer and from hearer to speaker. There it is constituted as a reflection upon transformation (conversion) and vocation (sanctification). The public and paradigmatic action of the community in its common liturgy (*leit*-urgia = action of the *people*) serves as a demonstration of call, transformation, vocation, etc. This demonstration or enactment occasions reflection upon the shape, form, or style of life that is displayed in concentrated and dramatic form. The reflection upon kerygmatic and doxological paradigms as normative articulation and enactment of forms of life produces "ethics." In Western (Latin and post-Latin) theology ethical reflection has regularly been associated primarily with the practice of confession, penance, and "satisfaction," but this sequence has often dropped out of liturgical practice to become a propaedeutic to worship. In the Eastern churches however the entire liturgical sequence of actions has been taken to be a paradigm for life and reflection. Accordingly, much greater attention has been given there to the 'doxological' character of ethical reflection. Since I take this to be a necessary and beneficial corrective to the "moral theology" or "Christian ethics" of Western Christianity, I have reserved my discussion of ethics for the discussion of doxological structures.

We should first notice that the connection between ethics and liturgical action is firmly embedded in biblical traditions. I will have to content myself with only two examples. In the summation of the law ascribed by Luke and Matthew to Jesus we have: "You shall love the Lord your God with all your heart, mind, soul, and strength and your neighbor as yourself." As is well known, the elements of this summary are present in Leviticus and the summary statement itself is anticipated in rabbinical literature. What is less often understood is the way in which this summation links doxological action (love of God) to 'ethical' action (love of neighbor). The demonstration of the doxological action is praise, the demonstration of the second is the 'overflow' of praise toward the neighbor. Praise is the articulation of 'abundance', plenitude, or affluence. Love of the neighbor is the enactment of this plenitude toward the other. This 'logic' of plenitude is seen in Jesus' otherwise puzzling parable of the Good Samaritan (Luke 10:29–37).[12]

The second illustration is from the prayer that, according to Luke and Matthew, Jesus taught his disciples to pray. I have in mind here particularly the clause "forgive us . . . as we forgive . . . " This formulation is also anticipated in Jewish literature, especially in the reflections of Jesus son of Sirach (Eccles. 28:2). Again it is remarkable in this connection on account of its specifically 'liturgical' character. In contrast to the summary of the law (which, of course, both abolishes and 'completes' the law) the situation here is not one of plenitude but of lack or need; specifically the petitioners' 'indebtedness' or need of forgiveness, liberation, and thus plenitude. But like plenitude in the love of the neighbor so also in the case of lack or need in the forgiveness of the neighbor, the turning toward God is executed as a turning toward the neighbor. Thus our need or desire for transformation and plenitude is redirected in such a way as to engender deeds of liberating transformation for the other.[13] 'Forgiveness', it must be said, refers not to an attitude but to an action, not to a superficial action but to a fundamental intervention and transformation.

Now these examples suggest the exceedingly close relationship between reflection upon 'prayer and praise' and reflection upon 'ethics'. The development of ethical discourse is the development of this interconnection. Where this connection is dissolved then we may no longer have a specifically theological ethic but rather a general moral discourse which explicates structures of exchange (duty) and calculation of ends. An explicitly theological ethical reflection orients itself to the elaboration of existence as an existence *coram deo*, an existence articulated as the absence (and call for) or the presence (and plenitude of) God in prayer and praise.

It is important to give some attention to the relation between doxological and kerygmatic structures of discourse, as it is apparent that there is a significant degree of overlap. I have maintained that ethical discourse is based upon liturgical language and thus the language of prayer and praise. The difficulty is that ethical discourse has a generally *prescriptive* structure, that is, a structure which we would normally associate with kerygmatic language. Does this mean that ethical discourse has here been displaced and belongs in our discussion of kerygmatic rather than doxological language? Or is this prescriptive structure only a surface, as opposed to a depth structure? Or must we speak here of a combination of structures? Or are we obliged to distribute ethical discourse across the spectrum of descriptive, prescriptive, and ascriptive modes of ethical discourse?

Certainly kerygmatic and doxological structures belong together. This is evident from the vocative structure they share, in contrast to the "objective" structure of descriptive discourse. This togetherness is further attested by the presence of proclamation in worship and by the liturgical use of Scripture. This togetherness should be exemplified in the various modes or levels of discourse that reflect and reflect upon these basic structures. Thus we may expect a mutual re-enforcement of kerygmatic and doxological structures at all levels, including the sphere of ethical discourse. This mutuality of interaction is articulated in the insistence (most forcefully and persuasively expressed by Karl Barth) that considerations of doctrine and ethics belong together.[14]

Nevertheless it remains, I believe, appropriate to insist upon the priority of a doxological structure for ethical reflection. Barth acknowledges this when he proposes an outline for a consideration of Christian ethics in which a consideration of baptism, Lord's prayer, and Eucharist supply the skeleton for distinctively Christian ethical reflection.[15] The basis of ethics in liturgy has been further stressed by Käsemann and by Moltmann despite their own heavy emphasis upon the kerygmatic language of liberation.[16]

If I am right in suggesting that Christian ethics is to be grounded in liturgy and thus in the language of prayer and praise, then the fundamental problematic of Christian ethics is not: 'what does the Lord require' but *what sort of existence is "ascribable" to God.* That is, in what way is existence to be lived so that it may anticipate the principal destiny of human existence as the glorification and enjoyment of God. There is no question but that this would entail a fundamental revision of the discipline of Christian ethics. But it is a revision that might untangle some of the traditional knots of moral theology and open up the prospect of fruitful dialogue with the theology and ethics of Eastern Christendom.

It is worth noting in this connection that in the fragments of an *Ethics* left by Dietrich Bonhoeffer we have just such a call for a fundamental revision of theological ethics.[17] The problem for a distinctively Christian ethics, he maintains, is the abolition of the principle of the discrimination between good and evil. This principle, so important to a philosophical or natural ethic, can have no place, he suggests, in Christian or theological ethics. The reason for this is supplied in his reflections upon the "Fall"[18] in which the fall is characterized as entry into this knowledge, this discrim-

ination. Now this may be reformulated from the perspective of our own
argument. Theological ethics does indeed abolish or at least render questionable the logic of morality, which involves above all a discrimination
between good and evil, righteous and unrighteous, pious and godless, sinners
and saints. The abolition of this discrimination and distinction is most
evident in the language of praise and thus of love. This has already been
demonstrated in our discussions of command here and in the preceding
chapter. In the attempt to develop an ethic along the lines suggested by
Bonhoeffer or in these pages, a significant contribution may be made by a
reflection upon Nietzche's in some ways quite similar call for an ethical
discourse that is "beyond good and evil."[19]

The Doctrine of God   The corollary to the question: what sort of existence
is ascribable to God?, is the question: to what sort of God is this form of
existence ascribable? It is in the course of pursuing this second question that
doxological discourse gives rise to a doctrine of God. Insofar as doctrinal
statements are statements 'about' God they identify the character of that to
which doxological speech is addressed. As a primary example of such movement we may consider the so-called "attributes" of God. The assertion of
the goodness of God, for example, identifies the antecedent condition of
praise and thanksgiving—ascribing this attribute to the being or essence or
reality of God. The movement of ascription (and thus of 'attribution') reflects
the typical structure of praise. Pannenberg, following Schlink, explicates
this movement of attribution/ascription as a 'sacrifice' of the adoring subject
and of "the conceptual univocity of his speech."[20] As such the ascriptive
naming of God is not simply analogical but is a "deliberate" (rather than
arbitrary) equivocation.[21] The doxological character of dogmatic statements
then renders impossible a straightforward (univocal or even analogical) de-
duction of God's nature from the attributes ascribed to God in this way.

Despite the importance of the observation of Schlink and Pannenberg
concerning the doxological generation of the attributes of God, it must
nevertheless be objected that they have failed adequately to understand this
'doxological' logic. Praise is by no means constituted on the basis of an
impoverishment of human being. We have seen that praise is the articulation
of reflected or anticipated plenitude or excess. It is on this basis (and not
by way of a "sacrifice of univocity") that the words of praise (and thus the
attributes of God) *exceed* language. Thus the ascriptive discourse by no means
depletes human being but articulates the excess of human being. This is
the logic of the *via eminentia* or the 'way of the superlative' for the attribution
of God.

The logic of ascription derivative from oralogical address may be similarly understood. Here the actual lack of human being serves as the negative basis for the generation of ascriptive attributes. To God is ascribed that plenitude which corresponds to our need, lack, or yearning. This is the logic of the *via negativa*.

It is when we understand the doxological (and oralogical) generation of the attributes of God that we are in a position both to understand and respond to Feuerbach's claim that the attributes of God are the alienated attributes of humanity. Feuerbach is quite right in sensing the correlation of the attributes of divinity to the articulation of the human condition. But this by no means entails the impoverishment of the human in order to enrich the attribution of God. These *attributes* are not *tribute* to a petty tyrant—a tax to be exacted. They are instead the anticipation of divinization as the goal or aim of human being. Feuerbach's critique is right only if the "identity description" of these attributes loses its doxological and/or apocalyptic character and assumes the form of a fixed and unalterable opposition. When this occurs, we no longer have the logic of ascription but the logic of description and thus the deformation of theological (and thus Christian) discourse. In short we have theism or one of its nearer or more distant cousins.

But the doxological (and apocalyptic) form of ascription anticipates the collapse of such fixed and opposed identities into the "all in all" of eschatological plenitude. This is precisely the meaning of the Orthodox understanding of 'deification' as the aim or goal of the divine economy or soteriology. (God becomes as we are in order that we may become what God is.) In Reformed dogmatics we find a similar formulation under the heading of "glorification" as the end or goal of human being. Even Wesley's notion of "perfection," although perhaps excessively moralized, corresponds to this 'logic' of the collapse of the ultimate distinction between the attributes of divinity and humanity.

The attributes of God then, insofar as they are generated ascriptively (rather than meta-explicatively), are a conceptual anticipation of the aim or goal of human being in the presence, plenitude, and "all in all" of the divine. Thus Pannenberg is correct in supposing that there is a proleptic structure to dogmatic statements concerning God insofar as they have an oralogical basis. But his view of attribution must be corrected from the standpoint of a fuller appreciation of the distinctive character of doxological ascription. The account I have given of the relationship of prayer and praise may clarify how doctrinal statements reflect both the presence and absence of God and so articulate the structure of prayer and praise.

It is possible that a closer attention to the ascriptive character of theological and dogmatic statements would illuminate many of the problems that arise from the attempt to understand these statements as merely descriptive (explicative and meta-explicative) in character. A brief illustration may be of help here. The assertion that God is both all powerful and beneficent has typically been understood as an explicative and therefore descriptive proposition. When these statements are understood in this way (as they are in theism) the well-known problem of "theodicy" emerges. This problem begins with the observation that not all things are good—there is evil in the world. But if God is "all powerful" then God is responsible (omnipotence as explication of what is). If God is responsible for evil then how is this to be reconciled with the goodness of God? Within this framework of descriptive and explicative discourse there are three possible moves: (1) deny the reality of evil (it is an illusion, it serves the good, etc.), (2) deny the omnipotence (as in "panentheism"), (3) deny the beneficence.

Quite a different picture emerges, however, if these "attributes" are understood ascriptively rather than descriptively. In this case the presence of "evil" does not contradict but in fact "motivates" the ascription of power and goodness as the basis for the invocation of that power and goodness as "God." Similarly the occurrence of the overcoming of evil (the healing of sickness or liberation of the masses or what have you) would give rise to ascription of goodness and power as the basis of praise and thanksgiving. In neither case is the assertion "God is good and powerful" being used to describe or to explain a structure, but rather to invoke or celebrate an event. The naive and 'ungrammatical' transposition of ascriptive into descriptive discourse has produced an artificial difficulty.

The development of the doctrine of God must be seen as the result of the interplay of kerygmatic and doxological discourse and of reflection upon them. The Trinitarian form of this doctrine then owes itself to this double origin of Christian god-language in the 'situation of address'.

The transformation of liturgical language into doctrinal discourse is determinative of the god-talk of doctrine. As our reflections upon 'ethics' have shown us, this god-talk is always co-related to talk of the human condition and human destiny. Yet the ascriptive nature of doxological language makes it inevitable that 'god' will be thematized here even more than in the case of kerygmatic or prescriptive language. In this ascriptive structure 'god' functions to indicate that alterity toward which human existence and discourse is oriented and directed. What is of concern for the doctrine of God is then not 'god' as a principle of explanation but as the goal of existence.

In terms of our earlier discussion of language and word we could then say that 'god' signifies the goal of the fundamental transformation or volatilization of language by word. Thus doctrinal discourse founded by the language of prayer and praise will inevitably stand in a relationship of irreducible tension to the explicative discourse that aims at the assimilation of word to language.

At this stage these proposals can be no more than plausible hypotheses no doubt requiring reformulation, elaboration, and testing. Yet even at this stage it is clear that an account of Christian use of 'god' will need to take into account the doxological 'motive' of god-talk in this tradition, a motive which will entail that this god-talk is not reducible to explicative discourse.

Dogma

When doctrinal language gives an account of itself, seeks to exhibit the fundamental structure of its discourse as a regulative 'grammar', we have the development of dogma. The peculiar status of dogma as 'mystery of the faith' owes not to the antiquity of its formulation but to the logo-logical function it performs.

In the development of dogma, doxological discourse with its ascription of attributes to God plays an indispensable function. Indeed the question of the divinity of Son and Spirit are originally posed as the question whether these are to be the object of praise or worship. The determination of the full divinity of the Spirit then regulates both doxological discourse (the Spirit is praised "together with" Father and Son) and the doctrinal discourse that reflects upon doxological and kerygmatic language.

Simply to notice these connections is to open up a host of issues for exploration. The task of a reconstruction of Trinitarian dogma, which I believe to be an urgent one, will include the clarification of the respective roles of kerygmatic and doxological structures in its formulation and the ways in which specific Trinitarian (and Christological) controversies are concerned with the fundamental structures of Christian discourse. In any case it is clear that what is at stake in the development and critique of dogma is not the addition or subtraction of an element of Christian discourse but its structure as a whole.

We cannot leave the subject of dogma without noticing its peculiar character as an 'act of praise'. The creedal formulations of dogma are situated by the community within its liturgy and their peculiar character indicated by the 'rubric' that they are to be "sung." This indicates that these dogma's 'exceed' language—not in the sense of glossalalia but in the sense of articulating the (hidden) base and goal of its articulation. The hymnic surface structure of dogmatic formulation is therefore not incidental to it but is rather symptomatic of its fundamental character.

III. Conclusion

Although we are still quite far from being able to articulate a full structural analysis of the grammar of doxological and doxologically generated discourse, we have been able to outline the direction in which such an analysis would take us. Thus far our analysis has shown us how kerygmatic and doxological (including oralogical) structures belong together as articulations of a fundamental vocative structure. The articulation and elaboration of these structures produces the genres of narrative, apocalypse, command (law), creed, proclamation, hymn, and liturgy. These genres are by no means simply a collection of accidental or unrelated forms but rather have a precise relationship to and are derived from the 'situation of address'. This 'situation of address' apprehends the rupture of the structures of experience as an address (speech-event) provocative of address (repetition, invocation, response).

Doxologically structured discourse then stands as an indispensable partner to kerygmatically structured discourse. The specific character of doctrinal and dogmatic god-talk derives from the interplay of these structures with one another. Above all it has become clear that this 'god-talk' functions ascriptively to designate the aim or goal of linguisticality transformed into hymnic address. In this context we may understand and appropriate the definition of the Westminister Catechism to the effect that "the chief end of man (the linguisticality of our existence) is to glorify God and enjoy God forever."

14
Conclusion

The path of exploration is seldom direct. The explorations we have undertaken in these pages have involved us in many turns of direction and an occasional retracing of our steps. In this final chapter we must attempt to give an account of the terrain we have covered and to suggest the direction of further exploration. Thus our task here is both retrospective and prospective, both a summing up and an opening out.

Each of the three major parts of this essay has considered the question of our way of speaking about God from a different perspective. In part one we viewed this question as occasioned by the rise and fall of theism as the form for the doctrine of God. The perspective taken there was historical and raised the question of a post-theistic way of speaking of God that would be generally intelligible.

In part two we approached the question from the perspective of a phenomenology of experience which sought to locate the generation of our speaking of God in the rupture of the structures of experience. These structures are, above all, linguistic, and their rupture occasions the use of god as an explosion into discourse of that which ruptures language, that is, as an expletive.

In part three we have approached this question as the question of the 'grammar' of our discourse. This grammatical and analytical approach has opened up a way of discriminating a variety of 'language games' within which the term 'god' has played its part. To the extent to which it has been possible to identify the rules of these various language games it has also been possible to give an intelligible account of the way in which that term functions within them.

The movement from an historical to a phenomenological to an analytical and grammatical perspective upon the question of god-language represents a movement from the exterior toward the interior of our problematic. The perspectives gained by this movement are by no means simply additive, leading up to a set of well-rounded 'conclusions' which it could now be our task to set forth as demonstrated theorems. For we have not reached the end of our inquiry but a point from which it may be possible to begin again.

Accordingly this concluding chapter will reweave the threads of our discourse. We shall be guided in this task not by a set of theses but by a set of questions which we address to the work as a whole. This will serve then as a kind of index to the chapters and parts of the essay. Thus the 'conclusion' reconstructs the text on the basis of these questions. (That is after all the function of an index.)

But the questions are by no means resolved such that their interrogative form is a mere rhetorical formula. Rather these questions also point forward to the work that lies ahead. We contend then not that these questions have been answered but that the text provides an opening in the direction of more fruitful responses to these questions.

I. The Question of Apologetics

We began this essay with the question of the 'meaning of god-language'. This question has been the impetus for a number of similar exploratory essays in the recent past and we have been guided often by the results of these earlier expeditions. Like them we have been persuaded of the importance of the crisis in language generally and the crisis in the use of god-language in particular. This crisis confronts us with both an apologetic and a confessional task. Apologetics must render the language of faith intelligible to those outside the Christian community so that whether they accept or reject this language their judgment will be an informed one. Dogmatics, on the other hand, must render the language of faith clear to those who do use it so that they may employ it in ways that do not destroy it. The many confusions and dilemmas regarding the ways in which we use 'god' and cognate terms have threatened to render faith unintelligible not only to those outside the community but also to those within it.

Thus, like others before us we have set out to clarify the language of faith, particularly the use of the term 'god'. But our exploration has diverged from others in several important respects. First, it has been necessary to qualify the conception of the task in two ways. Unlike previous explorations into the character of god-language we have not assumed that god-language stands alone in its presumed 'oddity' or in its alleged 'unintelligibility'. Talk of god is only one of the ways in which Christian discourse may be characterized and is only one of the points at which the question of intelligibility may be raised and will have to be answered. The justification for undertaking an inquiry into 'god-language' then is not that it is the sum of all Christian discourse, but that it is the focus of questions regarding the intelligibility of that discourse as a whole. Failure to recognize this limitation of an inquiry into god-language results in the near total neglect of other aspects of Christian discourse and in the artificial abstraction of 'god-language' from the concrete discourses in which it is embedded and by which its meaning(s) is (are) determined.

But if the starting point of the inquiry must be brought into question and qualified, so also must its aim or goal. Any apologetic undertaking must have clearly in view the limits of its objective. It cannot aim at the demonstration of the 'self-evidence' of faith or its language. It can only demonstrate the intelligibility of that language.[1] Failure to take this limit into account may make us too hasty in identifying the language of faith with some other language of the intelligibility or plausibility of which we may believe other persons to be more easily persuaded.

The careful delimitation of the aim and scope of an inquiry of this sort is crucial to its success or indeed to the determination of how far it has either succeeded or failed.

That faith requires articulation and that the proximate aim of this articulation is intelligibility are theses which have become gradually more clear in the course of these reflections. Our reflections upon the vocative structure of the language of faith has exhibited the internal necessity of this articulation as repetition and response to the call, claim, and promise of a gracious alterity. The refusal of articulation is a refusal of that which calls faith into being. But this articulation is an address and as an address to, and in the presence of, other persons it must become intelligible—it must be capable of being heard, understood and appropriated. At this inner core of the linguisticality of faith there is no final distinction between "apologetics" and "dogmatics." The discipline of theology is entrusted with the special task of ensuring this intelligibility both for those within and those without the community of faith. Thus insofar as the task we have undertaken in these pages is a theological task, we have aimed at displaying, not the necessity but the intelligibility of the language of faith insofar as this language is also god-language.

The aim sketched in part one is taken up into the question of experience in part two by insisting that the event of the rupture of the structures of our linguisticality must be intelligible from the character of that linguisticality itself. This is the meaning of the insistence upon the 'generic' character of the events in question. That analysis does not found the language of faith as such but rather shows how that language shares a common foundation with a variety of other kinds of discourse both 'religious' and 'secular'. That common foundation is the event of the rupture of the structures of linguisticality.

In part three the aim of intelligibility is manifested not by the question of 'generically human experience' but by the question of the grammars of disparate language games. What any language game must have, in order to be intelligible (either 'language' or 'game'), is a regulating grammar by means of which it is possible to determine in how far it is 'rule-governed', 'mean-ingful', and so to determine in particular instances whether it is properly or improperly articulated. A discourse is not made intelligible by being replaced by another discourse but by the exhibition of its basic structure.

Thus the intelligibility of Christian (or Jewish or Islamic) talk about 'god' is not demonstrated by replacing that discourse with another (explicative or meta-explicative) but by the exhibition of its generative grammar—thus the display of the vocative structure of kerygmatic and doxological discourse in chapters twelve and thirteen.

II. The Question of Theism

Beyond these initial clarifications and delimitations but clearly related to them has been the disavowal of theism as either an intermediate link in an apologetic strategy or as its goal. It has been necessary to identify the par-ticular features of theism, the way in which it has been formed and the difficulties to which it has been subjected in order to show that it is a particular form of the conception of God, involving particular ways of construing the meaning of god-language, and subject to characteristic di-lemmas consequent upon these particularities. The uncritical appropriation of theism has been a major factor in what I believe to be the ultimate failure of many previous attempts to give an account of god-language. This mistake occurs when it is simply assumed that features of god-language peculiar to a particular historical epoch are determinative for all uses, and indeed that the occurrence of 'god' in discourse is a sign of a latent or manifest theism. This is a completely unhistorical and therefore uncritical approach. It is unhistorical (1) in that it fails to take into account the fundamental variations in god-language and (2) in that it fails to recognize the 'cultural', economic, and social rootedness of particular conceptions.

By the uncritical adoption of a particular theistic conception (which then 'forgets' its particularity) a host of confusions are introduced into the discussion of god-language. The 'over-selling' of the centrality of the problematic of god-language, for example, is produced by the characteristic separation of 'god-world' conceptions from soteriological, anthropological, and eschatological conceptions, a separation characteristic of theism. It is this same factor that results in what I have termed the comedy of the reverse apologetic, which sets itself up to invent and defend an 'unknown god' as a way-station of the apologetic task.

A further though related confusion introduced by uncritically adopting the presuppositions of theism is that god-language is treated as a unitary phenomenon for which some single account is supposed to be adequate. Thus the oddity of god-language is assumed to associate with the term itself, so that wherever the term is employed we are supposed to be confronted with the same phenomenon, the same meaning, the same peculiar 'logic'. This approach is doomed to complete failure. It is not the appearance of the term 'god' that determines the meaning of the discourse in which it appears. It is the discourse, its structure, its function, its specific relations between terms, that give this term its meaning. Language games differ not on account of their lexicon but on account of the ways in which the lexicon is deployed. To put the matter bluntly: there is no such thing as god-language, there are only language games that deploy 'god' in ways determined by the respective rules of each of these games or kinds of discourse.

Continued blindness to this fact despite the work of Wittgenstein on the one hand and structural linguistics on the other is largely the result of an uncritical assumption of the presuppositions of theism. The results obtained in this way are predictable. Since theism is characterized by the explicative use of 'god' (together with a usually unclearly differentiated meta-explicative use) the inquiry into god-language completely ignores the statistically most widely employed uses of this term: expletive, predicative, kerygmatic, and doxological. Thus, despite talk of 'ordinary language' or 'functional analysis', these analyses focus upon an artificially restricted sample, which itself cannot be clearly described because it is not seen in relation to and distinction from alternative (and more prevalent) language-games.

But the question *of* theism and *to* theism becomes even more acute on account of the reflections upon the vocative character of the language(s) of faith. For here it becomes clear not only that theism is a discredited and currently implausible form of talk about god (chapter two), not only that it is a replacable and unnecessary form of explicative and meta-explicative discourse (chapter ten), but also that it is profoundly antithetical to the basic character of the articulation of faith.

Theism is inherently a stabilizing, consolidating, and thus explicative (and meta-explicative) form of discourse. As such it stands opposed to the interruption of the structures of our linguisticality that is articulated in the vocatively generated discourse of faith. It is precisely on this account that theism has been incapable of withstanding the critique of modernity launched by Marx, Freud, and Nietzsche. It allied itself with a cultural status quo and so stood opposed to any (prophetic) critique of that status quo. But this is no historical accident that a reformulated theism could have averted or could still avert. It is rather a symptom of its deeper antagonism to the language of faith.

The language of faith is the articulation of the rupture of the structure of our linguisticality, the sounding and resounding of the word that shatters all past and fixed identities and volatilizes discourse as the repetition of and response to this transformative word. A discourse that opposes or seeks to prevent or render harmless this rupture, this event, this transformation, can in no way serve as the 'bearer' of this word, as that which conveys its intelligibility. It is for this reason that post-modern theologies have to one degree or another had also to be anti-theistic as the examples of Tillich and Barth, Ebeling, Moltmann, and Altizer have shown.

III. The Question of (the Linguisticality of) Experience

The rejection of the confusion attendant upon an uncritical appropriation of a theistic point of view is one of the ways in which this essay is distinguished from a number of other attempts to clarify the meaning of god-languages. To this primarily negative principle a positive one may be added. It is that any inquiry into the linguistic oddity of god-languages must orient itself by the problematic of linguisticality as such. Thus we cannot separate the question of the 'experiential referent' of 'god' from the question of the linguisticality of experience or from the problems of the function and structure of particular discourses. The importance of this positive principle in conjunction with the negative principle (that theism is not the proper point of departure or goal of an analysis of god-language) may be seen in a brief review of some of the perspectives gained in this way.

(a)   The question of the relation of various uses of 'god' to our experience has recently been developed under the heading of 'transcendence and mystery'. But this inquiry has been characterized by a bewildering set of methodologies and of results. By orienting this inquiry to the linguisticality of experience a number of important results are obtained. First it becomes possible to develop a clear set of criteria for events that 'rupture the (linguistic) structure of experience'. These criteria are determined not by some particular conception of 'god' (monotheistic, polytheistic, etc.) but by the character of language (viewed as a structure and a structuring of experience). Thus this inquiry receives a far more secure foundation and stable procedure than would otherwise be possible. Moreover it is possible on this basis to show how these experiences are on the one hand extraordinary and on the other 'embedded' in the most general characteristics of universal human experience. Thus the understanding of language as the structure of experience makes clear how linguistic experience may be ruptured, as well as the ways in which this rupture is, in most cases, avoided, circumscribed, or erased. This makes it possible to bracket the distinction between the religious and the secular, the sacred and the profane, and thus to get at a more precisely phenomenological description of experience.

Since we are not bound by the presuppositions of theism it is possible to attend more carefully to the character of experience itself rather than attempting to argue directly from this experience to that which, by hypothesis, causes it. These experiences need not be treated as 'effects' the antecedent cause of which (the being of God, the activity of the unconscious, or what have you) it is our principal business to establish. Instead we are concerned with the experience itself as a linguistic experience and thus with the sort of god-language that it may generate. We are concerned not with the 'being of God' which by hypothesis stands behind the experience, but with the 'talk of God' which comes after it, or may be coordinated with it. Only by keeping this direction of analysis clear will it be possible to avoid the 'fallacy of misplaced concreteness'.

(b)   This approach has resulted in the discrimination of a series of experience-events (which are also called here word-events in order to stress the linguisticality of experience) organized into subsets on the basis of the region or mode of experience to which they belong. What is most important here is the relation of these events to the general structure of language and experience. The details of enumeration (why ten and not six or fifteen such types of events) and of nomenclature (why despair rather than dread) and of organization (are there only three regions or, alternatively, can't these be reduced to two: e.g., onto-aesthetic and historico-ethical) are of less importance at this stage of our inquiry. What is important about this 'table of radical affections' is that it shows that there are such experiences, that they are embedded in the general characteristics of linguisticality which they also rupture, that they are distributed across cultural lines, and that they correspond to particular uses of 'god', i.e., expletive and predicative uses.

(c)   Beyond this, the table of word-events or experience-events gives us a tool to employ in developing a 'taxonomy' of religious and 'secular' discourse. Thus we may use this table to characterize religions by the relative centrality or marginality of particular types of experience-events and by the way in which these are related to one another. Of course this use is not restricted to religions for we have seen that there are also non-religious ways of articulating, valuing, and relating these kinds of experience. Since we have been in no great hurry to establish the credibility of theism (or the necessity of religion) it has been possible to give more scope to non-theistic and non-religious articulations of these experience-events than might otherwise be possible. Thus we have not had to claim either (i) that everyone in fact has such experiences (only that they are possible for us by virtue of the linguisticality of our experience), or (ii) that when one has such an experience one must use 'god' to name the quality of this experience (only that expletive/predicative uses of 'god' do so), or finally (iii) that such a use of 'god' is prototheistic; in fact it stands in some considerable tension to theism, focusing as it does the rupture rather than the structure, the predicative or adverbial rather than the nominative or substantive.

(d)   But we must reckon here not only with the question of experience but with the questionableness of experience. The discussion of part two simply takes for granted the intelligibility and necessity of this category of "experience" and this has led to a taxonomy of affections (chapter nine). But how is this talk of experience related to the talk of language-games in part three? The significance of the reflection upon experience for the reflection upon language lies in the development of the notions of event and structure, of Word and Language, rather than in the development of a 'description' of subjective, or interior affectivity. This affectivity is no more than a symptom or a 'trace' of the rupture of the structures of linguisticality.

It is important to notice this first, because of the way in which the talk of interiority, subjectivity, and thus affectivity has become problematic in our time. Already in chapter three I have indicated how the context of plausibility for theism was the self-evidence of an appeal to personalistic categories and metaphors. But it is precisely this context that has become problematic in the twentieth century as the disappearance of the human face from modern (or rather post-modern) painting, literature, ballet, and music attest. Thus the attempt to use the interior landscape of affectivity as a point of contact for theological discourse with the culture generally may be doomed to failure.

In this connection it is worth remembering that the secularized world of descriptive psychology has little place for what we have termed the 'radical affections'. Thus instead of terror we have phobias, instead of dread we have guilt feelings, in place of despair, anxiety. Similarly love becomes attachment, peace becomes adjustment, and joy, "happiness." Thus radical affections elude the descriptive matrix to take up their fleeting abode in the laconic diction of poetics and a distantly remembered poetics at that.

The language of the radical affections serves then not to map our interior but as an index of the rupture of the structures of our linguisticality. The discussion of the radical affections like that of the root metaphors of chapters five through nine points to the generation of a lexicon. This lexicon is by no means simply to be identified with religious language or with god-language or with the language of faith. Each of these kinds of language may deploy these lexical items—words like abyss or ground, peace or despair—but the mere presence of these terms tells us little about a discourse save that it has some relation to the event of the rupture of the structures of our linguisticality. They are the traces of the occurrence of a final or radical alterity.

But it is with this occurrence and with the form of the discourse generated from this event rather than with these lexical traces that we are concerned in part three of our reflections. This aim is anticipated by the discussion of linguisticality, language (structure), and event (word-event) which is already embedded in part two. The result of that discussion is not the reestablishment of theism as the correlate of our experience but an analysis of expletive and predicative uses of 'god'.

IV. The Question of "Natural Theology"

Precisely this distinction between an expletive/predicative use of 'god' and the uses to which we have grown accustomed in theism (and other forms of god-language) raises the question of the character of these other uses of 'god'. To raise this question at all is possible only when one has abandoned the illusion fostered by uncritically assuming theistic presuppositions. What now comes into view is the particular character of the use of 'god' not to name the rupture of structures but to name or to protect and legitimate linguistic structures in the face of their actual or possible rupture. Thus we are able to give an account of the particular features of an 'explicative' use of 'god' and to discriminate this use from expletive and predicative uses as well as from what we have termed the meta-explicative use. This discrimination has far-reaching consequences. It enables us to account for the difference between science and metaphysics, to account for the peculiar features of a metaphysical use of god (for example, its apparent 'emptiness'), to account for the collision between explicative uses of god and the quest for a 'scientific' explanation. Moreover these discriminations enable us both to account for and to prevent confusions in language that arise when meta-explicative language is substituted for explicative, or when expletive-predicative language is introduced into explicative discourse. Finally despite the very clear differences between these discourses (and thus the use of 'god' in each of them) it is also possible to account for the relation among these discourses. Thus we are able to describe a series of transformations by which expletive becomes predicative, predicative is transformed into explicative, explicative is transformed into meta-explicative. Thus we do not have simply a collection of separate language-games, but an ordered sequence of language-games in at least one of which (the explicative) the use of 'god' appears to be illegitimate or at least productive of confusion and without current plausibility. This is, of course, the very sort of language-game within which theism is to be located.

These reflections place us in a far better position to understand the complaint of theologians like Bultmann and Buri concerning "objectifying language" (chapter four). For it appears that the rupture in the structures of language is inexorably sealed over by its opposite—the explication and legitimation of those structures that 'ward off' any rupture. Yet the true or radical opposite to objectifying language is not the discourse of subjectivity and interiority, but the discourse that is generated by and articulates this volatilization of language in the occurrence of alterity. The discourse of subjectivity is the reiteration of 'the same'. But the articulation of the vocative is the annunciation of the other. The language of the same inevitably assumes the monological character of descriptive discourse and so becomes "objectifying." But the discourse that repeats and responds to the call of the other is vocative rather than 'objective'. Thus kerygmatic and doxological discourse do not so much "express" subjectivity as "provoke" the transformation of the subject. In this sense we may say with Lacan that the subject is summoned out of the endlessly circulating discourse of desire (*parole vide*) toward the utterance of a true word (*parole pleine*).

V. The Question of the Articulation of Faith

The discrimination of expletive, predicative, explicative, and meta-explicative discourses and the identification of their respective ways of using 'god' still leaves us quite far from an adequate account of those uses of 'god' that most abound in Christian (as well as Jewish and Islamic) discourse. The languages of prayer and praise, of prophet and proclaimer, are not readily assimilable to the paradigms of explicative or meta-explicative discourse. This problem is seldom even noticed so long as it is assumed that the explicative or meta-explicative uses of god are the only ones in question—an assumption characteristic of theism (because of its exclusive use of 'god' as a principle of explanation). In order to make good this assumption, all other uses of 'god' are thought of as vaguely 'symbolic' by which is usually meant that they are pre-explicative (or pre-meta-explicative). But these uses of 'god' are not adequately accounted for as deficiently conceptualized forms of explicative or meta-explicative discourse. Their stability, their continued existence alongside explicative and meta-explicative uses of language, and their vigor in the face of the weakening of explicative and meta-explicative uses of 'god' show that they must be reckoned with as relatively autonomous 'language games'. At the very least then an attempt must be made to determine their particular characteristics, the rules by which these uses are governed.

In attempting to do just this we have discovered that these ways of using 'god' have in common what we have termed the metaphor of 'voice'. They all employ the paradigm of address, they are all 'vocative' in character. What this means is that these ways of employing 'god' do so by locating 'god' in the situation of concrete address. The situation of address is this: that A calls B. This situation is quite different from A and B discussing x, or A describing x to B. These latter situations are most readily understood as descriptive in contrast to the prescriptive and ascriptive character of the vocative language of address.

This vocative structure is already anticipated in the development of part two, both in our reflections upon Word and Language (chapter four) and in our reflections upon the historical region of experience. Thus the vocative structure that generates kerygmatic and liturgical discourse may be understood as the radicalization of word and the volitalization of language through the articulation of that word. That we speak as those who have been addressed is not an evasion of our common linguisticality but is the meaning of that linguisticality itself.

This is particularly evident in respect of what we have termed the historical region of experience (chapter eight). There we noted that the advent or absence of the other is, as well, the word of promise or judgment which announces the giving or withholding of a future. It is the correlation of the question of the other and that of the future which constitutes this region.

Thus address both ruptures and founds the linguistic structuring of this region. To be sure this address may be simply deflected or effaced. The question of future and of other may be deflected to some other region of experience or it may be effaced by incorporation into the structure of exchange and of expectation. But it may also itself generate or provoke our speaking. In this case our speaking has itself the character of an address (kerygma) or of the response to such an address (prayer and praise).

But it would be a misunderstanding to suppose that this vocative structure is heard only in specifically Christian discourse. This vocative structure is to be encountered not only in Christianity but, I believe, in Islam as well and in their common ancestor, the prophetic discourse of Judaism. Indeed it may also be heard in the secular prophets of late modernity, especially in Marx and Nietzsche. Of course we must distinguish between what Derrida has called a Marx of the Left and a Marx of the Right, as well as a Nietzsche of the Left and a Nietzsche of the Right. On the Right we have the legitimation of totalitarian structures (state communism or national socialism) whereas on the Left we find permanent critique of all structures—especially totalitarian ones. It is in the latter rather than the former that the call to alterity resounds. Faith in these instances means relying upon and permitting one's thought, language, and action to be provoked by this call. It is within this arena of a shared commitment that we may inquire how best to articulate this call. But a far more important question is this: how may we in each of our traditions more clearly and responsibly articulate this call? Our intention has been to show how the language of the Christian community is, and may yet more clearly be, an articulation of this vocative structure.

Undoubtedly much work remains to be done to more precisely clarify this vocative both within and outside the discourses of Christian faith. Our reflections have only served to indicate the potential fruitfulness of such work.[2]

By attending to the situation of address it becomes possible to account for the character of much of Christian discourse. Thus we are able to show the character of prophetic language as the repetition of address. In prophetic discourse 'god' names the original speaker of the address that addresses, claims, and thus alters the existence of the hearer (hence the talk of vocation, election, and covenant). So fundamental is this alteration that it is possible also to speak here of an address that constitutes or creates the hearer. As we have seen, the 'content' of address is the identity of speaker and hearer. It is thus an obvious elaboration of this address to provide an extended identity or character 'description' in narrative form. Thus prophetic annunciation is elaborated in narrative, and this connection, far from being fortuitous, is intrinsic. The prophetic annunciation founds a narrative discourse just as it also founds an apocalyptic discourse that anticipates the transformation of all separated identity into the "all in all" of apotheosis. This apocalyptic discourse prevents narrative from becoming merely descriptive by displaying the end or goal of narrative as eschatological consummation. Narrative, on the other hand, prevents the premature identification of any present attainment with such apocalyptic transformation.

This situation finds an analogy in the way in which the call for God (prayer) or the ecstatic response to God's word (praise) founds a liturgical language. In this doxological discourse we remain within the sphere of vocative language but the 'position' of God is reversed. Instead of being the author of address, God is now the one addressed, the hearer rather than the speaker. Accordingly god-language is here ascriptive rather than prescriptive. The elaboration of these ascriptions then does not function to explain 'the world' or to explain 'God' but to invoke or to celebrate the advent of the one whose coming is known in the transformation of all things.

We have noticed a similar juxtaposition in the relationship of command and grace summarized in the "law of love." The tendency of the articulation of command to take the form of legalism or moralism is interdicted by the summation or completion of this law as 'love.' Conversely the tendency of talk of love to become only a decorative supplement to the way things are is itself interdicted by the form of command.

The juxtaposition of narrative and apocalyptic, of prayer and praise, of law and gospel is not by any means fortuitous but corresponds to the inner necessity of a vocatively generated discourse. It is by this juxtaposition, supplementation, correction, and completion that the discourse of faith stands over against those discourses which prevent or silence the rupture of the structures of our linguisticality. Thus the discourse of faith is continually volatilized through this juxtaposition to exceed or transgress every structure of the self-evident possession of the other or the future. In this it corresponds to the call that it articulates.

VI. The Question of Doctrine

While a great deal of work remains to be done to clarify the peculiar status of doctrinal language, the clarification of the vocative situation that gives rise to kerygmatic and doxological language (elaborated in narrative, liturgy, creed, etc.) does shed light on important features of doctrinal discourse. This discourse is to be understood as the attempt to develop an adequate conceptual formulation of the articulation of character (or 'identity') displayed in narrative and liturgical language. Thus the 'theme' of character is transposed from narrative to conceptual discourse. In this way the characteristic preoccupations of doctrine (theological anthropology and Trinitarian economy) are generated by a reflection on the characterological narrative upon which doctrine is a meditation. The prescriptive structure of kerygmatic language results in a focus upon theological anthropology (for which god-language serves to elaborate the basis) whereas the ascriptive structure of doxological language results in a focus upon 'god' (Trinity) for which the anthropological language (e.g. ethics) serves as a base.

(a)   One of the 'results' of this analysis has been the substantiation of the thesis that 'god-talk' cannot be clarified in isolation. So for example we have seen that in the vocatively based discourse of faith the elaboration of 'god' is always co-relative to the elaboration of anthropological terms. In kerygmatic discourse 'god' names the 'speaker' in relation to the hearer. In doxological discourse 'god' names the one addressed in correlation to the one who addresses. The language of prayer coordinates the emptiness, lack, or neediness of the speaker with the absence of the one addressed. The language of praise coordinates the presence of God with the fullness, exuberance, or vitality of the one who speaks. This coordination and correlation does not entail a reduction of theology to anthropology but, on the contrary, their interdependence. The severance of one from the other must necessarily produce incoherence and unintelligibility. We may term this the logo-logical significance of Christological dogma. The attempt to isolate (and then justify) god-talk cannot function as a clarification of Christian god-talk but must instead result in the production of a very different sort of 'god-talk', namely theism. Conversely the apparent untenability of theism still leaves open the question of the intelligibility of the language of faith.

Doctrinal discourse is produced by the attempt of faith to give a generally intelligible account of its proclamation, and of the narrative, apocalyptic, liturgical, and 'ethical' articulation of this proclamation. Precisely as this reflective-critical account this discourse makes contact with the explicative and meta-explicative discourse of its era. The 'explication' of faith however stands in irresolvable tension with the 'logic' of the explicative or meta-explicative logos. This tension may not be overcome either through an evasion of the explicative logos or through a mere adaptation to it. Faith must be articulate, and this articulation is precisely to occur within (though also over against) language. This exigency corresponds to the vocational character of vocative discourse. Yet if it is to maintain its character as generated by an 'address' this account may not simply surrender itself to the logic of a structuring discourse. To the extent to which it does so it becomes simply an alternative 'science' (creationism vs. Darwinism) or a 'natural theology' that legitimates and sanctifies a given order (deism, theism, etc.). In either case it has abandoned its own vocative structure and thus becomes its own opposite and opposition. It has assumed the position of Dostoyevsky's Grand Inquistor.

Thus the intelligible account both of the human subject and of the divine that doctrine is charged with rendering will exhibit a characteristic tension with explicative discourse generally. A theological anthropology is concerned not with a 'given' subject but with a subject in transformation. Accordingly summary formulas for the characterization of this subject are necessarily paradoxical (image of God, original sin; *simul justus et peccator*, etc.). Similarly its characterization of God will exhibit a typical tension between absence and presence, *via negativa* and *via eminentia*, as well as the fundamental tension between a radical alterity and an apocalyptic "pantheism."

(b) On this basis it also becomes possible to acquire a better understanding of the character and function of dogmatic language. Dogma is not to be understood as a particularly arcane or privileged doctrine—still less as one that is to be maintained without or in the face of evidence. Dogma is rather to be understood as the logology of doctrine, that is, as the making explicit of the fundamental grammatical structure of doctrinal discourse. This function explains the especially fierce controversy out of which these dogmas are born and the tenacity with which they are maintained. What is at stake in their formulation or transformation is the structure of Christian discourse as a whole.

Part of the difficulty associated with dogma is its attempt to serve as a kind of 'meta-language'. Of course its terms remain within the sphere of the language it purports to govern. This is a not uncommon difficulty with language that functions both concretely and categorically. It has been identified by Levi-Strauss as *"bricolage."* One of the imperative tasks of theology is to clarify how this process of bricolage occurs in the development of doctrine and dogma and then, on that basis, to clarify the function of these kinds of discourse and the position of basic terms within these discourses. The identification of the logo-logical character of dogma is an important step, though only a step, in this direction.

The identification of the structure of address as that which generates the language of faith, and thus also the doctrinal reflection upon and elaboration of that language, has the further advantage of suggesting why dogmatic language concerns itself with the category of 'person' (three persons, one nature or two natures, one person). The clarification of the situation of address, even at the level of regulation, is concerned with the identification of a who, a subject, a speaker.

This characteristic of the god-language of the Christian tradition may be the particular focus of Trinitarian (including Christological) dogma. Yet this can be no more than a hypothesis until we acquire a much better understanding of logo-logical discourse generally and of a Trinitarian logic in particular. It is in any case clear that a mere theism can by no means extricate itself from the counter-logic of explicative and traditional meta-explicative discourse. It is also clear that the 'point' of Trinitarian discourse is to internalize the transformation in the divine 'subject' attested in the proclamation concerning the cross[3] and to internalize the corresponding transformation in the human subject toward apotheosis.[4] Yet an investigation into the character of Trinitarian discourse can by no means become an activity of mere restoration. Rather than looking for such a discourse in the fourth or fifth century it would be more accurate to say that such a discourse does not yet exist. The formulation of this discourse is not so much a matter of coming to terms with a privileged past as it is an urgent task for the future of theological discourse.

In summary then our inquiry into the language of Christian faith proposes the discrimination of a double series of discourses or language games. Kerygmatic and doxological discourses derive from what we have termed a situation of address or a vocative structure. These are elaborated in narrative and liturgy respectively. In doctrine they are transformed into conceptual, reflective and critical forms, the most fundamental regulation for which is provided by the logo-logical formulas of dogma.

But this proposal opens to view a host of questions and possible investigations. The field of religious discourse generally and of Christian discourse in particular may now be investigated with the intention of testing the hypotheses that have been advanced in these pages concerning the status of narrative and apocalyptic, command and annunciation, prayer and praise, doctrine and dogma. The advantage gained by our analysis is that this array of discourses no longer appears as a sheer multiplicity but as an ordered, regulated, intelligible series. Only when this has happened is it possible to launch an inquiry with any prospect of success. Our reflections have not led us to the end but to the real beginning of such an inquiry.

VII. The Question of the Relation of 'Natural' to 'Kerygmatic' Theology

It is possible to view the reflections of parts two and three of this essay as producing a taxonomy of discourses within which to situate the term 'god'.

Thus by focusing upon language, its function and structure, we can develop an outline of a coherent and comprehensive account of the various kinds of discourse characteristic of the Christian community and of the way in which talk of God is located in these ways of speaking. But this is of course only an outline. Much work would remain to be done for us to feel that we had produced a fully reliable map of the terrain which has been covered. The initial 'results' of this exploration are quite encouraging. They suggest that the way may be open for a satisfactory account of the intelligibility of these uses of god-language—an account which will make it possible to clear up a good many of the confusions attendant upon the careless use of this language.

If the proposals of the second and third parts of this essay hold up under critical scrutiny then we would have at our disposal a relatively sophisticated instrument for identifying the use of 'god' with which we are confronted in a particular text. It should then be possible to locate such discourse both with respect to the table of radical affections and with respect to its location in a descriptive, prescriptive, or ascriptive series. This would put us in a position to identify far more precisely the sort of god-language under discussion. This more precise identification would make it possible for us to avoid the confusions attendant upon the conflation of quite different discourses and usages into a single "god-language." Employing careful distinctions and discriminations would also make it possible to work out the relationships among quite different kinds of discourse—neither confusing them nor arbitrarily isolating them from one another. Working in this way will undoubtedly increase our understanding not only of the ways in which 'god' is used in language but of language itself and thus of the most intimate workings of human intelligence.

But despite the important contribution which such a taxonomy of discourse may make to the clarification of a number of otherwise perplexing problems, we must also be aware of the limits of such a taxonomic procedure. For we are not dealing here with a set of neatly categorizable bits of discourse which we may arrange in neat tables and series. Such an arrangement, while it may clarify certain problems, may also obscure a more fundamental one. This more fundamental issue is the struggle or contest for discourse itself.

This problem is most acute at the point of the interaction of descriptive discourse with the doctrinal discourse engendered by reflection upon kerygmatic and liturgical ways of speaking. Certainly doctrinal discourse presents inevitable analogies to, and affinities for, explicative discourse. As an attempt to give a generally intelligible account of the speech of faith it inevitably appropriates the language of explicative (and meta-explicative) discourse—just as liturgical or prophetic speech assimilated the lexicon and, at least, the surface grammar of cognate discourses. Faith has no "native tongue" in which it may 'express' itself without struggle and controversy. Rather faith always acquires speech through the appropriation of an 'other' language.

But this appropriation is also an expropriation, for language is forced to obey a different law—the law of the vocative. In order to be clear about this it is necessary first to eliminate a number of false difficulties. These are difficulties which arise from supposing that there is some single god-language whose 'oddity' may be accounted for by a single principle. Indeed when we gain some provisional clarity concerning the sort of discourse within which 'god' appears, we see that the term follows the 'rules' of that discourse. Thus the use of 'god' as an expletive has the same function as any other expletive. Where it is not simply "colorful" it marks the rupture of the structure of our linguistically ordered existence in the world.

The cases of explicative and meta-explicative language are similar. Where 'god' is used as a metaphysical principle it functions in exactly the same way as any other metaphysical principle—that is, it functions to identify the antecedent conditions of explanation. It has been adapted to this use on account of its use in a variety of other contexts to name that which is 'most real', and so confers upon the metaphysical principle the sense of that which is more real than superficial or phenomenal appearance. Presumably a Buddhist metaphysics would find a different term more satisfactory in this regard. Since meta-explicative discourse in necessarily a product of "*bricolage*" we must suppose that the selection of terms here is entirely a matter of convenience—terminology may be expropriated from ordinary (for example, explicative) discourse for meta-explicative purposes. In any case the oddity of this god-language owes entirely to the special characteristics of meta-explicative language generally.

In the case of explicative discourse the term 'god' may also function in ways analogous to other explicating and legitimating terms. Thus 'the will of God' may function here in exactly the same way as 'the history of *geist*' or 'historical determinism'. Or in the sphere of nature, talk of God's providence or 'law' will have the same function as talk of 'laws of nature'. That this is so is shown by how readily god-talk is replaced in the spheres of explicative discourse with the emergence of "secularization."

Thus with respect to the forms of discourse elaborated in chapter eleven we may say that the oddity of the use of god corresponds exactly to the oddity or particularity of the language game itself. Where other difficulties arise we may suppose that these are generated either by the unwitting transposition of 'god' from expletive to explicative, from explicative to meta-explicative, from meta-explicative to explicative (etc.) modes of discourse. Careful attention to the distinctive characteristics of these discourses should serve to eliminate confusions within this sphere of descriptive discourse.

But when these difficulties occasioned by a confusion or conflation or kinds of discourse are resolved, a more fundamental tension and opposition comes into view, for the doctrinal discourse of faith enters into conflict with the explicative Logos of language. Language as explicative discourse seeks to heal the wound caused by the rupture of language in the advent of a radical alterity. But the discourse of faith attempts to articulate this rupture within and against language. Here it is not simply a question of 'god'—but of the entire lexicon. This entire lexicon (derived we recall from language generally) is deployed in accordance with a coherent strategy—the articulation of the vocative.[5]

In taking on the form of doctrine and of dogma this vocative discourse risks its own subversion by the logos of explication, legitimation, consolidation—a risk which is, of course, the same for liturgical discourse or the prophetic discourse itself. Yet as the articulation of this vocative, as the vocation of articulation, faith cannot refuse this risk.

Nor can it finally accept a truce or a partition of discourse such that it can leave an explicative logic of discourse in peace, claiming for itself only some "religious sphere." The articulation of faith is the volatilization of discourse, not only some discourse but discourse as such. For it speaks of the Word that sets free and makes true. Thus it seeks to articulate the truth of our linguisticality in such a way as to liberate and transform that linguisticality.

What is finally at stake here is the proper function of word. Is the word for naming, ordering, controlling? Or is it instead for claiming, promising, calling, asking, thanking? In chapter one I noted that the crisis of god-language is situated within the crisis of language as a whole. We live, after all, in the world of mass propaganda and of advertising. Words can kill, and language has become a cemetery containing the bones and ashes of too many "final solutions." What is language for? And how may it become a word of life and not the law of sin and death? This is not an ecclesial question. It is the question of our linguisticality itself—for atheist and Christian, Moslem and Jew alike.

It is by no means the case that Christendom has consistently articulated the call toward a true and liberated linguisticality. Often enough its discourse has been appropriated to legitimate a status quo, to guard against any word that disrupts the secure possession of a structure.

And we also hear the prophetic utterance of a transforming and indeed radically transforming word from outside of Christendom. We hear it first in the prophets of Israel and perhaps, had we ears to hear, would hear it in the prophets of Islam. But more and more we hear it in the words of those who stand outside, unlegitimated by any 'religious' tradition. We hear it today in the call for a critical theory, for a liberating praxis, for deconstruction and dissemination. We hear it wherever there is the call for a word that sets free and makes true—which, within and against language, struggles for the word, for the truth of word.

But if this is so, have I not ended by proposing a new 'natural' theology? If so it is one that does not seek to accommodate faith to modernity (a kind of revisionism or reductionism) nor to cast about faith the borrowed cloak of a dubious prestige acquired from a perennial philosophy. Rather the discourse I have here proposed is one that seeks only to articulate faith in accordance with its own inner necessity within whatever lexicon may be available.[6]

If it is the case that other discourses too seek a mode of articulation that struggles against language to speak the rupture of dead or deadly structures this should not occasion too great a surprise. For as a Christian, I by no means suppose that the word announced by faith is any other word than that which calls Earth and all humanity into and toward being. It is certainly not to be supposed that the divine advent is for us alone. Rather it is for all.[7] Only on this basis is an intelligible proclamation possible. That the shock waves of this advent should be felt outside the church, and perhaps even more strongly there, is not strange. The great astonishment of early Christianity was how gladly those 'outside' and 'far off' heard the news of the liberating word. It would be strange if that were not also true today—especially if we have subverted our own language into a way of being 'at home' and 'at peace' with the way things are, with the structures of exchange and of expectation.

A fully historical linguisticality cannot abide within the received structures of the tradition—even when this is the *depositum fidei*. Yet at the same time it does not exist apart from this tradition, in inarticulate splendor. Rather it continually reverses, transgresses, deconstructs, and disseminates it. It is then not a 'hermeneutical' but a 'constructive' task that such a linguisticality sets itself.

The rupture of the structures of our language "makes room for thought" and provokes discourse toward the advent of that other which is our common destiny. The articulation of that rupture must continually be contested lest it become, against itself, its own opposite, a new prison for thought and life.

If natural theology is the name of every attempt to consolidate and control, and kerygmatic theology the name of every call into a volatilized discourse then the contest between natural theology and kerygmatic theology is not a contest between those outside and those inside the church. It is rather the common struggle within and against language for a true and liberating word.

Notes

Chapter One

1. Among the most useful such summaries we may include Frederick Ferré's, *Language, Logic and God* (New York: Harper and Row, 1969), Langdon Gilkey's *Naming the Whirlwind: The Renewal of God-Language* (New York: Bobbs-Merrill, 1969) especially part one, "The Challenge to God-Language", pp. 1–230. Some of the most important essays in this discussion are collected by Antony Flew and Alasdair MacIntyre in *New Essays in Philosophical Theology* (London: SCM Press, 1955) and by John Hick in *The Existence of God* (New York: Macmillan, 1964).

2. For a presentation of views which serve as the background to Ayer's challenge, cf. J.O. Urmson, *Philosophical Analysis: Its Development Between the Two World Wars* (Oxford: Clarendon Press, 1956).

3. A.J. Ayer, *Language, Truth and Logic* (New York: Dover, 1946). (Cf. Hick, *The Existence of God*, p. 219.)

4. Anthony Flew puts the challenge in terms of "the simple central questions, What would have to occur or to have occurred to constitute for you a disproof of the love of, or of the existence of God." (In Hick, *The Existence of God*, p. 227.)

5. Cf. Ferré's discussion of this position, "The Logic of Encounter, *Language, Logic and God*, pp. 94–104. Unfortunately missing in this debate is a consideration of William Ernest Hocking's *The Meaning of God in Human Experience* (New Haven: Yale University Press, 1912, 1963).

6. The most forceful critique of the argument from religious experience is found in Ronald W. Hepburn, *Christianity and Paradox* (London: C.A. Watts & Co., 1958). The particular value of this book is that it applies the methods of analytic philosophy to the work of major contemporary theologians, rather than restricting itself to the rather narrow group of philosophical theologians who have taken a professional interest in language philosophy.

7. John Hick, *Faith and Knowledge* (Ithaca, New York: Cornell University Press, 1957). See also "Theology and Verification," in Hick, *The Existence of God*, pp. 253–273.

8. For an expansion of this argument, cf. Ferré, *Language, Logic and God*, pp. 53–55.

9. Wittgenstein's formula in its entirety is "For a *large* class of cases—though not for all—in which we employ the word 'meaning' it can be defined thus: "the meaning of a word is its use in the language". *Philosophical Investigations*, 3d ed. (New York: Macmillan, 1958), pp. 43, 20.

10. Further elaboration of this relationship between modern theism and moral values will be found in the following chapter.

11. R.B. Braithwaite, "An Empiricist's View of the Nature of Religious Belief," in Hick, *The Existence of God*, pp. 229–252.

12. Paul van Buren, *The Secular Meaning of the Gospel* (New York: Macmillan, 1963). Van Buren's contention is that God-language is, in Christianity, subordinant to Christ-language (a move dependent upon Barth) and that Christ-language is understandable in terms of the "contagiousness of Jesus' freedom." A revision of this analysis which takes into account the relationship of theological language to diverse forms of discourse is to be found in his more recent book, *The Edges of Language: An Essay in the Logic of a Religion* (New York: Macmillan, 1972).

13. A good summary of this discussion may be found in *Language, Logic and God*, pp. 126–129.

14. Wittgenstein, *Philosophical Investigations*.

15. Among those influenced by Wittgenstein whose work is cited in these pages are J.L. Austin, Paul van Buren, Fredric Ferré, and Langdon Gilkey.

16. The literature on 'Transcendence and Mystery' has now grown rather large. One of the most interesting works of this kind remains Alistair Kee's *The Way of Transcendence* (New York: Penguin, 1971). Representative essays on this theme may be found in: *Transcendence*, ed. Herbert W. Richardson and Donald E. Cutler (Boston: Beacon Press, 1969).

17. Schleiermacher's initial and 'romantic' formulation is to be found in the *On Religion: Speeches to its Cultured Despisers* (1799) and receives a more formal and systematic formulation in *The Christian Faith* (1821/22, 1830), trans. and ed. H.R. Macintosh and J.S. Stewart (New York: Harper and Row, 1963), vol. I, pp. 3–18.

18. Rudolf Otto, *The Idea of the Holy*, trans. John W. Harvey (London: Oxford University Press, 1923).

19. For a discussion of the place of this notion in the thought of Paul Tillich, cf. Theodore H. Runyon, Jr., *The Immediate Awareness of the Unconditioned and the Interpretation of History in the Theology of Paul Tillich*, unpublished dissertation, Göttingen, 1958.

20. Perhaps the most influential argument against these mystical and metaphysical tendencies is to be found in Harvey Cox, *The Secular City* (New York: Macmillan, 1965).

21. Gordon D. Kaufman, *God the Problem* (Cambridge: Harvard University Press, 1972), esp. pp. 41–71.

22. Schubert M. Ogden, *The Reality of God* (New York: Harper and Row, 1966). A fair statement of the thesis is found in the following assertion: "one can only conclude that faith in God as the ground of confidence in life's ultimate meaning is the necessary condition of our existence as selves," p. 43.

23. John B. Cobb, Jr., *God and the World* (Philadelphia: Westminster Press, 1969). The core of the argument may be found in pp. 42–66. A similar case is made by John A.T. Robinson in *Exploration into God* (Stanford: Stanford University Press, 1967).

24. Peter L. Berger *A Rumor of Angels: Modern Society and the Rediscovery of the Supernatural* (Garden City, New York: Doubleday, 1970), esp. pp. 49–75.

25. Langdon Gilkey, *Naming the Whirlwind*, pp. 305–413.

Chapter Two

1. "The answer, however, is given, three 'persons', not that it might be spoken, but that it might not be left unspoken". *On the Trinity*, Book V, ch. IX (NPF, vol. III, p. 92).

2. So, for example Augustine notes "What therefore remains except that we confess that these terms sprang from the necessity of speaking, where copious reasoning was required against the devices or errors of the heretics." *On the Trinity*, Book VII, ch. IV (NPF, vol. III, p. 110) Basil gives a similar reason in *On the Holy Spirit* XXX, 79.

3. I have described this aspect of the language of faith in my *Introduction to Theology* (Philadelphia: Fortress, 1976), pp. 22–82.

4. The thesis that theology is to be understood as "reflection upon the Christian mythos" and so upon the figurative language of faith I have elaborated in *Introduction to Theology*, pp. 88–106.

5. This notion of a "grammatical rule" will be elaborated in part two.

6. The notion that Trinitarian language is a formal and regulative principle echos the traditional description of doctrine as the "rule of faith." Augustine anticipates this when he describes Christological dogma (and, by extension Trinitarian dogma as well) as "this rule for interpreting the scriptures." *On the Trinity*, Book I, ch. I, vii.

7. *On the Trinity*, Book I, ch. VI. Augustine can so strongly insist on this distinction that he is led at one point to speak of "the person of that Trinity"

(Book II, ch. X), a phrase which threatens to produce a quaternity rather than a trinity.

8. In Aquinas' *Summa Theologica*, questions 2 to 26 deal with "the one God" while questions 27 to 43 deal with "a triune God."

9. This discussion of the displacement of "the triune God" from its proper place and function is heavily indebted to Karl Rahner's remarkable essay *The Trinity*, trans. Joseph Donciel (New York: Seabury Press, 1974).

10. In the *Summa Contra Gentiles* Aquinas' discussion "of the one God" begins Book I and dominates the whole. The discussion of the Trinity appears only in the concluding Book IV after the intervening discussion of creation and providence. This ordering is clearly related to the apologetic purpose of the treatise. The *Summa Theologica* has as its aim the 'catechetical' instruction of theologians and a correspondingly different structure. Despite the difference in aim and structure however it is noteworthy that the earlier placement of the treatment of the Trinity (before creation) has no effect upon the elaboration of the discussion of creation, etc., which might just as well proceed directly from the discussion "of the One God." Cf. Rahner, *The Trinity*, pp. 21–24.

11. The dependence of Thomas Aquinas' arguments upon Aristotle's analysis of causation is most evident in *Summa Contra Gentiles*, Book I, ch. XIII. This discussion is summarized and given systematic expression in the *Summa Theologica* I, Q.2, articles 2,3. The "five ways" of article 3 are summarized in article 2 as "two ways": One is through the cause . . . the other is through the effect."

12. I owe to Prof. Ivor Leclerc of Emory University the characterization of medieval Christian philosophy as preoccupied with the attempt to introduce a conception of absolute transcendence into a monistically oriented philosophical vocabulary derived from Greek philosophy.

13. In this connection it is important to notice that *no* economic function is assigned to "the Father" by Aquinas to compare with the quasi-economic designations of Son as Word and Image or of Spirit as Gift and Love. This is but a further indication of the collapse of "Father" into "God" and of the loss of economic pertinence for the doctrine of the Trinity as a whole.

14. I have in mind here chiefly the development of nominalism.

15. Philip Melanchthon, *Loci Communes Theologici*, ed. Wilhelm Pauck, The Library of Christian Classics (Philadelphia: Westminster Press, 1969), p. 21.

16. The concern for peace in Europe took on not only the political tenor of the question of toleration but also was of fundamental concern for philosophy. Kant's treatise *On Perpetual Peace* (1795) indicates the level of concern which this question evoked. We may also cite in this connection the attempts of Leibniz to develop the basis for harmony between nations and competing confessions to illustrate the connection between early forms of modern theism and the quest for peace in Europe.

17. John Locke, *The Reasonableness of Christianity* (1695).

18. The Lisbon earthquake of 1755 is best remembered for its effect upon Voltaire,

whose *Candide* made of this natural catastrophe a problem for theism as then understood.

19. It is of course true that the problem of pain or of evil has been with us for a long time. I am distinguishing this general issue from the way in which this issue has been formulated on the basis of theism with its characteristic concentration upon the relation of God to the world and its definition of God as omnipotent beneficient creator (cause) of what is. It is a very common error to suppose that this way of setting up the question is universal and to suppose that all responses to the fact of evil, innocent suffering, etc., are responses to the question *as thus formulated*. The point is that this formulation is by no means universal but depends upon a particular conception of God characteristic of modern theism.

20. The nearest approximation to this modern formulation is to be found in stoicism which, however, is distinguished from the modern problematic by its greater emphasis upon practical rather than theoretical approaches to such issues, its relatively impersonal conception of providence or deity and its monistic world-view.

21. This is true, of course, only as long as a degree of cultural isolation separates the expressions of American black Christianity from the Enlightenment-influenced "mainstream" of American Christianity. Where this isolation is broken down there is the tendency to appropriate the Enlightenment ethos with its concommitant formulations of theism and theodicy. I am indebted to Prof. E. Brooks Holifield of Emory University for drawing my attention to the way in which this cultural isolation broke down earlier than I had previously thought for a significant minority of black Christian leaders.

22. A very suggestive illustration of this point may be found in the essay by Ronna L. Case, "When Birth is Also a Funeral," in the *Journal of Pastoral Care*.

23. Jürgen Moltmann, *The Crucified God*, trans. R.H. Wilson and John Bowden (New York: Harper and Row, 1974), pp. 200–290. See also the study of Trinitarian responses to protest atheism in W. Waite Willis, Jr. *Theism, Atheism and the Doctrine of the Trinity*, Ph.D. dissertation, Emory University, 1983).

24. Kant's *Fundamental Principles of the Metaphysics of Morals* (1785) and *The Critique of Practical Reason* (1788) are the fountainhead of this alliance between theism and moral values which continues in the proposals of Braithwaite and van Buren described in the previous chapter.

25. One of the most famous cases of such disillusionment is that of Karl Barth whose outrage at the support given the German war effort by Germany's leading theologians helped to fuel the devastating critique of that theology in his commentary on Romans.

26. The notion of a 'context of plausibility' derives from the 'sociology of knowledge'. See Peter L. Berger and Thomas Luckmann *The Social Construction of Reality: A Treatise in the Sociology of Knowledge* (New York: Doubleday, 1966), esp. pp. 19–128.

27. Roderick Seidenberg, *Post-Historic Man: An Inquiry* (Boston: Beacon, 1957).

Seidenberg's thesis, in brief, is that the movements toward rationalization, bureaucratization and collectivization combine inexorably to produce a "posthistoric" form of humanity.

28. Michel Foucault concludes his stunning analysis of the emergence of structures of knowledge with these words: "As the archaelogy of our thought easily shows, man is an invention of recent date. And one perhaps nearing its end." *The Order of Things: An Archaeology of the Human Sciences* (New York: Random House, 1970). Foucault has demonstrated that "man" as the self-evident centering of the episteme emerges at the end of the eighteenth century and that it is possible to see already the signs of the disappearance of this organizing principle.

29. The disappearance of "person" as the root metaphor of modern thought naturally raises the question of the root metaphor of "post-modern" culture. It is, as Hegel aptly remarked, at the end and not at the beginning of an era that we are able to acquire a knowledge of its most fundamental character. It is not impossible however that the categories of event and structure, of relation and transformation will come together as the major elements of this emergent metaphor. It is, in any case, with caterories such as these that the present analysis will proceed.

30. For an examination of the notion of narcissism as a way of categorizing contemporary American society see Christopher Lasch's *The Culture of Narcissism* (New York: Norton, 1978).

31. In this discussion of post-theistic perspectives I am leaving out of account the more nearly Trinitarian responses to the collapse of theism, Among these we may number the proposals of Karl Barth, Jürgen Moltmann, and Thomas J. J. Altizer. These are not so much revisions as they are refusals of theism, The direction in which these proposals have moved, insofar as that direction is not one of repristinization, seems to me to hold the greatest promise for future work on the doctrine of God. A consideration of the deconstruction and possible re-construction of Trinitarian dogma must be postponed however until greater clarity is reached concerning the character of the language within which faith comes to expression and so falls outside the scope of this inquiry.

32. Among the most influential statements of the personalist perspective are: Edgar S. Brightman, *Person and Reality: An Introduction to Metaphysics*, ed. P. A. Bertocci (New York: The Ronald Press Company, 1958); P. A. Bertocci, *Introduction to the Philosophy of Religion* (New York: Prentice-Hall, 1951); L. Harold DeWolf, *A Theology of the Living Church* (New York: Harper and Bros., 1953). A still useful summary statement and critique may be found in John B. Cobb's *Living Options in Protestant Theology* (Philadelphia: The Westminster Press, 1962), pp. 60–90.

33. John B. Cobb Jr.'s development of a process theology begins with the very influential *A Christian Natural Theology: Based on the Thought of Alfred North Whitehead* (Philadelphia: The Westminster Press, 1965). The basic themes of this position are amplified and made more accessible in *God and the World*

(Philadelphia: The Westminister Press, 1969). In the more recent *Christ in a Pluralistic Age* (Philadelphia: The Westminister Press, 1975) Cobb develops his reformulation of Christological doctrine. For a critique of process theology see Robert C. Neville *Creativity and God: A Challenge to Process Theology* (New York: The Seabury Press, 1980).

34. Briefly stated this revision consists in modifications of the notion of transcendence—so as to be able to speak of a real and reciprocal relationship between God and the world, thus correcting for the difficulties of a medieval notion of God's transcendence as absolute (i.e., as without real and reciprocal relations). Thus, in common with personalism, God is understood as 'a' being rather than as 'Being'.

35. The theodicy problem is addressed by reducing the scope of God's omnipotence, thus making resistance to God a plausible explanation of evil. Presumably, however, this resistance is limited both by the persistence and pervasiveness of divine influence and by the vision, taken more or less seriously, of a kind of 'Peace' as the telos of divine action. A full statement of a process perspective upon the theodicy question is to be found in David Griffith's *God Power and Evil: A Process Theodicy* (Philadelphia: The Westminister Press, 1976).

36. The most consistent interest in the question of proofs for the existence of God has been displayed by Charles Hartshorne. For a statement of his position see *The Logic of Perfection* (La Salle, Illinois: Open Court, 1962), esp. pp. 28–117.

37. While it is impossible to go into detail here, the following points may be noted: (1) that only actual entities are to be envisaged as units of perception, (2) that all other 'beings' are derivative and abstractions from these, (3) that actual entities 'prehend' only those actual entities which are no longer actual. From which we must conclude either (a) God is not *an* actual entity but an abstraction (i.e., a 'personal order') of a succession of such entities or (b) God is not 'prehended' in any way and so can have no influence upon (relations with) other actual entities. Attempts to resolve this question on the basis of a distinction between actual entities and actual occasions threaten to violate Whitehead's dictum that God must not be understood as an exception to but the chief exemplification of the categorical obligations which specify the 'nature' of actual entities. Attempts to answer this objection are legion, but among the most important is William Christian's *An Interpretation of Whitehead's Metaphysics* (New Haven: Yale University Press, 1959). In my own judgement a more fundamental recasting of the notion of actual entity is required and has been proposed by Ivor Leclerc in *The Nature of Physical Existence* (New York: Humanities Press, 1972).

38. For the defense and restatement of this liberal tradition on the part of a process theologian see John Cobb's *Liberal Christianity at the Crossroads* (Philadelphia: The Westminister Press, 1973).

39. For an important attempt to develop a process Christology see John Cobb's *Christ in a Pluralistic Age* (Philadelphia: The Westminister Press, 1975). This

very provocative treatment of the question relies so heavily upon the notion of the 'spirit of Christ' that one cannot help wondering whether it is not more successful as a pneumatology than as a Christology.

40. It is difficult to escape the impression that process theology is intent upon becoming a form of scholasticism, preoccupied with the prestige of 'the philosopher' (in this case Whitehead) and with the attempt to maintain at all costs the compatibility of a particular metaphysic with Christian faith. It does not have the advantage of previous forms of scholasticism however of having at its disposal a metaphysical system of universal prestige. This is not because of the weakness of Whitehead's philosophy but because of the pluralism of philosophical perspectives on the one hand and rather restricted influence of any of these on the other. This problem will be addressed in the next chapter.

41. The notion of God as 'Being' is therefore the obverse of the proposal of process thought. While there is no simple correspondence, the notion of Being is closest to Whitehead's notion of 'creativity' which is *not* a divine attribute as such but the most general feature of all actuality.

42. Paul Tillich's classic statement is his *Systematic Theology* in three volumes (Chicago: University of Chicago Press, 1951, 1957, 1963) of which the first volume remains the most influential. In some ways a more radical, though less systematic, statement is to be found in *The Courage to Be* (New Haven: Yale University, 1952). John Macquarrie's theology may be characterized as an appropriation and creative reinterpretation of perspectives from Heidegger and Bultmann.

Chapter Three

1. Cf. chapter one.
2. Acts 17:22–31.
3. John Macquarrie, *Principles of Christian Theology* (New York: Scribners, 1966), p. 42.
4. Ibid. p. 110.
5. Barth's attack upon religion in the name of faith is concentrated in his commentary on *The Epistle to the Romans*, trans. E.C. Hoskyns (London, Oxford University Press, 1933), pp. 229ff. This argument by no means exempts Christianity from the critique of religion but it does insist that Christian faith is not to be understood as a form (even the highest form) of religion.
6. Bonhoeffer's call for a nonreligious interpretation of faith is found in scattered fragments in his *Letters and Papers from Prison*. It is the fragmentary character of these suggestions which have made it possible for so many disparate theological programs to legitimate themselves by reference to these suggestions.
7. Among the calls for a secular understanding of Christianity we may recall John A.T. Robinson's *Honest to God* (Philadelphia: The Westminster Press, 1963) and *Exploration into God* (Stanford: Stanford University Press, 1967) and Harvey Cox's *The Secular City* (New York: Macmillan, 1965).

8. Conrad Simonson, *In Search of God* (Philadelphia: United Church Press, 1974).
9. Cf. Karl Barth, *Church Dogmatics* I, 2, pp. 333ff.
10. This culture critique has more recently taken the form of theologies of revolution, liberation etc.
11. Martin Buber, *The Eclipse of God: Studies in the Relation Between Religion and Philosophy* (New York: Harper, 1957).
12. Thomas J.J. Altizer, *The Gospel of Christian Atheism* (Philadelphia: The Westminster Press, 1966).
13. Jacques Ellul, *Hope in a Time of Abandonment* (New York: The Seabury Press, 1973).
14. Gabriel Vahanian *The Death of God* (New York: George Braziller, 1961). The character of Vahanian's position is better conveyed by the title of his second book: *Wait without Idols* (New York: George Braziller, 1964).
15. In his early work, *The Secular Meaning of the Gospel*, Paul van Buren is inclined to reduce god-talk to talk of freedom evoked by Jesus. In the more recent *The Edges of Language* his approach is less 'reductionistic' as he seeks to give an account of the oddity of god-language.
16. This is the argument of J.A.T. Robinson in *Honest to God* (Philadelphia: The Westminster Press, 1963).
17. So, for example, Schubert Ogden maintains that: "Rightly understood the problem of God is not one problem among several others; it is the only problem there is." *The Reality of God* (New York: Harper and Row, 1966), p. 1. A similar claim is put forward by Gordon Kaufman: "The central problem of theological discourse, not shared with any other 'language game' is the meaning of the term 'God'." *God the Problem* (Cambridge: Harvard University Press, 1972). What are we to make of this assertion? Certainly the term 'god' is shared with a good many other 'language games': cursing, pledging, metaphysics, praying. These may be relevant to theological discourse but scarcely are that discourse or language game itself.

Chapter Four

1. *Large Catechism* commentary on the first commandment.
2. This turn to the relationship between God and experience both characterizes the major developments in theism and carries within itself the seeds of its own destruction. This later was exposed by Feuerbach whose notion that the idea of God was to be understood as a projection, a weapon against the tradition of modern liberal theology while still maintaining the necessity of the theological task. For Barth's assessment of Feuerbach, cf. *Protestant Theology in the Nineteenth Century: Its Background and History* (Valley Forge: Judson Press, 1973), pp. 534–540.
3. Kant, *Critique of Pure Reason*, p. 225.
4. "As regards the identification of absolute dependence with 'relation to God'

in our proposition: this is to be understood in the sense that the *Whence* of our receptive and active existence, as implied in this self-consciousness, is to be designated by the word 'God' and that this is for us the really original signification of that word." Schleiermacher, *The Christian Faith*, vol. 1, p. 16 (para 4).

5. The problem of the relationship of time and eternity dominates Kierkegaard's writings but is particularly focused in the *Philosophical Fragments* and in *The Concluding Unscientific Postscript*. In the introduction to the latter he summarizes the problem of the *Fragments* as the problem of the *Postscript*: "Is an historical point of departure possible for an eternal consciousness . . . is it possible to base an eternal happiness upon historical knowledge?" trans. Swenson and Lowrie (Princeton: Princeton University Press, 1941), p. 18.

6. An excellent recent discussion of this issue may be found in Gordon Kaufman's *An Essay on Theological Method* (Missoula: Scholars Press, 1975).

7. It is Jacques Derrida who has most clearly formulated the consequences of linguisticality for the phenomenological project of Husserl. Cf. *Speech and Phenomena* (Evanston: Northwestern University Press, 1973).

8. Of incalculable importance in tracing the historical impact of shifts in linguisticality is the work of Walter J. Ong, *The Presence of the Word* (New York: Simon and Schuster, 1970), esp. pp. 17–110.

9. The linguistic structure of the unconscious is the theme of Jacques Lacan's reflections in the *Discours de Rome*, trans. Anthony Wilden as *The Language of the Self: The Function of Language in Psychoanalysis* (Baltimore: Johns Hopkins University Press, 1968). This is the edition which will be cited in subsequent references in this text. The essay is also available in *Ecrits: A Selection*, trans. Alan Sheridan (New York: Norton, 1977), pp. 30–113.

10. Robert Funk, *Language Hermeneutic and Word of God* (New York: Harper and Row, 1966).

11. Lacan, *op. cit.*, p. 39: "It is the world of words which creates the world of things."

12. The work of J. L. Austin has been especially fruitful in uncovering the performative character of certain uses of language. Cf. *Philosophical Papers*, 2d ed. (London: Oxford University Press, 1970) pp. 233–252 and *How to Do Things with Words* (New York: Oxford University Press, 1962).

13. Lacan, *op. cit.* p. 42.

14. The problem of objectifying language is a recurrent theme for Bultmann. Cf. *Jesus Christ and Mythology* (New York: Charles Scribner's, 1958). The question is already formulated in the 1925 essay "Welchen Sinn hat es, von Gott zu reden" *Glauben und Verstehen*, vol. I (Tubingen: JCB Mohr, 1933), pp. 26–37. Fritz Buri's formulation of the problem of objectifying language may be found in *How Can We Still Speak Responsibly of God* (Philadelphia: Fortress Press, 1968).

15. The distinction between *Rede* (address) and *Gerede* (talk) is fundamental for Heidegger. Cf. *Being and Time*, para 35, trans. J. Macquarrie and E. Robinson

(New York: Harper and Row, 1962) pp. 221–4. The distinction between *parole vide* and *parole pleine* is developed by Lacan to designate the difference between a discourse wholly ensnared by the imaginary (*parole vide*) and a discourse in which the subject utters a true word concerning himself (herself) to an other who is not only imaginary. This last is the goal of the relationship between the therapist and the 'subject'.

These distinctions are different from that of Saussure and structural linguistics between *Langue* and *parole* in which the first (language) designates the formal structure and the second (speech or discourse) designates the activity governed by this structure.

If we place these distinctions together we have the following: Language is the structure of speaking or discourse; this speaking may be falsifying (*Gerede, parole vide*) or may be the coming to expression of (intersubjective) truth (*Rede, parole pleine*). But this alternative is 'loaded' in favor of falsification by the structure (*Langue*) itself, i.e., in its objectifying of what pertains to a subject (Heidegger, Bultmann, Buri) or in its entrapment in the sphere of the imaginary (Freud, Lacan). This requires that we apply what Ricoeur has called a "hermeneutic of suspicion" in relation to discourse.

16. Thus the determining theme of Barth's reflections upon "the word of God" is indicated by the regularly repeated phrase "God speaks." Cf. *Church Dogmatics*, vol. I, pt. 1, pp. 150ff.

17. This turn from 'general' to 'special' revelation is analogous to the turn from structure to event, from 'Language' to 'Word'.

18. Unfortunately there is very little in English on Ferdinand Ebner, the Viennese thinker to whom Karl Heim attributed a Copernican revolution in modern thought. A brief introduction may be found in my dissertation *Man as the Subject of Existence: A Study of Post-Hegelian Anthropologies in Continental Theology* (1971), pp. 66ff. References to Ebner's work in succeeding footnotes are to the collected works: *Schriften*, 3 vols., ed. Franz Seyr. (Munich: Kosel-Verlag, 1963). Volume 1 of this collection includes the most important of Ebner's writings.

19. The 'mysticism' of Buber is far more pronounced in *I and Thou* than in *Between Man and Man*, which represents a more mature presentation of his thought. Indeed, in the latter work Buber accuses Feuerbach of a "pseudo-mystical construction." *Between Man and Man* (New York: Macmillan, 1963), p. 17. For Buber's response to the charge of mysticism cf. P. A. Schilpp and M. Friedman, eds., *The Philosophy of Martin Buber* (La Salle, Illinois: Open Court, 1967), pp. 707ff.

20. *Schriften*, I p. 231.

21. *Ibid*, pp. 96–97.

22. Buber's contention that God is the 'eternal Thou' is in *I and Thou* (New York: Scribners, 1958), p. 75. Ebner's insistence that God is the 'first person' is in *Schriften*, vol. I, p. 97, though he is also able to speak of God as a Thou. Cf. *Schriften*, pp. 708–718, 911–918.

23. *Ibid*, p. 128.
24. *Ibid*, p. 158, and *passim*.
25. *Word and Faith*, Eng. trans. (London: SCM Press, 1963), p. 326.
26. *Ibid*, p. 361.
27. *Ibid*, p. 324.
28. *Ibid*, p. 325.
29. *Ibid*, pp. 325–6.
30. *Ibid*, pp. 326–8.
31. The development of structural linguistics has its origin in the lectures of Ferdinand de Saussure compiled in *Course in General Linguistics*, trans. Wade Baskin (New York: McGraw-Hill, 1959). A useful summary of structural linguistics may be found in Jonathan Culler's *Structuralist Poetics* (Ithaca: Cornell University Press, 1975) pp. 3–112. Claude Levi-Strauss is primarily responsible for demonstrating the far-reaching importance of structural linguistics for the human sciences generally. Cf. "Structural Analysis in Linguistics and Anthropology" in *Structural Anthropology* (New York: Basis Books, 1963), pp. 31–54.
32. Ebeling, *Word and Faith*, pp. 347–53.

Chapter Five

1. Ian T. Ramsey, *Religious Language: An Empirical Placing of Theological Phrases* (New York: Macmillan, 1957), p. 24.
2. While these two prohibitions, the use of 'God' in false statement (Exod. 20:7) and the later rabbinic prohibition of the pronunciation of YHWH, may not have been directly related one cannot help noticing that the conjunction of these prohibitions corresponds tolerably well to the late modern suspicion that ordinary discourse is deceitful. This suspicion is the hallmark of Marxist and Freudian analysis and is given philosophical form in the language philosophy which follows Heidegger.
3. The prohibition which Matthew attributes to Jesus (Matt. 5:33–37) is represented as an intensification of Exodus 20:7. This prohibition of the legitimation of 'truthful' speech by reference to 'God' may be understood as a desacralization of discourse *and* as an insistence upon the authority of the ordinary speaker who, like Jesus, is to speak with authority rather than on the basis of a borrowed supernatural authority.
4. A number of avenues for exploration open up here which can only be briefly indicated. We may notice that when we study a foreign language we are unlikely to find in our standard grammars and vocabularies much in the way of useful information concerning expletives. Yet the expletive is that which is studied most avidly, learned most quickly, and retained when all else is forgotten. Is this attributable only to the accidental features of schoolboys' (or schoolgirls') mischief or is there here a clue to what is at stake for us in language itself?
    In relation to the prohibition attributed to Jesus we may inquire whether

the use of 'God' to certify the conformity of our speech to the demands and expectations of Language is the radical or fundamental character of profanity in the sense of profanization. That is, it is the profanization of that which must forever elude these structures and whose actual occurrence shatters them. This may be connected with the way in which the normalization of religious language in Victorian culture makes it less available for expletive use. It becomes so ordinary (profane) as to be unavailable for 'profanity'. Hence the ascendancy of scatological/erotic expletives and the decline of 'religious' ones.

5. Bonhoeffer cites the words from Euripides' *Helen* "So then to meet again is a god" in *Letters and Papers from Prison* (Letter for 8 July 1944), enlarged ed. (New York: Macmillan, 1962), p. 344.

6. See chapter four.

7. In "The Problem of a New Testament Theology" Braun concludes "God would then be a definite type of relation with one's fellow man." (Robinson *et al.*, *The Bultmann School of Biblical Interpretation: New Directions* (New York: Harper and Row, 1965), p. 183. In *Jesus of Nazareth: The Man and His Time* ET (Philadelphia: Fortress Press, 1979) Braun makes a number of similar suggestions. Speaking of forgiveness and self-acceptance he writes "God is the event that here occurs" (p. 135). He suggests that God may be spoken of "as the process by which the wicked and hopeless person receives a future and hope" (p. 136). These suggestions are clearly at some variance with one another but they suggest something of the possible richness of a predicative use of 'god'.

8. I am indebted to Prof. Ivor Leclerc of Emory University for his exceedingly helpful emphasis upon the way in which the problematic of transcendence introduced into monistic Greek thought characterizes medieval thought including Jewish and Moslem philosophy.

9. For Husserl on the intentionality of experience cf. *Ideas: General Introduction to Pure Phenomenology*, trans. W.R. Boyce Gibson (New York: Collier Books, 1962), pp. 107–110, 222–225.

10. A relatively accessible discussion of this theme is to be found in Whitehead's *Adventures of Ideas* (New York: Macmillan 1933), pp. 177ff.

11. Whitehead uses this phrase in his Lowell lectures of 1925 *Science and the Modern World* (New York: Mentor Books, 1948), p. 161.

12. Cf. Lacan, *The Language of the Self, op. cit.*, p. 13.

13. The formal notion of region and of the fundamental categories constitutive of regions is developed by Husserl in *Ideas, op. cit.* pp. 57ff. The approach which I will take in the next three chapters is by no means a simple replication or application of Husserl's method but is a rather free adaptation of it.

14. For an elaboration of the procedure and necessity of a hermeneutical phenomenology, see Paul Ricoeur, *The Symbolism of Evil* (Boston: Beacon Press, 1967), pp. 3–24, 347–357.

Chapter Six

1. This illustration is adapted from Peter Berger's *A Rumor of Angels* (Garden City: Anchor, 1970), pp. 54–55.

2. The initial statement of Schleiermacher's position is to be found in his *On Religion: Speeches to its Cultured Despisers*, trans. John Oman (New York: Harper Torchbooks, 1958). Especially relevant is the "Second Speech," pp. 26–118).

3. Cf. Runyon, *op. cit.*

4. In the early *Speeches* (1799) Schleiermacher's position is not yet clearly distinguished from a Spinozistic pantheism. But Schleiermacher attempts to distinguish his view more sharply in *The Christian Faith* (2d ed., 1830), trans. H. R. Mackintosh and J. S. Steward (New York: Harper and Row, 1963), vol. I, pp. 16–17.

5. Without question Paul Tillich wants to focus attention upon Being-itself as distinct from the sum of beings (ensemble). Cf. *Systematic Theology*, vol. I, pp. 163–210.

6. In speaking here of an experiential basis for the question of the whole I am in disagreement with Gordon Kaufman's contention that experience is not a source for but is rather a means of validating theological judgments. Cf. *An Essay on Theological Method*, p. 8. In other perhaps more fundamental respects, the argument of this chapter has a number of important points of agreement with the Kaufman's argument. Among these, attention may be drawn to Kaufman's notion that God (at least in the sense of this chapter) is a concept without a corresponding percept (p. 23). Kaufman's very clear distinction and correlation between the notions of 'world' and 'God' (pp. 41–45) is also very valuable.

7. Cf. *Systematic Theology*, vol. I, pp. 110–115. Tillich uses interchangeably the terms: ontological shock, metaphysical shock, and the shock of non-being.

8. Cf. *Systematic Theology* and *The Courage to Be* (New Haven: Yale University Press, 1952), pp. 32–56.

9. The uses of notions like 'ecstatic reason' and 'essentialization' shows that Tillich is not content with the disjunction which he has posited between Being and beings. This may be due to the way in which soteriological interests overcome ontological ones.

10. It is interesting to note that the 'direction' of this ontological experience is for Tillich inward and *downward*. This appears to be characteristic of Teutonic and Romantic mystical traditions. Mediterranean mystical traditions typically use the metaphor of inward and upward. Thus instead of 'Ground', the metaphor for that by virtue of which the whole is, is 'Heaven'. The difference in spatial and directional metaphor does not seem to be crucial to our inquiry. Both involve the positive apprehension of the whole as founding or establishing the existence and meaning of the parts. Although in their original cultural settings these metaphors may have designated immanent principles, their appropriation by the Judeo-Christian (and Islamic) thinkers has resulted in their being understood as external to, thus transcendent of, the whole as ensemble.

11. With respect to Ogden's argument, it is not clear that he has sufficiently noted the difference between whole as ensemble and whole as the principle by virtue

of which the parts are constituted as a whole. The persuasiveness of his argument appears to depend upon moving back and forth between these notions. That the parts (myself included) are parts of a whole is plausible but this does not itself legitimate the notion of a *ground* for that unity (god). The confidence with which we approach our tasks does not 'imply' more than an ensemble. Thus it would be necessary to distinguish between an unreflective confidence which presupposes (perhaps quite dimly and only implicitly) that everything is a part of a whole (an ensemble) and the ontological confidence which is dependent upon the disruption of this unreflective confidence. It is only in this latter case that we could say that experience warrants talk of God (as opposed to world). But we cannot claim that we all have such an experience because we all act as if we had reason to be confident. On the contrary, these are antithetical modes of experience; one of the reliability of the whole as ensemble, the other of the collapse of the whole as (mere) ensemble. It is possible to translate these distinctions into Whiteheadian categories. Thus for Whitehead 'world' designates the ensemble of actual entities exclusive of God who functions as the principle (subjective aim) by virtue of which the ensemble has coherence. Beyond this God and the world may be understood as units (exemplifications) of 'creativity' which then becomes the most fundamental character of reality (though it itself is 'real' only in its exemplifications). But if we follow this procedure we will have to claim that the ontological 'Ground' is not God but is Creativity as such. It is creativity which is the cognate of "Being-itself" and which answers to the radical question of the whole. This surprising result helps to account for the confusion which follows from an attempt to use Whiteheadian terminology to account for the problem of the 'whole'. The god-talk of Whitehead does not function on the same level as the god-talk of, say, Tillich or the Heideggerians.

12. For discussions of this problem see Paul Tillich, *Systematic Theology*, vol. I, pp. 18–189, and Karl Barth, *Church Dogmatics*, vol. II, pt. 3, pp. 289ff.

13. Langdon Gilkey, *Naming the Whirlwind, op. cit.* p. 329.

14. *Ibid*, p. 327.

15. There is something unsatisfactory about the term 'despair' in this connection. It is appropriate for the immediate purpose of identifying 'word-events' which may give rise to expletive and even predicative uses of 'god'. But it has far too 'romantic' a ring to it. In religious and philosophical traditions which appear to give greater importance to a category like 'nothingness' rather than 'being' (e.g., some Asian traditions) the use of a term like despair would be clearly out of place. Indeed we might have to say that there we should reverse the terms, using peace to designate the apprehension of the whole as nothingness with despair then being the sense that the phenomenal world was anchored in Being. It is certainly possible to read the narrative accounts of the enlightenment of Gautama Buddha in this way. My fundamental contention is that the apprehension of the world as plenum or as vacuum, as ground or abyss, as Being or as nothingness are equally fundamental.

16. For a useful overview of this view of language based upon Saussure (*of. cit.*) cf. Terence Hawkes, *Structuralism and Semiotics* (Berkeley: University of California Press, 1977), pp. 17–27.
17. Plato's *Sophist*, 260a.
18. *Ibid*, 259d.
19. *Ibid*, 253.
20. See especially Jacques Derrida, *Speech and Phenomena*, trans. David B. Allison (Evanston: Northwestern University Press, 1973), pp. 129–160.

Chapter Seven

1. When the aesthetic region is the subject of explicit theological inquiry this tends to occur within the framework provided by a concern for the ontological region. Schleiermacher and especially Tillich illustrate this tendency; cf. "Protestantism and Artistic Style" in *Theology of Culture* (New York: Oxford University Press, 1964) pp. 68–75. However this situation may be changing. The very interesting work of Gerardus van der Lenaw: *Sacred and Profane Beauty: The Holy in Art* (Eng. trans. New York: Holt, Rinehart, 1963) is an important contribution in this area. The increased dialogue between Eastern Orthodox and Protestant theology in the area of liturgical theology provides yet another impetus for a consideration of this region. Much more in the public eye of late have been works such as Harvey Cox's *Feast of Fools* (Cambridge: Harvard University Press, 1969), Jürgen Moltmann's *Theology of Play* (New York: Harper and Row, 1972) and Gerhard G. Martin's *Fest: The Transformation of Everyday* (Philadelphia: Fortress, 1976). Perhaps the most ambitious attempt to develop a theological interpretation of aesthetic experience is Hans Urs von Balthasar's monumental *Herrlichkeit: Eine Theologische Asthetik*, I–II (Einsiedeln, 1961–1967). The present chapter remains heavily indebted to Tillich.
2. These issues are most sharply foccused in Tillich's *The Courage to Be* (New Haven: Yale University Press, 1952), pp. 32–63.
3. 'Meaning' in structural linguistics refers to the locus of an element (phoneme, grapheme, etc.) within a system of differentiations. This principle is established by Ferdinand de Saussure *Course in General Linguistics Eng. trans.* (New York: Basic Books, 1963), cf. esp. pp. 31–97.
4. The question of the compatibility of novelty and order is one of the dominating themes of Whitehead's philosophy. Cf. *Process and Reality*, pp. 514–518, for a summary statement.
5. For a further elaboration of the notion of presentational immediacy in contrast with discursiveness, cf. Suzanne K. Langer *Philosophy in a New Key* (Cambridge: Harvard University Press, 1942, 1951).
6. One of the most striking illustrations of the way in which art figures or prefigures social organization is to be seen in the correlation between the appearance of the individual (as opposed to stylized) human visage in Renaissance art and the inauguration of the social ideal of the individual and 'personality'

in the early modern period culminating in the institutions of democracy and laissez-faire capitalism. The twentieth century is inaugurated in the arts by the disappearance of the human visage with a concentration upon form, line, color. This may then be correlated to the emergence of a social order variously described as beauracratic, technocratic, managerial or even totalitarian in all of which the images of individuals become at best, irrelevant. The widespread supposition that 'art' is separate from the sociopolitical order represented by such slogans as "art for art's sake" is only thinkable for a culture which segregates art from culture through such innovations as museums, theater districts and 'art shows'. The perplexity which the segregation occasions when one seeks to distinguish 'primitive art' from 'primitive craft' is but one indication of the artificiality of this arrangement. The separation is itself an indication of the character of our own historico-cultural ethos reflective of the now-waning ages of individual and empire.

7. In the work of Robert A. Nisbet we find an extended argument that the study of society emerges as an effect of the disappearance of social experience. Cf. *The Sociological Tradition* (New York: Basic Books, 1966).

8. The connection between nihilism and totalitarianism was made most effective by Hermann Rauschning in his reflections on the rise of Nazism in *Revolution of Nihilism* (New York: Longmans, Green's Co, 1939). That totalitarianism is produced by the fear of freedom (nihilism) is the thesis of Erich Fromm's *Escape from Freedom* (New York: Rinehart, 1941). These theses are not necessarily mutually exclusive, since we may think here of a spiraling interdependence of these contrasting phenomena. What is most important is to recognize this interdependence of superficially contrary phenomena: nihilism and totalitarianism.

9. Still one of the best analyses of this tendency of technology understood as an all-encompassing phenomenon in our era is Jacques Ellul's *The Technological Society* (Eng. trans. New York: Alfred A. Knopf, 1964).

10. See the monumental work of Eric Vögelin, *Order and History.* 3 vol. (Baton Rouge: Louisiana State University Press, 1956–).

11. Cf. Jürgen Moltmann's critique of "intimism" in culture and theology in *Theology of Hope, op. cit.*, pp. 311–32.

12. Max Müller, *Natural Religion* (London: Longmans Green's Co., 1889).

13. For a time the notion of 'mana' was widely interpreted as an 'impersonal' and 'free floating' force. It has since become clear that it does not have this "nominative" character but is instead adverbial or adjectival in character (i.e., predicative).

14. This is most clearly represented in the *Oresteia* of Aeschylus.

15. Hermann Rauschning, The Revolution of Nihilism (New York: Longmans, Green's, Co, 1939).

16. Jean Paul Sartre, *Nausea.*

17. For further elaboration of the notion of '*doxa*' cf. Hans Urs von Balthasar's *Herrlichkeit: Eine Theologische Aesthetik,* I–II (Einseideln, 1961–7).

18. Michel Foucault in his *The Order of Things*, Eng. trans. (New York: Random House, 1970) demonstrates the way in which alternative ways of ordering or classifying phenomena is constitutive of the modern episteme. Similarly Claude Levi-Strauss in *The Savage Mind* (Chicago: The University of Chicago Press, 1966) demonstrates the function of totemism to provide a system of classification by which aspects of nature and culture are both sorted and interrelated.

19. Obviously the Appollonian tradition will discern in the ecstatic transports of the Dionysian experience not the presence of power as 'spirit' but the presence of power as chaos. Similarly the Dionysian will detect in the Appollonian illumination the life-destroying Law. These opposed attitudes constituitive of the aesthetic region seem destined to misunderstand one another not just in detail but also fundamentally.

20. For an illustration of Hartshorne's polemic at this point see *Man's Vision of God* (Hamden, Connecticut: Archon Books, 1941), pp. 1–141. This polemic is regularly (one might almost say routinely) repeated by exponents of process philosophy and theology. That this critique only mystifies the upholders of the medieval tradition only further illustrates the mutual miscomprehension with which Appollonian and Dionysian perspectives confront one another.

21. Confirmation of this suggestion has recently come from comparative zoology. The study of vocalizing primates (gelada monkeys) by Bruch Richman, "Did Human Speech Originate in Coordinated Vocal Music?" in *Semiotica* (vol. 32, nos. 3–4, 1980), has resulted in the hypothesis that human language derives from the melodic and antiphoned 'chant' or 'chorus' whereby social cohesion is articulated. From complexities of pitch and rhythm come the complexities of inflection, conjugation, and declension. The anticipation of eschatological existence as an anthem or chorale (epaenon) of praise in Ephesians 1:12 may then be a volatilization of linguisticality which 'restores' and 'exceeds' the origin of speech in song.

22. Cf. Immanuel Kant, *Critique of Judgment*, trans. J. H. Bernard (New York: Hafner, 1968). Kant regards the object of this critique as the 'combination' or synthesis of the critique of "natural concepts" and the "concept of freedom" which correspond tolerably well both to what we have termed the ontological and the historical regions of experience and to what we have identified as the fundamental constituents of the aesthetic, i.e., order and Energy, or the question of meaning and vitality (pp. 7–15). The first part of the *Critique of Judgment* (Critique of the Aesthetical Judgment) has numerous points of contact with the analysis of this chapter.

23. That questions of temporality enter in by way of this essentially aesthetic issue may help to explain the sense that for all its prominence the thought of both Heidegger and Whitehead on this question of time never really succeeds in becoming historical/ethical. For both Heidegger and Tillich the question of the future is the question of death as the loss of energy or power. If this observation is anywhere near the mark then it would appear that only the work of Ernst Bloch (and perhaps that of the exponents of "critical theory") are fully historical in their interest in temporality.

Chapter Eight

1. This is the view of time most closely associated with the critical philosophy of Immanuel Kant for whom temporality is neither illusory nor 'objective' but an a priori condition of the subject's experience of the world.

2. This second view of temporality is more closely akin to Heidegger's notion of time as the horizon for the question of being, the inescapable horizon since dasein ("This entity which each of us is himself," *Being and Time*, p. 27) is constituted as a being toward death.

3. In *Process and Reality* (New York: Harper and Row, 1960) Alfred North Whitehead remarks upon the sense of time as "perpetual perishing" which he then contrasts with the sense of time as "the moving image of eternity" (pp. 513–514). The latter sense however, tends quite far in the direction of a abrogation of time, at least in this writer's view.

4. The 'longing for the eternal' as a flight from time was characterized by Kierkegaard as the 'aesthetic'. His subsequent working through of modes (or stages) of existence is determined by increasing the tension between, and coincidence of, 'the eternal' and 'time'. It is in this connection that the notion of the coincidence of the eternal with the temporal moment is developed in ways which were to be subsequently appropriated by Tillich, Barth, Bultman, and Gogarten, making use of such notions as kairos, krisis, the eternal now, and so on. Characteristic of these theologians is the association of this notion with eschatology (a theme for which Kierkegaard does not have a highly developed sense). For a critique of this notion of the eternal now, see Jürgen Moltmann, *The Theology of Hope*, Eng. trans. (New York: Harper and Row, 1967), pp. 50–69.

5. As in the case of the 'whole' so also in the case of the 'future' there is no 'percept' which corresponds to the 'concept'. This is why we speak here of 'apprehending' rather than 'perceiving'.

6. The connection made by Marx between misery and hope is elaborated by Ernst Bloch and Jurgen Moltmann and has become one of the principle themes of liberation theology.

7. The difference between hope produced by contrast to the present and hope produced by analogy with the present largely determines the characteristic differences between the theology of Jürgen Moltmann and Wolfhart Pannenberg. The latter is characteristically more concerned with the resurrection while Moltmann is more concerned with the cross as the 'key' to the understanding of history. The difficulty in Pannenberg's position is that by understanding the radical future by way of analogy he runs the considerable risk of simply and quickly 'redomesticating' the future as an extension of or extrapolation from the present, thus weakening the distinction between hope and 'optimism'.

8. Cf. Vittorio Lanternari *The Religions of the Oppressed*, Eng. trans. (New York: Alfred Knopf, 1963) for a fascinating account of "third-world" forms of this anticipation of the future as the advent of an era of justice and prosperity.

9. In her *The Human Condition* (Chicago: The University of Chicago Press, 1958) Hannah Arendt remarks upon the problem of guilt occasioned by the Greek emphasis upon 'mighty words and deeds' (see pp. 188ff and pp. 236ff).

10. An especially interesting example of the use of language to neutralize the threat of the future is the construction of the future tense on the basis of the past tense. Thus I may say "In 1982 I *will have finished* writing this book." An awareness of the fragility of this attempt to secure a hold upon the future is illustrated by the custom, widespread in Judeo-Christian and Islamic cultures, of appending to such statements some version of Jacob's condition: "if God wills and I live," thus further warding off the threat of the future to rupture the structure of expectation and projection.

11. In the discourse of the prophets and apocalypticists, examples of the contortions produced by the attempt to articulate hope within the self-evident temporal structure of language. Bultmann has identified two structures typical of this distortion in New Testament and especially Pauline literature: the tension and alternation between 'already' and 'not yet' and the similar tension between 'indicative' and 'imperative'. Thus the interruption of the temporal structure by hope produces a characteristic counter-structure which remains in permanent tension with (because it does not simply replace) the structure of temporal succession. See Rudolf Bultmann, *The Theology of the New Testament* (New York: Charles Scribners, 1951).

12. That human relationships are determined by the dynamics of desire and thus by the attempt to secure possession of the object of desire is a perception given a new basis by the work of Freud and the psychoanalytic movement. An especially provocative discussion of this dynamic is to be found in the work of Ernest Becker, *The Denial of Death* (New York: The Free Press, 1973) and *Escape from Evil* (New York: The Free Press, 1975).

13. Levi-Strauss has shown in *Elementary Structures of Kinship* (Boston: Beacon Press, 1969) that a system of relational exchange depends upon an incest taboo. But since the prohibited relationship varies from culture to culture what is incest for one culture is 'normal' for another and vice versa. Thus an alternative system of exchange is directly or indirectly a violation of this taboo for the old system.

14. Granger Westberg, *Good Grief* (Rock Island, Ill.: Augustana Press, 1972) for an illustration of this perspective. I by no means intend to dismiss this approach, only to show how it it related to the fundamental structure of our experience.

15. The development of a theory of attachment is one of the most important advances in contemporary psychology. In this connection we should particularly notice the work of John Bowlby, esp. *Attachment* (New York: Basic Books, 1969). This work makes clear that we have to do here not with an incidental aspect of our experience but with its fundamental structure.

16. The literature on grief is, by now, quite extensive but these characterizations of the effect of grief on the sense of self are fairly typical.

17. While it may seem strange to speak of a relationship which is both reciprocal

and hierarchical, it is nonetheless appropriate. A "master-slave" relation is reciprocal if both are engaged by the relationship. A nonreciprocal relation would be one in which one of the parties to the relationship remains oblivious to or unaffected by the relationship. For the still classic discussion of the reciprocity of master-slave relations, see Hegel *The Phenomenology of Mind*, trans. G. Lichthein (New York: Harper and Row, 1976), pp. 228–240.

18. See my article "Human Sexuality: A Theological Perspective" in *The Journal of Pastoral Care*, vol. xxxiii, March 1979, pp. 3–16.

19. Ronald Hepburn, *Christianity and Paradox* (London: C.A. Watts & Co., 1958).

20. The introduction of the motif of I and Thou into philosophical discourse occurs in the context of a protest against the monological logos. See Ludwig Feuerbach, *Principles of the Philosophy of the Future II* (New York: Bobbs-Merrill, 1966). This protest is then taken up and given even sharper focus by Ferdinand Ebner in *Schriften*, vol. I, ed. Franz Seyr (Munich: Kosel-Verlag, 1963).

21. In *Fear and Trembling*, Eng. trans. (Princeton: Princeton University Press, 1941).

22. Of course 'salvation and damnation' can be (and regularly are) incorporated into the system of exchange through being transposed into a system of rewards and punishments. It is precisely characteristic of the Judeo-Christian tradition (and certainly not of Christianity only) that it is engaged in continual conflict at this point; that is, in contesting the domestication of salvation and damnation as simple reward and punishment while still maintaining that there is no abrogation of the historical-ethical sphere as such.

23. In Anselm of Canterbury: *Trinity, Incarnation and Redemption*, ed. and trans. J. Hopkins and H.W. Richardson (New York: Harper and Row, 1970), pp. 81–134.

24. These recent studies tend to focus on the early and presumably formative writings of Hegel. Hans Küng's recent work *Menschwerdung Gottes* (Freiburg: Herder, 1970) is representative of this research.

25. Martin Heidegger, *Being and Time*, trans. John Macquarrie and Edward Robinson (New York: Harper and Row, 1962). The phrase is taken from the title of part I of the projected work which was never concluded.

26. The work of Ernst Bloch finds fullest expression in the massive work *Das Prinzip Hoffnung* (Frankfurt-am-Main: Suhrkamp Verlag, 1965). A more accessible source is A *Philosophy of the Future* Eng. trans. (New York: Herder and Herder, 1970).

27. Thomas J.J. Altizer, *Total Presence* (New York: The Seaburg Press, 1980).

Chapter Nine

1. For a brief review of the history of this issue see chapters one and four of the present essay.

2. If, as we maintained in chapter four, language presides over experience, then it is clear that without the metaphors which are the residue of these experience-events there would be no way of articulating them or drawing attention to them. Thus we may expect that language regularly conspires against the recognition or articulation of these experiences.

3. See Theodore W. Jennings, *Introduction to Theology: An Invitation to Reflection upon the Christian Mythos* (Philadelphia: Fortress, 1976) for a further elaboration of this perspective. Readers who have also read my *Introduction to Theology* may be puzzled by the relationship between these two texts. Despite the difference in theme and aim (reflected in the focus upon 'imagination' in the *Introduction*, in contrast to the focus upon linguisticality in this essay), they were begun at the same time. Thus the concentration upon linguisticality by no means entails an abandonment of the theme of imagination. The genres generated by the vocative structure are, in their mutual interrelationship, the Christian mythos. The reflection upon this material is theology as doctrine. The discrimination of the basic structures regulative of doctrine is theology as dogma. In both cases I have maintained that theology is derivative from and dependent upon antecedent modes of discourse (narrative, liturgy etc.). In both cases I have been guided by the belief that theology belongs within the broader field of human inquiry and is to be clarified in relation to this field and not in isolation from it.

4. See Jonathan Edwards, *On Religious Affections*, ed. John E. Smith (New Haven: Yale University Press, 1959).

5. In his *Two Sources of Morality and Religion*, Henri Bergson Eng. trans. (New York: Henry Holt, 1935) distinguishes between essentially individual and creative sources on the one hand and collective and noncreative ones on the other. The association of individuality and creativity is to my mind a mistake deriving from the cult of the individual characteristic of modernity. If we understand individuality and collectivity as independent variables then we may appropriate Bergson's analysis as pointing to the difference between religious traditions which focus most strongly upon alterity and those which focus more strongly upon structure. Since the former are, in Bergson's view, more closely related to "emotion," the connection between his perspective and the one I have been suggesting with respect to the radical affections is clear.

6. It is of course quite possible that the vulnerability of the structures of our experience to the irruption of this alterity has a physiological foundation similar to the difference in characteristic function of the left and right side of the brain or in the different functions of the R-complex and the neocortex. We certainly cannot take this to be in any way already established however. If it were it would not detrimentally affect the notion of the *imago dei* in this connection however since even for ancient Israel the earthling's likeness to God at least included physiological or somatic characteristics.

7. I do not wish to argue that theology is obliged to interpret the *imago dei* in terms of this capacity—only that this capacity would be properly related to the

imago dei or some other anthropological category rather than used as an argument for the reality of God. It goes without saying that interpreting this capacity in terms of the *imago dei* would already presuppose rather than establish the reality of God.

8. Feuerbach's analysis and critique of religion is in fact an analysis and critique of just this alienation of experience by means of projection and reification. See Ludwig Feuerbach, *Lectures on the Essence of Religion* Eng. trans. (New York: Harper and Row, 1967), esp. the third lecture, pp. 17–24, and pp. 178–198.

9. For Feuerbach's concern with experience, see *Principles of the Philosophy of the Future* (New York: Bobbs-Merrill, 1966).

10. It should be observed that most contemporary discussions of the experiential basis of god-talk tend to presuppose, without arguing for, a monotheistic paradigm for the interpretation of this data. This is due, I think, not merely to the presupposition of the Christian language about God (which is after all Trinitarian rather than monotheistic) but to the assumption of the theistic form of that doctrine characteristic of the modern period. Whatever its source, such a monotheistic paradigm would have to be justified rather than simply presupposed. Those who, like Schubert Ogden, find only one radical affection (e.g., ontological confidence) would have somewhat less difficulty at this point than those who find several. Among those who find several radical or "transcendent" kinds of experience, Peter Berger's approach seems most justified in acknowledging the distance separating these experiences from the theistic paradigm. For Berger this distance is inscribed in his title: *Rumors of Angels*.

11. For David Miller's position see *The New Polytheism* (New York: Harper and Row, 1974).

12. It is by no means my intention to suggest that the triplicity of the regions of experience functions as a kind of "vestige" of the Trinity, as Augustine argued for the triple character of the mind (*On the Trinity*, Books IX, XIV). On the other hand it does seem to me to be possible to use some of the formal characteristics of Trinitarian dogma (e.g., the unity of a multiplicity) as a heuristic device for illuminating our experience, so long as we are clear that this can in no way constitute an argument for the cogency of the dogma materially.

Chapter Ten

1. *Philosophical Investigations*, p. 116, para. 373. In the text this phrase stands alone, unexplained and unelaborated, an enigmatic sign of perplexity or of purpose, in parenthesis.

2. That theology through the use of 'paradox' entails a suspension of logic is a much debated notion. I believe that this contention arises from a failure to attend to differences in language games rather than from an inherent anti-logic in theological language. This is evident from the fact that theologians'

arguments for paradoxical assertions employ the same canons of argumentation used to establish unparadoxical ones. There is certainly no suspension of such (logical)/argumentation on the part of such theologians of paradox as Tertullian, Luther, or Barth.

3. After Wittgenstein the most influential discussion of this issue, and one from which these illustrations are borrowed, is that of J.L. Austin. *Philosophical Papers* (London: Oxford University Press, 1970).

4. A similar outline is employed by Gerhard Ebeling in his *Dogmatik des Christlichen Glaubens* (Tubingen: J.C.B. Mohr, 1979) vol. I, pp. 158–261. It was published after these chapters were written and so too late to provide more than general confirmation of the procedure which I have followed. Ebeling's order is somewhat different both from that which I have employed and from that which I would expect to be appropriate for a systematic account of the language of faith. Ebeling's order is: speaking *about* God, speaking *to* God, speaking *from* God (proclamation). It seems to me that for the purposes of an account of Christian faith this order should be reversed: speaking from God, speaking to god, speaking about God. In any case, talk about God is, for faith, clearly derivative from the other modes of discourse.

Chapter Eleven

1. See Mircea Eliade, *The Sacred and the Profane* (New York: Harcourt Brace and Co., 1959).

2. Emile Durkheim, *The Elementary Forms of the Religious Life*, Eng. trans. (New York: Macmillan, 1915).

3. Jürgen Moltmann makes reference to this three-fold division in his *The Crucified God* (Eng. trans. New York: Harper and Row, 1974), p. 65, and cites M. Poblenz, *Die Stoa* I, 1964.

4. Precisely because of this explicative use of 'god' to stabilize political order the denial of this civil or political religion may be perceived as subversion of the state. Thus the refusal of the early Christians to worship the Roman state gods was punished as subversion. More recently 'atheism' has often been regarded as subversive by the "secular" democracies of the modern era. This may explain why *'godless'* communism was the object of such fear in the McCarthy era of the 1950s in the United States.

5. The best representative of the attempt to understand contemporary civil religion is the work of Robert Bellah. See *The Broken Covenant: American Civil Religion in time of Trial* (New York: Seaburg, 1975).

6. See Hannah Arendt's essay *On Revolution* (New York: Viking Press, 1963), pp. 13–52.

7. For a discussion of the way in which fairy tales serve this function see Bruno Bettleheim's *The Uses of Enchantment* (New York: Random House, 1976). A somewhat different case is made by René Girard in his argument that religion, especially as it comes to focus in sacrifice, serves the function of a restraint of

violence. Classical drama which leads to catharsis is in his view a further development from this religious function. *Violence and the Sacred*, Eng. trans. (Baltimore: Johns Hopkins University Press, 1977). Girard's argument tends to confirm the connection suggested here between certain kinds of religious expression (poetic theology), the stabilizing of emotional conflict, and poetics generally.

8.   It would appear then that 'secularization' in the sense of an atrophy of explicative god-language strikes first in the area of poetical theology and only subsequently in the spheres of political and natural theology.

9.   Northrop Frye, *The Anatomy of Criticism* (Princeton: Princeton University Press, 1957) esp. pp. 131–242.

10.   So, for example, each of these ways of employing explicative god-language may be understood from the standpoint of our discussion of the aesthetic region. On the other hand, poetic theology is at least as closely related to the issues discussed under the heading of the historical region of experience as to those of the aesthetic region. Nor should we expect to find any correspondence for, on the one hand, we were discussing regions or modes of experience, and on the other, types of religious or theological discourse.

11.   'Secularization' has a double meaning. Most fundamentally it refers to the use of language to structure the 'everyday' and thus to a concentration of attention upon the ordinary and the structure of the ordinary rather than upon the extraordinary and the rupture of this structure. The second sense of secularization is the atrophy of god-language, especially in explicative discourse. The first prepares the way for the second. Once 'god' functions to explain, then 'god' may be supplanted by other terms of explanation. Thus in Christian theology Thomas Aquinas' fateful move of giving 'god' a principally explicative and (as we shall see) meta-explicative meaning—a move associated with his concentration upon the doctrine 'of the one God' (chapter two)—opens the way for secularization.

12.   From the perspective of a consideration of the explicative use of 'god' it may appear that the predicative use is transitional between expletive (rupture) and explicative (structure). It would then appear as a step toward the domestication of 'word-event' into language. Yet that which mediates also separates. The use of 'god' as a substantive is quite different from the use of 'god' as a qualifier (predicative).

13.   *Metaphysics*, Book VI, 1025b–1026a.

14.   *Summa Theologica* I, Q.2, article 3. The 'five ways' of demonstrating the existence of God are derived from Aristotle's reflections upon causation in the *Metaphysics*.

15.   Thus Pascal is correct in supposing that there is a fundamental difference between the "god of the philosophers" and the "God of Abraham, Isaac and Jacob." This will become more clear in our discussion of kerygmatic and doxological discourse in the next two chapters.

16.   If I am correct in maintaining that the metaphysical use of 'god' is meta-

explicative then it does not seem to make much sense either to try to bring this way of talking about god into harmony with religious language or, in the name of religious language to oppose the metaphysical enterprise. It is important to keep these distinct if we are not to produce considerable confusion. Theism with its various blends of religion and philosophy fails to attend to this fundamental distinction, lumping together explicative and meta-explicative uses of 'god' as well as kerygmatic (chapter twelve) and doxological (chapter thirteen) uses.

17. Ludwig Feuerbach, *Principles of the Philosophy of the Future*, p. 12, para 9.

18. For an attempt to trace the notion of the existing subject from the notion of the knowing subject and to distinguish various models of the existing subject see my dissertation *Man as the Subject of Existence: A Study of Post-Hegelian Anthropologies in Continental Theology*, Emory University, 1971.

19. This is one of the aims pursued by Wolfhart Pannenberg in his *Theology and the Philosophy of Science* (Philadelphia: The Westminster Press, 1976).

20. Kenneth Burke, *The Rhetoric of Religion: Studies in Logology* (Berkeley: The University of California Press, 1970), p. 1.

21. The relation of metaphysics to physics as an instance of the relation of meta-explicative discourse to explicative discourse raises the question of meta-explicative discourse which corresponds to the domains of political and poetical theology. Is there a meta-politics or a meta-poetics? A meta-politics would be an attempt to account for the antecedent conditions for any social order whatever. Perhaps the best example of such an attempt in contemporary thought is the "Frankfurt School" with its elaboration of a post-Marxian "critical theory."

A meta-poetics on the other hand would be the attempt to account for the antecedent conditions for a comprehension of intra-psychic and inter-psychic conflict. The development of psychoanalysis is certainly one illustration of this attempt as is also Heidegger's analysis of *Dasein*.

The task of developing a meta-politics or a meta-poetics appears to be far more difficult than that of developing a metaphysic—owing perhaps to the impossibility of separating the investigator from that which is to be investigated.

Chapter Twelve

1. See chapter eight, "V. The Historical Regions and the Other Regions," for a discussion of the appropriation via apocalyptic of ontological and aesthetic lexicons into the historical region.

2. Perhaps the most important attempt in recent theology to uncover the implications of this predominance of 'voice' is in Thomas J. J. Altizer's *The Self-Embodiment of God* (New York: Harper and Row, 1977). Through a meditation upon 'voice' and thus upon speech Altizer seeks to break through "to a new theological language, a language that will be biblical and contemporary at once and altogether" (p. 6). That this entails an identification of faith "with a speech which is both speech and listening at once" and the proposal that

"when we name God as God we name the finality of otherness" (p. 34) are but two indications of the way in which I find my own work to be congruent with his, even if we use very different language and method.

3. Emmanuel Levinas has proposed a similar view in "La révélation dans la tradition juive" in *La Révélation*; P. Ricoeur, E. Haulotte, E. Cornelis, Cl. Geffré (Brussels: Facultés Universitiarias Saint-Louis, 1977), pp.–77. While his proposal concentrates upon the Old Testament and upon an imperative structure, thus requiring revision and amplification to account for the complexity of biblical utterances, it is nevertheless an important essay making a 'turn' in the thought of this philosopher. For a helpful overview of Levinas' thought see Edith Wyschogrod, "God and 'Being's Move' in the Philosophy of Emmanuel Levinas," in the *Journal of Religion*, vol. 62, no. 2 (April 1982), pp. 145–55.

4. Karl Barth, *Church Dogmatics* I, 1, "God's Word is God Himself in His Revelation," p. 339.

5. See chapter four.

6. Hence the notion of creation by the word of Genesis 1:1–2:4.

7. That all become 'speakers' in this way is the meaning of the prophecy of Joel 2:28–31 which is then appropriated by Acts 2:18–19: "I will pour out my spirit upon all flesh and your sons and daughters shall prophesy. . . . "

8. Jürgen Moltmann, *The Theology of Hope*, pp. 95–105, 139–148.

9. If, as von Rad suggests, the YHWH is to be translated as "I will be with you."

10. A reasonably representative evaluation of the Jubilee laws (Lev. 25:8–17, 23–55) may be found in Roland de Vaux, *Ancient Israel: Its Life and Institutions* (New York: McGraw Hill, 1981), pp. 175–7. De Vaux does not, however, realize the significance of this 'Utopian' law for an understanding of legal texts generally.

11. The question of the law will be further clarified in chapter 13, "Law and Grace."

12. The analysis of such linkages is the work of tradition criticism (identification of the elements linked) and redaction criticism (analysis of the linkages proper to determine the principles by which disparate materials are brought together). Undoubtedly these two approaches require one another. Unfortunately the tendency of the practitioners of both methods to focus upon isolated fragments regularly obscures the narrative structure itself.

13. This accounts for the inclusion of the "historical books" of the Old Testament and 'Acts' in the New Testament in the 'canon of Scripture'.

14. The problem is brought into focus by the analysis of Paul's self-referential assertions in the work of E. Guttgemann's *Der leidende Apostel und sein Herr* (Gottingen: Vandenhoeck and Ruprecht, 1966).

15. Northrop Frye has recently maintained that the 'rhetorical' or vocative character of language underlies biblical narrative as myth. *The Great Code: The Bible and Literature* (New York: Harcourt Brace Jovanovich, 1982), pp. 27–30. He does not develop this insight further although his reading of the Bible as (also) a literary work is suggestive in a great many additional ways.

16. The abolition of identity within an apocalyptic perspective is one of the most consistent and important themes in Altizer's work. His *Oriental Mysticisms and Biblical Eschatology* (Philadelphia: The Westminister Press, 1961) articulates this theme in relation to Eastern religious traditions as well as Western traditions. The subtitle of *The Descent Into Hell: A Study of the Radical Reversal of Christian Consciousness* (Philadelphia: Lippincott, 1970) restates this theme by reversing the traditional meaning of resurrection. His most recent book, *Total Presence: The Language of Jesus and the Language of Today* (New York: Seabury, 1980), returns to this theme and demonstrates its pertinence for a consideration of the character of Jesus' proclamation and of modernity. It is in correlation to this theme of the abolition of fixed identity that the theme of the 'death of God' is to be understood.

17. That "creedal formulas" are embedded in biblical material has been long recognized. Among the most famous examples are the Shema, the "Philippians Hymm," and the summary outlines of early Christian preaching in Acts. My point here is that these formulations are not to be simply opposed to narrative as another genre alongside narrative and in competition with it but are to be understood as outlines of narrative material. Conversely the narrative material must be understood as confessional in character, governed by proclamation.

18. Gerhard Ebeling, *The Word of God and Tradition* (Philadelphia: Fortress Press, 1965), pp. 11–31. As will become evident below, I do not really agree with Ebeling's understanding of theology as a strictly hermeneutical discipline (note 22).

19. The theology of Karl Barth and the in many ways quite different theology of Gerhard Ebeling are both characterized by an attention to the event of proclamation as the critical determinant of theological work. For Barth the emphasis falls upon the dogmatic basis of this event (God speaks) while for Ebeling it falls upon the concrete situation of address (word-event). For brief and readable summaries see Karl Barth, *The Preaching of the Gospel* (Philadelphia: The Westminster Press, 1963) and Gerhard Ebelings' *God and Word* (Philadelphia: Fortress Press, 1967).

20. For a further elaboration of the way in which theology is necessitated in these ways see my *Introduction to Theology* (Philadelphia: Fortress Press, 1976). See also my essay "On the Construction of Doctrine" in *The Vocation of the Theologian*, ed. Theodore W. Jennings, Jr. (Philadelphia: Fortress Press, 1985).

21. Book I, 1.

22. The internalization of alterity in doctrinal discourse will mean that this doctrine can by no means be 'perennial' or merely 'revised'. Rather it is continually constructed, deconstructed, or critically reconstructed. There is certainly no revealed doctrine. There is instead only doctrine which gives a conceptual account of kerygmatic address. See below, chapter fourteen, "The Question of Doctrine."

23. The discussion of "fundamental theology" has brought into focus the significance of a formal theological reflection upon the structure of conversion.

See Avery Dulles, "Fundamental Theology and the Dynamics of Conversion,"
Thomist, vol. 45 (1981), pp. 175–93. Matthias Neumann, "The Role of Imagination in the Tasks of Fundamental Theology" *Encounter,* vol. 42 (1981),
pp. 307–327; Donald Gelpi *Experiencing God* (New York: Paulist Press, 1978).
For an overview of the discussion of fundamental theology, see Randy L.
Maddox, *Toward an Ecumenical Fundamental Theology* (Chico, Calif.: Scholars Press, 1984).

24. In a similar fashion Karl Barth takes the assertion "God speaks" to be the
source or ground of Trinitarian formulation in *Church Dogmatics* I, 1, pp. 349–
383.

Chapter Thirteen

1. See my essay "Prayer: the Call for God" in *Christian Century,* April 18, 1981,
for a further exposition of this contention.

2. Many of the suggestions made in this chapter concerning the language and
significance of prayer and praise are elaborated and substantiated in a separate
essay: *Life as Worship: Prayer and Praise in Jesus' Name* (Grand Rapids: Eerdmans, 1982). That essay is intended as the first in a series of reflections upon
the life of the community of faith as that life is concentrated in the words and
actions of the community's worship. Thus the proposals made here concerning
the understanding of this discourse are actually worked out and tested within
the community of faith itself. This is the advantage a theologian has over the
philosopher of religion. The advantage is also a limitation since the theologian's
proposals must survive testing against the actual practice of the community
and the 'self-understanding' of that community. I hope to follow the *Life as
Worship* book with a study of confession and forgiveness of sins which will
explore the relation between oralogical and kerygmatic discourse within an
ecclesial context.

3. The still classic study of the charismatic character of earliest Christianity is
Hermann Gunkel's *The Influence of the Holy Spirit,* Eng. trans. (Philadelphia:
Fortress Press, 1979; original German edition published in 1888).

4. So, for example, Augustine in letter CXXX "To Proba" regularly explains
prayer as self-admonition. Similarly, Aquinas writes "we need to pray to God
not in order to make known to him our needs and desires but that we ourselves
may be reminded of having recourse to God's help in these matters" (*Summa
Theologica* II, Q. 83, article 2). These reflections have the effect of undermining
the otherwise penetrating analyses of these theologians. This undermining
occurs when oralogical language is subordinated to explicative language.

5. See Rudolf Bultmann's *Jesus and the Word,* Eng. trans. (New York: Scribners,
1958) for a similar analysis of 'law'.

6. For further discrimination of the character of ritual, see my essay "On Ritual
Knowledge," *Journal of Religion,* April, 1982.

7. It is, however, also the case that the liturgical cycle contains within itself a

counter-tendency. The season of Advent which articulates Christian hope contrasts sharply with the seasonal cycle of approaching winter with which it coincides (in the Northern hemisphere where the liturgical cycle originates). Similarly, the season of Lent culminating in Good Friday with its liturgical emphasis upon repentance and renunciation stands in marked contrast to the seasonal approach of spring with which it coincides. See also my article on "Liturgy" in the *Encyclopedia of Religion*, ed. Mircea Eliade (New York: The Macmillan Press, forthcoming).

8. To be sure, this view of sacrament as anticipation of apocalyptic reality requires a fundamental reworking of the notion of sacrament in traditional theology. Such a 'deconstruction' has already begun. Of interest in this regard is the demystification of sacrament undertaken by Barth (*Church Dogmatics* IV; 4 fragment on baptism), whose position that Christ is the only true sacrament is already anticipated by Ambrose in the early fifth century. A more conservative but still fundamental revision of sacramental theory has been proposed by Karl Rahner (for a brief description of Rahner's view see *Meditations on the Sacraments* (New York: Seabury, 1977) pp. ix–xvii). More recently the suggestions of Jürgen Moltmann (*Church in the Power of the Spirit*, New York: Harper and Row, 1977) suggest a more fully eschatological and thus radical deconstruction of the notion of a sacrament. See also my article on "Sacraments" in the *Encyclopedia of Religion* (New York: Macmillan, forthcoming).

9. A new translation of this treatise is now available: *Of Basil the Great On the Holy Spirit* (Crestwood, St. Vladimir's Seminary Press, 1980). The occasion for the treatise as a controversy concerning a doxological formula is discussed in 1.3 (p. 17).

10. Cabasilas, *The Life in Christ* (Crestwood, New York: St. Vladimir's Seminary Press, 1974).

11. Alexander Schmemann's *Introduction to Liturgical Theology* (London: Faith Press, 1966) and *For the Life of the World* (New York: National Student Christian Federation, 1963) are two of his most important works. See also the work of Geoffrey Wainwright, especially *Doxology: The Praise of God in Worship, Doctrine and Life* (New York: Oxford University Press, 1980).

12. This parable is discussed at some length in my *Life as Worship*, pp. 116–7.

13. *Ibid*, pp. 72–74.

14. *Church Dogmatics*, II, 2, pp. 509ff.

15. *Church Dogmatics*, IV, 4 (fragment), p. ix. Barth only completes the first part of this project—the reflection upon baptism. Notes for the continuation of this reflection have recently been published as *The Christian Life* (Eerdmans, 1981).

16. For Käsemann, see "Worship in Everyday Life: A Note on Rom 12," *New Testament Questions of Today*, Eng. trans. (Philadelphia: Fortress Press, 1969), pp. 188–195. For Moltmann, cf. *The Church in the Power of the Spirit* (New York: Harper and Row, 1977), p. 271.

17. Dietrich Bonhoeffer, *Ethics*, Eng. trans., ed. Eberhard Bethge (New York: Macmillan, 1962).

18. *Creation and Fall* (London: SCM Press, 1959).
19. Nietzsche, *Beyond Good and Evil* (Chicago: H. Regnery, 1965).
20. "Analogy and Doxology," *Basic Questions in Theology*, vol. I (Philadelphia: Fortress Press, 1970), pp. 212–235. The quoted passage appears on p. 216.
21. *Ibid*, p. 227.

Chapter Fourteen

1. For a description of recent changes in the conception of apologetics, see Johannes Metz, *Faith in Church and Society* (New York: Seabury, 1979). For a survey of apologetic proposals and the move toward a fundamental theology see Randy L. Maddox, *Toward an Ecumenical Fundamental Theology* (Chico, Calif.: Scholar's Press, 1984).
2. Movement in the direction of such a clarification of the vocative structure is inaugurated by Barth's reflections on the phrase "God speaks" (*Church Dogmatics* I, 1, esp. pp. 349–38) and is undertaken from quite a different perspective by Karl Rahner in *Hearers of the Word* (New York: Herder & Herder, 1969). More recently, Ebeling's reflections upon word-event cited in chapter four as well as in his *Introduction to a Theological Theory of Language* (Philadelphia: Fortress Press, 1973) have forwarded this discussion significantly. It is the project which he adumbrates in the latter volume to which I hope these pages have made a contribution. That this movement toward a theological theory of language is not a merely European phenomenon is shown by the work of Th. J. J. Altizer in *The Self-Embodiment of God* (New York: Harper and Row, 1971) and in *Total Presence* (New York: The Seabury Press, 1980). The fascinating work of Leahy, *Novitas Mundi* (SUNY Press, 1981) came to my attention too late for work on this essay. The development of such an analysis of 'address' and of a theological theory of language must always orient itself at one and the same time to biblical (and liturgical) discourse and to the universal features of linguisticality.
3. Work in the direction of a reformulation of Trinitarian discourse as the basis of kerygmatic discourse has been undertaken by Jürgen Moltmann in *The Crucified God* (New York: Seabury, 1974) and in the more recent *The Trinity and the Kingdom* (New York: Harper and Row, 1981).
4. For a classical statement of the argument for Christological theses on the basis of 'apotheosis' of the human subject see Athanasius, *On the Incarnation of the Word*.
5. It is important to bear in mind that 'god' is not the invention of a kerygmatic address. Rather this term is expropriated from language generally and is deployed in ways often contrary or opposed to ways in which it is employed in mythological, explicative, or meta-explicative discourse. Much confusion arises from the supposition that terms like 'god', 'christ', resurrection, sin, salvation are "religious" or "Christian." They are not. They have been expropriated from other discourses and then volatilized in accordance with a vocative struc-

ture. Hence the plausibility of the charge against early Christians that they were impious, blasphemous, or atheistic—charges made by the guardians of an explicative and meta-explicative discourse.

6. Thus the first test of this theory of vocative discourse must be the extent to which it offers a satisfactory account of the distinctive and 'normative' articulations of faith. In this sense dogmatic clarification precedes apologetic validation.

7. Despite appearances to the contrary I suppose that the view worked out in these pages is by no means contrary to Barth's famous opposition to "apologetics." While I would obviously formulate my position in different terms, I agree in principle with the opposition to an accommodationist apologetic and with the insistence that theology develop its major categories from attention to its own discourse. I may however take more seriously than Barth the methodological implications of his doctrine of election and am disposed to take Bonhoeffer's way of developing a Christocentric position more into account. The clarification of these connections and tensions are perhaps best left to others.

Name Index

Aeschylus, 246n.
Altizer, Thomas J.J., 35, 121, 214, 235n., 250n., 255n., 260n.
Anselm, St. 118, 250n.
Aquinas, St. Thomas, 16, 29, 118, 155, 179, 182, 233n., 254n.
Arendt, Hannah, 249n., 253n.
Aristotle, 155, 182, 233n., 254n.
Augustine, St., 15, 16, 159, 178, 232n., 252n.
Austin, J.L., 231n., 239n., 253n.
Ayer, A.J., 7–8, 230n.

Balthasar, Hans Urs von, 245n.
Barth, Karl, 23, 33, 34–35, 37, 51, 53, 156, 157, 169, 182, 203, 234n., 235n., 238n., 240n., 248n., 253n, 257n., 258n., 259n., 260n., 261n.
Becker, Ernest, 249n.
Berger, Peter, 11, 232n., 234n., 252n.
Bergson, Henri, 99, 251n.
Bertocci, P.A., 235n.
Bettelheim, Bruno, 253n.

Bloch, Ernst, 118, 247n., 248n., 250n.
Bonhoeffer, Dietrich, 33, 203, 237n., 261n.
Bowlby, John, 249n.
Brathwaite, R.B., 9, 231n., 234n.
Braun, Herbert, 61, 242n.
Brightman, S., 235n.
Buber, Martin, 35, 169, 238n., 240n.
Bultmann, Rudolf, 49, 54, 55, 105, 117, 174, 239n., 240n., 248n., 249n., 258n.
Buri, Fritz, 49, 240n.
Burke, Kenneth, 159, 255n.

Camus, Albert, 87
Christian, William, 236n.
Cobb, John B. Jr., 11, 27, 127. 232n., 236n.
Cox, Harvey, 232n., 245n.

Darwin, Charles, 158, 223
Derrida, Jacques, 46, 55, 86, 121, 220, 245n.

Subject Index

Abandonment and loss, 111–112
Aesthetic region, 91–93, 94, 245n., 247n.,
 254n. *See also* Art and poesis; Culture
Affectivity, 151, 216–217
Annihilation. *See* Dread and annihilation
Anthropomorphism, 151
Apocalypse, 174, 200
Apollonian vs. Dionysian perspective,
 247n.
Apologetics, 162, 210–212, 260n.
 abandonment of, 34–35
 post-Theistic, 29–39
 secular, 33–34
Art and poesis, 121, 150–52, 245–246n.
Assertions
 eschatological, 8
 meaningful, 141
 verifiability of, 8–9
Attachment, theory of, 249n.
Awe, 98

Being, vs. Non-being, 84
Bible. New Testament, 60, 164, 173, 174,
 176, 199, 249n.

Epistles of St. Paul
 Corinthians I, 174, 192
 Romans, 106
 Gospel according to John, 96
 Gospel according to Luke, 192, 200–202
 Gospel according to Mark, 112
 Gospel according to Matthew, 171, 200–
 202
Bible. Old Testament, 60, 165, 174, 200–
 202, 256n.
 Exodus, 120
 Genesis, 96, 115, 159, 179, 249n.
 Leviticus, 201
 Samuel, 165, 171
Blacks, Christianity and, 234
Boredom, 92
Buddhism, 85, 131

Chaos, 94–95
Christian community, 162, 163, 170, 180,
 190, 195, 201
Christianity. *See specific subjects*
Church Dogmatics (Barth), 182

267